Reflections of a Cold Warrior

RICHARD M. BISSELL, JR.

with Jonathan E. Lewis and Frances T. Pudlo

Reflections of a Cold Warrior

From Yalta to the Bay of Pigs

Yale University Press New Haven and London

Designed by Sonia Scanlon
Set in Minion type by Keystone Typesetting, Inc.
Printed in the United States of America by
BookCrafters, Inc. Chelsea, Michigan

Library of Congress Cataloging-in-Publication Data
Bissell, Richard M. (Richard Mervin), 1909–1994
Reflections of a cold warrior : from Yalta to the Bay of Pigs / Richard M. Bissell, Jr. ; with Jonathan E. Lewis and Frances T. Pudlo.
p. cm.
Includes bibliographical references and index.
ISBN 0-300-06430-6
1. United States. Central Intelligence Agency—History. 2. Bissell, Richard M. (Richard Mervin), 1909–1994. 3. Intelligence. officers—United States—Biography. I. Lewis, Jonathan E., 1962– . II. Pudlo, Frances T., 1948– . III. Title.
JK468.I6B55 1996
327.1273—dc20 95-43084

CIP

A catalogue record for this book is available from the British Library.

The paper in this book meets the guidelines for permanence and durability of the Committee on Production Guidelines for Book Longevity of the Council on Library Resources.

10 9 8 7 6 5 4 3 2 1

Contents

Acknowledgments

The interest and active support of many colleagues, friends, and family members helped make this project possible. The following people were kind enough to allow themselves to be interviewed or else provided valuable criticism or moral support when it was needed: Stanley Beerli, McGeorge Bundy, Lloyd Emerson, General Leo Geary, Ted Geiger, General Andrew Goodpaster, Lincoln Gordon, Richard Helms, Lawrence Houston, Leo Janos, Robert King, Herman "Fritz" Liebert, Arthur Lundahl, Michael Lutzker, Doris Mirage, Paul Nitze, James Reber, Ben Rich, Eugene Rostow, Walt Rostow, Arthur M. Schlesinger, Jr., Melbourne Spector, Evan Thomas, and Ted Thomas.

The CIA's history staff was supportive of this project, and Gerry Haines in particular was very helpful. Gerry gave an early version of the draft a critical read that greatly assisted us in making subsequent revisions. Evan Thomas also gave a hard and clearheaded appraisal of the draft. Walt Rostow was especially generous in giving us not only his support and counsel but a valuable reading of the draft as well.

David Haight at the Eisenhower Library should be considered a national treasure. His encyclopedic knowledge of the library's holdings and his dedication to helping researchers are greatly appreciated. Suzanne Forbes at the Kennedy Library was always highly responsive to requests for guidance and information. In locating one especially critical document, she kept searching well beyond the point when many others would have stopped with a clear conscience.

Thanks to the guidance of Michael Hunt, we decided to approach Yale University Press to publish this work. We are deeply appreciative of the support Charles Grench at Yale gave the project, as well as of the hard work of our editor, Roslyn Schloss.

Our families were very understanding of the long hours we devoted to the project. Fran wishes to express gratitude to two people in particular who will always hold a special place in her heart—Richard M. Bissell, Jr., her boss, teacher, mentor, surrogate father, and dear friend of twenty years, who made everything possible; and Ann Bushnell Bissell, whose courage, strength, perseverance, and humor continue to be an inspiration.

Jonathan is especially grateful to his father, Robert J. Lewis, who instilled in him a lifelong love of history, and Nancy Lewis, who, along with Robert, gave him the confidence to follow his instincts. He would also like to thank his brothers, Steven and Richard, and his nephew Jeremy, who now knows a good deal more about intelligence history than most elementary school children. Most of all, deep thanks go to the understanding and patience of his wife, Laura, who always supported this project with all her heart, even when her husband spent weekends at a computer or on research trips.

If Mr. Bissell were still alive, he would want us to thank the many historians whose probing questions over the years challenged him to recall events long past and forced him to rethink his positions on a variety of issues. He would especially want to thank John Ranelagh, who prodded him a number of times to begin work on these memoirs and whose support and interest Mr. Bissell greatly appreciated. Most of all, he would want us to thank his wife, Ann, and his children, Richard, Ann Harriet, Winthrop, and Thomas.

We owe a great debt to Mr. Bissell for allowing us to participate in the research and writing of his memoir. To have had the opportunity of working closely with him was priceless. Mrs. Bissell also deserves a great deal of thanks. She provided us with guidance and counsel after Mr. Bissell's death, when many of the most important decisions regarding the book had to be made. Without her support, the publication of this book would not have been possible.

CHAPTER ONE

The Early Years

Bissells have deep roots in Connecticut soil. According to my grandfather George F. Bissell, the first Bissell settled in Windsor, Connecticut, having arrived from England in 1636, and "the family became an influential one and played a conspicuous part in public matters, in founding of churches, and in conflicts with the Indian tribes that harassed the Colony."[1] One ancestor, Sergeant Daniel Bissel, also from Windsor, was a spy for General George Washington. In August 1781 he was assigned to penetrate British lines in New York City and obtain information about British operations. Enlisting in the British army, he found himself in the same regiment as Benedict Arnold. Bissel spent months gathering the information Washington needed, but just as he was about to make his way back to American headquarters he was stricken with fever. The British physician who attended him through his delirium discovered his mission but chose not to unmask him as a spy. Instead, he helped him escape. Bissel returned to Washington's headquarters in Newburgh, where he provided crucial information and maps. He was awarded the Badge of Military Merit for his efforts, one of only three officers so honored.[2] Irony would have it that part of my career would be conducted in the intelligence field and that I, too, would be labeled a spy.

My paternal grandparents originated from either Manchester or South Windsor, Connecticut, but at a young age they decided to relocate to the Midwest, first to Dubuque and then to Chicago. My grandfather made his career with the Hartford Fire, serving the company for more than forty years. Considered "perhaps the most outstanding insurance executive in the Middle West in the greatly booming period following the Civil War," he also had the distinction of being the first fire insurance manager in Chicago to open an office after the Great

Fire in 1871.[3] A man of unusual ability, my grandfather became one of Chicago's leading citizens, involved in numerous civic and charitable enterprises. He left an impressive legacy and one in which his son, my father, was to play a major role.

Richard Mervin Bissell, Sr., was born in Chicago in 1862. Following his graduation from Yale in 1883, he began at the bottom of the fire insurance ladder, first at Moore & Jaynes in Chicago and shortly thereafter at the Hartford. He filled subordinate positions there until becoming vice president in 1903 (necessitating a move to Hartford) and president in 1913, a position he held with distinction for more than twenty-five years.

My father was an exceptional man and a great influence on my life, even if he was a somewhat distant figure at home. As one might expect, he was absorbed in a demanding job and deeply committed to the institution he was building. Many years later I came to know that presiding over and building an organization is a very satisfying activity, especially if one believes in what the organization is doing. He clearly did, and with good reason.

My parents met when my father was still based in Chicago. Marie Truesdale, born in Terre Haute, grew up in St. Paul, Minnesota, where her father, William H. Truesdale, was a railroad executive. Like my father she was a role model whom I have aspired to emulate throughout my life. After my father's death in 1941, she went to Washington and began working for the Red Cross, eventually becoming its national director of volunteer services, with responsibility for the performance of about three million workers.

My parents' move to Hartford from Chicago provided the setting for the warm and congenial family life I enjoyed along with my older brother and sister, William and Anne-Carolyn. I was born in the Mark Twain House on Farmington Avenue on September 18, 1909. The property, designed and constructed to Clemens's specifications, had remained his family's residence for seventeen years. It was there that I spent the first nine years of my life. With its queer little balconies and curiously shaped closets under the eaves, the house was a world unto itself. My mother, who had exquisite taste in decorating, updated the interior to eliminate its Victorian darkness. I particularly remember the conservatory at the rear of the house, which she transformed into a fernery with a small pool and a stream of water that could be turned on and off. For Bill, it was the perfect habitat in which to raise his pet baby alligator.

Of her three children, I was the one who tested my mother's maternal responsibilities to the fullest. Although healthy in other respects, I was born with severely crossed eyes. I wore glasses from the age of six months and had to undergo countless hours of therapy until, when I was about eight years old, the problem was alleviated for the most part by surgery. One benefit I derived from the whole unpleasant experience was being read to by my mother.

Each year we summered in Maine. My parents usually rented a furnished house in Dark Harbor from the middle of June until just after Labor Day. My mother was responsible for engineering the details of this great expedition, and our house would ring with activity for days as steamer trunks were brought down from the attic and filled with all the necessary items for a three-month stay. Including my mother, three children, a cook, and perhaps two maids, we made quite an entourage. To my great delight these trips were always made by train and I had a full day to indulge in the sights, sounds, and smells of the railroad. Since my father could break away from work and join us only for about two weeks in August, my mother commanded this convoy alone. I can still see her standing on the station platform counting to make sure that every member of her party was present, as well as every single piece of luggage—no small feat, since it was not unusual for us to travel with more than twenty steamer trunks. She would not budge from her position until all was in order and everything had been checked off her list.

It was in Dark Harbor that I learned to sail. My parents bought a gaff-rigged sloop for Bill, and he would take me along as his crew. One summer my parents rented me a twelve-footer that I used to race against the gardener-handyman. By then Bill led a much different life from mine, so our paths did not cross very frequently. It was my mother who volunteered to crew for me, helping me gain self-confidence and a taste for the role of captain. Later we chartered a Manchester seventeen-footer. Sailing marked the beginning of a passion that provided many pleasures and near-disasters with my family and friends over the years.

During World War I, Father served as chairman of the Connecticut Council on Defense, a coordinating body formed to mobilize the state. His responsibilities required that he travel to Washington almost every week. My mother's contribution to the war effort was to head up a local volunteer organization that sold postage stamps; these were meant to be pasted into a little booklet that, when full, could be converted into a defense bond.

In addition to being a highly respected businessman, my father took a keen interest in politics. He was a staunch Republican and favored Charles Evans Hughes over Woodrow Wilson in the 1916 presidential election. On election night, my parents hosted a large party. Father rented a telegraph line and instrument and hired an operator to receive up-to-the-minute results. By the time the California results came in at 1:00 or 2:00 A.M., everyone had already gone home, jubilant that Hughes, the early leader, had won. My father's experiment with modern technology did not meet his expectations or produce the effect he had hoped for.

My parents recognized the value of foreign travel, and our family made many trips to Europe. I'm told that I took my first steps at a French beach resort on the English Channel and did my first sustained walking at the Villa d'Este on Lake Como, one of my parents' favorite places. My father especially loved Venice, and partly for that reason I became fond of it myself.

Our family trips usually ended in Paris, where we lived in several different small hotels near the Place de la Concorde. On one trip, in about 1919, we drove out to see the battlefields of northern France. The July heat was intense, and the scene was dreary. The ruin of the war had been cleaned up pretty completely—roads were fixed, railroads ran, and power came on when one threw a light switch—but there were very few trees. All had been destroyed by the war. I formed the impression of World War I as a cataclysm. The sights surely spurred my interest in history; they may also have contributed to my becoming increasingly isolationist in the 1930s, when I was horrified at the idea of America's being involved in a war like that again.

In 1921, the year before I went off to boarding school, my mother thought it would be a good experience to have all three children live in Europe. We spent the winter in Rome while my father conducted his business back at home, coming to see us at Christmas and again for a couple of weeks in early spring. In March or April we left Rome and went to stay in a villa outside Florence that had been lent to my parents. I was bored stiff during this spell. I had more interest in Rome, because there I had begun reading ancient history and could visit the Forum and the Palatine and see where the buildings had stood. Ancient history comes through in a direct and simple fashion, unclouded by the ambiguities that surround the history of periods closer to our own, where there may be more evidence available. This appealed to me. I was enormously impressed with the Romans' accomplishment, as well as their power and organization.

That fall we moved into a house in Farmington that my parents had built. Colton Hill, as my mother called it, was comfortable and very beautiful, a special place to all of us and to many of my friends as well. When we moved, my parents leased the Mark Twain House, which had become extremely expensive to maintain, to a boys' day school called Kingswood that they had been instrumental in founding. It had started on the top floor of the house as a nursery school for me and a small group of other children but had expanded to another building, which also became too small.

It seemed very odd to me to attend school in the house where I was born and raised. The boys' entrance was at the rear of the house in the cellar; we were forbidden to use the front door, something I had been privileged to do for years. I didn't like Kingswood much and I was not a very good student. My main recollection is of failure—low marks, poor relations with my fellow students, inadequate performance in sports. This state of affairs was worrisome to my parents, who planned for me to follow Bill to Groton, the highly regarded preparatory school in Massachusetts. They felt that Groton offered academic excellence and a basis from which to form valuable and lasting friendships. I eventually found this to be the case as well.

Although I did not shine scholastically, the headmaster of Kingswood, George Nicholson, generously pointed out in his letter of recommendation that I was "still a little boy who, of course, has had no opportunity to contribute much to the life of the school, but who gives unusual promise of achievement in the future."[4] My parents were delighted when I was accepted at Groton, but boarding school was not an easy transition. In the first year or two especially, I suffered a great deal from homesickness. Instead of returning each day to a warm and friendly family setting, I went to a dormitory after evening school and had to live with boys my own age, most of whom I didn't like and most of whom didn't like me. I was shy, I wasn't a good athlete, and I was scared of them.

Life at Groton seemed to me austere; our time and space were rigorously structured. Each dormitory had a row of cubicles down either side. One's cubicle was the only place one had privacy, and that was minimal, as the partitions were only about seven feet high and the curtains across the inner end were rarely drawn. Each cubicle had a window and contained a bed, a bureau, one stiff wooden chair, and some hooks for clothes. There was a common washroom with black stone sinks along the walls. Each boy had a tin basin and a small space on the shelf for toilet articles. Rising time, announced by the bell on the schoolhouse, was five minutes before seven. A cold shower was obligatory. There was about twenty minutes of free time after breakfast, then chapel at eight-thirty and classes and study periods from nine to one. Athletics took place in the afternoon, which for me was the most disagreeable part of the day. I hated organized sports and was especially incompetent at baseball. I rarely caught a ball that came my way and I doubt if I scored three good hits in the course of four or five years of compulsory practice. In my last few years at Groton I was able to escape from baseball by taking up rowing, which, although vastly harder work, was a sport where I could compete more or less on even terms, get a letter, build a little self-esteem, and derive real enjoyment.

Whenever circumstances allowed, I would evade athletic activities by claiming to have a cold. The rules prescribed that if one could not engage in a regular organized sport one could instead walk for an hour and a half. Especially in winter, Joseph Alsop and I frequently arranged to be "off exercise" and would go on long walks together. I enjoyed walking (as I have all my life) and we had many interesting conversations. There was, however, a running argument between us on these occasions. For reasons that I couldn't quite make out, I would always be three or four steps ahead of Joe. He claimed that it was because I went faster at the start to establish a lead. I countered that it was because he went slower at the start and didn't keep up. This debate was never resolved.

I found solace in my long and warm friendship with Joe Alsop. He notes in his own memoirs that our mothers had been good friends for years and that as a result we grew up together. By the time we arrived at Groton, we were good friends as well.[5]

Groton was a church school, and its rector, the Reverend Endicott Peabody, was a very devout man. Averell Harriman once observed of him that he "would be an awful bully if he weren't such a terrible Christian."[6] Nevertheless, he reached out to me in a way that I still marvel at today. At the time I used to say that I was an atheist. I don't know how he heard about my pronouncement, but in my last year he sent for me one evening and we talked in his study. In effect, he said to me, "Boy, I know you think you are an atheist. You know that I am a deep believer in God and I am convinced that you will change your mind in due time. I want to ask you just one favor. If, as, and when you do change your mind, please let me know." His statement clearly implied trust in my judgment. He wasn't making little of it; the last thing he was trying to do was to order me to change. I left that session feeling great respect for him. Regrettably, I never followed up on the conversation.

I did, though, have another encounter with him. One cold February evening, my classmate Charles Stockton and I concocted a powerful stink bomb from hydrochloric acid and an iron salt. Although Stockton aided and abetted the effort, he counseled against activating it in Joe Alsop's study, as I had planned. Undeterred, I placed it in Joe's room and waited for the results. It took effect immediately, driving the entire school out into the snow.

Peabody quickly discovered who was responsible. He summoned me into his presence and delivered a lecture, the main thrust of which was that what I had done was not evil but mischievous. A punishment was delivered: I wasn't to go into the chemistry laboratory for a specified time, and there were some other things, long since forgotten. Again, his distinction between evil and mischief was sensible, and once more I had to respect him for his insight.

There has been speculation in recent years about the friendships established at schools like Groton and Yale and their impact on organizations like the Central Intelligence Agency. I think there *was* an Ivy League establishment in the sense of a body of men who had similar backgrounds and knew one another well, and the existence of that group had a good deal of influence on public affairs. It was not a self-conscious or exclusive grouping. If positions were available in various public institutions and members of that establishment were invited to fill them, I think it was more because these men knew one another than because of a deliberate policy of selecting only from a particular social group.

The question can also be raised whether the ethical training colored the formation of the agency in any way. This is difficult to answer. Many of us who joined the CIA did not feel bound in the actions we took as staff members to observe all the ethical rules that we would have observed and regarded as valid before we joined. But in a larger sense, the patriotism, the belief in the need for the United States to play an important role in the world had some of their roots in our upbringing and education, and they certainly did affect the atmosphere in the agency.

Two Grotonians with whom I would have a close relationship during my CIA years were Tracy Barnes and John Bross. They were a grade removed from me and I didn't know them terribly well at school, but our friendship grew when the three of us were colleagues during the 1950s and 1960s. Almost all the friendships I formed at Groton were lasting ones. Although the class of 1928 was small, among its twenty-four members several remained lifelong friends. Sargent Cheever and Joe Alsop were my best friends, but others were important to me as well—Dwight Morrow, Charles Stockton, William Marvel, William Thompson. My friendship with Dwight Morrow was especially rewarding. It was through him that I came to know his sister Anne and her husband, Charles Lindbergh. In the winter of 1927 Bill Marvel and I were invited to spend

Christmas vacation with the Morrows in Mexico City, where Dwight's father was the American ambassador. Traveling by train, we left Groton for New York's Pennsylvania Station, where we boarded the *Spirit of Saint Louis*. Then we transferred to a Missouri Pacific train and a private car chartered by the Morrows. I had been a train buff since childhood—no doubt through the influence of my grandfather Truesdale—and I was fascinated as I sat on the car's rear platform and watched the undulating countryside of the Midwest give way to the flat desert of Mexico. When we reached Mexico City, it seemed to me a most beautiful place.

We were met and driven to the embassy upon our arrival. It turned out that Charles Lindbergh was also a guest and he was quartered with Dwight, Bill, and me in a building across the court from the embassy. There was a Morrow cousin present named Richard Scandrett, who was very pleasant and entertaining. With our help, Lindbergh made him the object of a low-grade practical joke—short-sheeting his bed.

One day when we were touring the floating gardens of Xochimilco, a Mexican gentleman approached, embraced me, and exclaimed with great emotion, "My hero." Since Lindbergh's solo flight across the Atlantic had taken place only months earlier, the man no doubt mistook me for him, as I, too, was tall and thin. The others teased me, and Anne Morrow later wrote about the incident in her book *Bring Me A Unicorn*. It was on this trip that Lindbergh met her.

Mexico City was memorable for another reason, my first ride in an airplane, an old Ford Trimotor. My memory is sketchy, but I know Lindbergh went to the airport before us and he may well have been behind the controls of the plane. Later, at the end of the trip, we flew from Mexico City to Brownsville, Texas, again in a Ford Trimotor. This was early in the days of commercial travel, when airplanes were still considered a curiosity, so it was a very exciting experience. A memento of this trip—an autographed photograph of Lindbergh standing outside the American embassy—hangs in my office.

The fall of 1928 saw me enrolled at Yale University as a history major. My fascination with ancient history might have led me to become a classicist, but that would have required reading knowledge of both Latin and Greek, a challenge I was not prepared to undertake. By senior year, my focus had changed to nineteenth-century British history.

The environment at Yale was one of complete intellectual and political freedom at a time when, nationally, there was a great intensification of interest in political developments and debates. Exposure to a lot of bright people, both faculty members and students, was highly stimulating. There was, inevitably, a growing tendency to identify a struggle between left and right and to take sides.

Great changes were taking place in the university. The plan for new residential colleges that could eventually house almost the entire undergraduate body had been approved and we lived in the middle of heavy construction as four or five of the buildings began to emerge at the core of the university, with more to come. At the same time, the university's general budget felt the impact of the depression, and decisions had to be made about where to cut back instruction and services. Concern with educational developments and with the appropriate social and educational environment for the undergraduate community competed with the unavoidable concern over public affairs.

Along with fellow students Herman "Fritz" Liebert, Eugene Rostow, Max Millikan, and Richard Childs, I became involved with an independent, student-run magazine called the *Harkness Hoot*. We viewed it as a means of changing the Yale establishment and injecting educational values back into the forum of the university discussion. For a time, Childs, who was my roommate, and I were the editors. With the collaboration of Gene Rostow and others, I produced a document called "The Yale House Plan." An excerpt from this paper gives insight into our thinking: "Every interference by the University with non-educational matters is a wasteful, if not obnoxious, deviation from its proper path. Every restriction on undergraduate freedom is extraneous to the business at hand. . . . Because Yale has a high ideal to live up to and an important duty to perform, the absence of this realization and its consequent dissipation of energies is nothing short of tragic."[7] Needless to say, the university did not take kindly to publication of "The Yale House Plan," especially since the name Yale appeared in it, but the authorities did not press their objections very vigorously.

One aspect of Yale campus life that disturbed me was the institution of secret societies. I resented a system that introduced a competition for social standing that was counterproductive to true education, labeling one select group of individuals as more acceptable and successful than the rest of their colleagues. The tapping ceremony in which members were selected was a rigid ritual. On a designated day each spring all the juniors would gather in a clump on the old campus. Representatives of each society, dressed in dark suits, would go out, approach a candidate the society wanted as a member, put a hand on his shoulder, and say, "Go to your room." Then the candidate trotted off to his room and the society representative trotted after him. Almost always the candidate knew which society had tapped him and presumably he would accept when an official invitation was extended.

I stayed in my room. Presently a dark-suited man from Skull and Bones tapped me vigorously on the shoulder as I sat at my desk. He said, "Go to your room." I did not have the wit at the time, or I was too timid, to respond that I was already in my room, but I did inform him that I could not accept election. He said, "Are you sure?" I said, "Yes," and he left.

A year later Gene Rostow faced the same dilemma. Although he, too, was opposed to the principles of Skull and Bones, he thought he should accept if tapped, in order to give honor to being the first Jew inducted into the society. I understood and supported his position. Early in the afternoon of Tap Day, Gene came to see me and said he had changed his mind. He really didn't want to join Bones after all and didn't want to be tapped. He asked if I would be willing to go for a drive in the country with him for two or three hours. I agreed and we went.

Although I personally did not wish to become part of a secret society like Skull and Bones, many men I have known and admired were Bonesmen. My brother, Bill, was one. Yet, adhering to the strict codes of membership, Bill never discussed the society with me and he kept its secrets until his death.

The crash of 1929 and the Great Depression brought a seriousness to life that redirected my views and ambitions. It was a feeling that almost everyone shared in the early 1930s—that the United States was on the verge of a kind of collapse. It is difficult to convey the severity of the Great Depression and the sense of helplessness it induced, but it was the deciding factor in my selection of economics as a postgraduate major. I wanted to understand what was happening, what could have been done to forestall it, what could be done to put an end to it, and how to prevent a recurrence. Very soon these questions became the central topics of economic analysis and investigation.

After graduating from Yale with a B.A. in history in 1932, I enrolled at the London School of Economics, where I received my first exposure to the principles of economics from F. A. Von Hayek, a great advocate of the free market, who had arrived from Vienna the year before. His course was very nearly incomprehensible.

My year of study in Europe affected my outlook considerably by giving me exposure to international affairs. Reading the *London Times*, the *Morning Chronicle*, and the *Economist*, I saw the policies of the U.S. government through British eyes, and that different lens made me more perceptive than I had been about political, as well as economic, developments. When I returned to Yale in 1933 to continue my study of economics, my political affiliation had changed. I went to London as a Republican simply as a matter of inherited political allegiance. Roosevelt's campaign and then his first few months in office had an impact. I felt very strongly that many of the things he did were constructive and necessary and I came to believe in the importance of that type of government intervention in the economy. This belief in the ability of an activist good government to achieve positive ends greatly influenced the rest of my life.

My activism at Yale continued to take the form of writing. My friend Lyman Spitzer was editor of the *Yale News,* and he induced me to write a weekly column on economic affairs under the pen name Ricardo. These articles were much influenced by my London experience and were quite pro–free market. My thinking changed from the enthusiasm about Roosevelt's activism that was common at the time, especially among those my age, to skepticism about a number of the specific arrangements, particularly the National Recovery Administration. I also conducted a sort of "black market" seminar in economics for my friends. These included Spitzer, Walt Rostow (Gene's brother), William Hull, and Max Millikan. We usually met in the evening in my rooms in Davenport College, where I would give what could technically be termed lectures, but with such a small group they were quite informal. As a result of these sessions, Millikan made a career change from physics to economics. I also very nearly converted Spitzer, but in the light of his brilliant career in astrophysics, that would have been a loss to the nation.

It had been easy to slip into this academic world, especially since it offered an opportunity to devise an economic policy for recovery, an effort that was both appealing and compelling. In my second year, I was invited to hold a graduate seminar on economic theory. The following year I initiated an undergraduate economics theory course on model building, the important and useful part of which was macroeconomics. It was the first attempt to teach Keynesian economics at Yale—twenty-five students signed up the first year and sixty the second, and by the third we had to go to two divisions. I taught the course myself for about five years, then enlisted Millikan, and later another man, to share the responsibility. It was so popular that after I left Yale in 1941 it was required for all economics majors. Some of my illustrious former students were Gene and Walt Rostow, McGeorge Bundy, his brothers William and Harvey, and Kingman Brewster.

This recital illustrates the process by which a graduate student could gradually become first a part-time and then a full-time faculty member. It was not difficult, and as staggering unemployment still existed and good business jobs were hard to come by, I settled happily into the academic life of New Haven and used the opportunity to make my mark in the field of economics.

Although I concentrated on economic theory, I knew I needed more contact with the real world, if only so I could better judge the relevance and utility of the macroeconomic model. My chance came through John Davenport, a man about six years older than I who had taken my course and become a good friend. He had gone to New York and joined the editorial staff of *Fortune*; his older brother, Russell, was managing editor. John undoubtedly told Russell that he should get hold of me, and that was how I began to work part-time as a consultant on the magazine. Everything went quite well until I came up with an utterly disastrous idea for a story and Russ accepted it. My proposal was to take a small town—the kind you pass through on the sleeping car of a train—and try to discover what that town lived on. My approach involved distributing questionnaires to the town's consumers as well as to its businesses and institutions and using the answers to estimate its balance of payments with the territory immediately surrounding the town and with the more geographically remote parts of the economy. Oskaloosa, Iowa, about twenty-five miles east of Des Moines and near Ottumwa, was selected as the subject town. The pattern I expected to find, and did find, was that the town ran a heavy negative balance of payments with the world twenty-five to thirty miles out while maintaining a bigger surplus in the area within a thirty-mile radius. In other words, the classic function of a town in the middle of the Iowa corn belt was to be the place where agricultural products were shipped to and where the agricultural population of the surrounding area came in to buy its goods and supplies.

The undertaking was very expensive, requiring the time of at least two people from the magazine in Oskaloosa for two to three months. I still think it was an interesting idea, but it did not attract a wide readership and the magazine lost money. My association with Russ Davenport continued to be cordial, and we almost undertook a similar story about Huron, South Dakota, but in the end both of us thought better of it.

The challenge and stimulation I found in teaching and writing I also sought in my personal life. I frequently spent weekends at Colton Hill with my family, often inviting friends to accompany me. One weekend in 1931 when Max Millikan was visiting, he and I decided to do some climbing on nearby Pinnacle Rock, which was not particularly dangerous and which I had climbed more than once before. This time, though, I was so unwise as to try to explore unroped a place on the cliff about twenty to thirty feet further south. Of course I fell—about seventy feet. I don't remember anything from an hour before the accident to at least two days following, but the account in the *Hartford Courant* helped: "His momentum, as he shot out into space, apparently saved his life, it was reasoned after a study of the scene. Had his body landed a few feet short of where he did strike, he would have fallen on a large boulder. It was nearly 30 feet from the point where he went over the cliff to where his body first struck in a tangle of undergrowth, upon loose earth, and stone. He rolled and tumbled another 40 feet or more down a steep incline before coming to rest."[8]

I suffered a severe laceration of the scalp, tore my collarbone loose from my sternum, and suffered numerous bruises. Although I was grateful that my close call had not ended in tragedy, the chapter was not quite closed. When I recovered (after some weeks in the hospital and several months at home), I returned to Pinnacle Rock and made the same climb alone and unroped and without informing anyone of my intentions. I remember my hands were shaking a great deal, and although I admit it was incredibly foolish, I was glad to have done it and to know that I didn't have to do it again.

Two major turning points in my life occurred during 1939 and 1940. First, in May 1939 I received my Ph.D. in economics from Yale with a dissertation entitled "The Theory of Capital under Static and Dynamic Conditions" (dictated and drafted at a rate of twenty pages per day), and then on July 6, 1940, I married Ann Cornelia Bushnell of New Haven. She was the younger sister of Elizabeth Kubler, the wife of my good friend George Kubler. We moved into an apartment in New Haven that I hated and Ann loved, and I continued my career as an associate professor of economics at Yale.

Toward the end of 1940, the rumblings of war became deeply unsettling. The senseless destruction I had witnessed as a boy after World War I had left its mark and I was, by conviction, opposed to our becoming involved in the European war. Although I did not like the Nazi ideology, I felt it posed no invasionary threat to the United States and it did not seem to me sufficiently upsetting to justify going to war. I thought the country's most important goals should be economic. I became an early and active organizer of the America First Committee at Yale and remained involved until early 1941. Among my friends and colleagues, the individual who was most strongly opposed to my view was Gene Rostow. He and I used to debate the issue fiercely, but it never impaired our friendship.

The climax of the America First Committee movement at Yale took place on October 30, 1940, when Charles Lindbergh was invited to give an address in Woolsey Hall. Details of his visit to Yale, which I helped organize, are dimmed in my memory, but Lindbergh wrote about it in one of his journals. He recalled that, along with Kingman Brewster and a few other campus activists, we had a "pleasant and informal" dinner at Professor Whitney Griswold's. After the meal we proceeded to Woolsey Hall, where "every seat was taken, and people were standing along the walls." The meeting began with a brief address by Brewster, who provided an overview of the committee's goals. Then it was my turn to speak. My remarks were short, meant to serve as an introduction to Lindbergh. When he began to speak he expected "considerable opposition and probably some heckling," but instead he received a warm response. Lindbergh believed "it was by far the most successful and satisfying meeting of this kind in which I have ever taken part."[9]

Soon after this momentous occasion, the righteousness of being an America Firster seemed increasingly difficult to maintain. Writing to R. Douglas Stuart, a committee leader, in January 1941, Griswold explained our growing ambivalence: "I am speaking now entirely for myself, though I imagine that I am also representing Bissell's views as well. Events have marched so rapidly in the last two months that I am frankly confused in my own mind as to exactly what course of policy to believe in."[10]

In the spring of 1941 I received a call from the Department of Commerce asking me to come down to Washington for an academic year to take a position in the department's National Economics Unit. Many economists my age had already done service in Washington, and it was crucial experience for moving ahead in the field. I accepted, and Ann and I left for Washington in October 1941, totally unaware of how the upcoming war would redirect our lives.

CHAPTER TWO

The War Years

I accepted the position in the Department of Commerce with every expectation that I would spend one year in Washington and then return to New Haven to resume my teaching career at Yale. The surprise attack on Pearl Harbor changed everything.

Late in December 1941, Franklin D. Roosevelt and Winston Churchill met in Washington to decide the structures that would run the Anglo-American war effort. Among these were a Combined Raw Materials Board, a Combined Production and Resources Board, a Combined Food Board, and a Combined Shipping Adjustment Board (CSAB). Each board served as a bilateral committee of British and American government officials who worked together to coordinate policies toward the war effort. The British delegation to the CSAB came from the Ministry of War Transport and was headed by Sir Arthur Salter, a widely respected economist who had played an important role in Allied shipping during World War I. His views were very much respected and his opinions carried great weight in the councils of war. The responsibility for marshaling America's merchant shipping resources and serving on the CSAB fell to Admiral Emory Land, the head of the Maritime Commission, which oversaw merchant ship construction, personnel, and shipping allocation. It was not long, however, before Roosevelt realized that Land's abilities, combined with the structure of the Maritime Commission, did not readily lend themselves to the task at hand. On February 7, 1942, Roosevelt issued an executive order establishing the War Shipping Administration (WSA).

Salter had an office in the Department of Commerce and, having heard of me, wanted me to move from the department and become an economist for the CSAB. I told him truthfully that I knew absolutely nothing about shipping. Undeterred, he asked if I had any general feel for the major flows of international trade, and once again I had to admit that I did not. At this point Salter became so exasperated that he told me to just take the position, which I did.

As an American I was concurrently a member of the WSA staff. I quickly surmised that economics had remarkably little relevance to wartime shipping and found a role for myself working for Lewis Douglas, the deputy administrator of the WSA. A new Requirements Division, staffed largely with academicians who had some competence in economics, had been formed to forecast the volume of cargo requiring shipment and the number of ships needed to move it. Many of my early assignments involved working with this group, whose procedures were logical but cumbersome and not easily translated to the language of the commercial world. As a result, it was not particularly effective as a basis for week-by-week decisions. Douglas made little use of it, and one of my duties was to monitor its activities and keep him informed.

The Maritime Commission continued to focus on ship construction. Admiral Howard Vickery served as deputy chairman of the commission and the czar of merchant ship building, but the country's direct involvement in the war required overseeing the operation of the whole American-controlled merchant fleet. Commercial shipping was on lease to the government, which meant the Maritime Commission. It was given broad executive authority and allowed to take virtually any actions consistent with mobilizing the American merchant fleet to achieve war aims. With this authority also came the power to allocate shipping in support of military activities. Since it would have been impossible to establish overnight a worldwide organization, including shipping representatives, these responsibilities were turned over to the War Shipping Administration.

The appointment of Lew Douglas to head the WSA (made largely at the insistence of lend-lease administrator Harry Hopkins) had the advantage of not ruffling too many feathers in the highly competitive shipping business and of providing an executive who had no vested interest in shipping matters. Like Vickery he reported to Land.

Douglas immediately found himself confronting a crisis. He wrote Averell Harriman, the lend-lease representative in England, that he was "deeply concerned with what seems . . . to be the overriding question for the year 1942. All the evidence . . . indicates the meager supply of shipping as the paramount problem.[1] He quickly focused on the core problem, which was that all Allied military plans were constrained by an ability to support the fighting troops logistically. Furthermore, with Hitler's domination of the Continent and the rapid Japanese conquest of the Pacific, it was essential that Great Britain and the United States make the most of their limited resources. The basic function of the War Shipping Administration was to allocate specific vessels to civilian and military programs each month.

The early months of the war were a period of great difficulty for the United States, both on the battlefield and at sea. A secret report prepared for President Roosevelt in April 1942 revealed the seriousness of the problem: "The shipping shortage is affecting the entire conduct of the war. . . . It has dangerously delayed the fulfillment of the Russian Protocol Requirements. . . . Shipments to Britain have been curtailed to the point that further reductions will not only seriously weaken British striking power against the continent, but may even dangerously threaten their morale. Ships are urgently needed for India, China, Australia, and New Zealand."[2] There was much criticism of the WSA's handling of the nation's resources, but under Douglas's leadership everything possible was done to improve the situation.

The initial losses in shipping were horrendous. In March, 788,000 tons of shipping were sunk, and by June the figure had worsened to 936,000 tons. Antisubmarine defense was inadequate, convoys were used on the North Atlantic but not on our own East Coast, and domestic ship production fell far short of offsetting these losses, let alone replacing them.[3] The WSA's highest priority was to provide the shipping required to move munitions and other supporting cargos from the United States to the theaters of operations. As military activity spread, ships were needed to load military cargos bound not only for North Africa and the United Kingdom but for the Indian Ocean and, on a massive scale, the Pacific. My role was to forecast shipping availability, review competing demands, especially for purposes other than direct military support, and negotiate, primarily with the army, ways of containing the requirements to fit the available supply.

By the latter part of 1942, as my forecasting techniques became more sophisticated, I began to have a better-defined job. Once a month I produced a three-month forecast of the availability of dry-cargo shipping from the United States and any other places where cargo important to the war originated. Allowances had to be made for new deliveries of Liberty ships (which were being produced at the rate of twenty to thirty per month) and also for sinkings (which in this early period were about as great as additions of new tonnage).

Allowances also had to be made for congestion in overseas theaters and for a standard turnaround time in U.S. ports. For the most part, ships would arrive in ballast and then would have to be cleaned up, repaired, and made ready for another trip.

My goal was to reach a point where three months in advance I had less than a 5 percent margin of error, something I was able to achieve. Our methods were very primitive since they were totally manual. The work was done by a female staff of four, supervised by a very good woman whom I persuaded to come over with me from the Department of Commerce for the duration of the war. Today's computers would have made this job seem routine, but our database was a card-file system that listed every ship under our control on a separate card.

The functions I was performing earned me the title of planner, and it was in this capacity that I accompanied Douglas and his deputy, Franz Schneider, to the Quebec Conference in 1943. My responsibility was to confirm whether the requirements for dry-cargo shipping in support of possible military operations set forth by the Army Transportation Corps and the navy (which would make the estimates) could be met. The successive monthly patterns that evolved included new and unforeseen requirements. Although our resources were strained, it was my job to find ships to meet these needs. More often than not, the number of ships available for loading would fall short of the forecast because ships would be held up awaiting unloading in the overseas theaters. Especially from my perspective, however, this period saw a rapid and inexorable increase in the scale of the operation and constant improvement in our knowledge of what was going on and of the availability of shipping resources and in our ability to exercise effective control over the allocation of shipping.

At the same time, the president and his advisers were devising new structures for organizing the war effort at home. Roosevelt's practice of creating a new organization if the current one didn't meet with his satisfaction was disruptive. Quite often he would leave both organizations operating simultaneously while he decided whether to shut down one, both, or neither. The result was an atmosphere of intense bureaucratic infighting, and government agencies were soon locked in heated battles that kept many individuals busy devising strategies to promote their own agendas.

When Douglas was brought into the WSA, it was because Roosevelt was dissatisfied with how Land had been managing shipping resources as head of the Maritime Commission. Rather than fire Land and appoint Douglas to head a new organization (which would have provided a clear command structure and dealt with the problem), he left Land in place and appointed Douglas as his deputy, a situation ripe for conflict. I became aware of the rivalry between Douglas and Land soon after I joined the WSA. Douglas had solidified his control of the WSA by spring 1942 and was operating it virtually as an independent agency. His communications with Land were minimal, and, to the best of my recollection, he neither wanted nor accepted policy guidance. Despite the coldness, however, my impression is that relations between the two men were superficially correct. Land must have greatly resented the situation, and it was clear to those of us who were close to Douglas that he had little respect for Land.

Two themes run through most of Lewis Douglas's tenure at the WSA: his efforts to unsnarl and rationalize the utilization of American and Allied shipping and his relations with the military over allocation, loading, and consignment. Regarding the latter, the military's requirements were met, but without its succeeding in enlarging its jurisdiction. What really annoyed the military leadership about allocation decisions was that they were made by a civilian agency that did not report to the Joint Chiefs and was independent of the military. There was a sort of abstract power struggle, and it was galling for the military to have to go through the War Shipping Administration for shipping, just as it had to go through the War Production Board for steel, nickel, copper, and so on.

The biggest turf war that I ever participated in personally was between the War Shipping Administration and General Brehon Somervell. The commander of the army's supply services, which comprised the administrative and logistical units of both the army and the air force, Somervell wanted to take over from the WSA direct control of docks in the United States. The conflict lasted for weeks. I remember that during this period Douglas would sit in his office for days at a big conference table covered with documents he would use as evidence to support his position. The subsequent decision was in his favor but the victory turned out to be short-lived, as the Joint Chiefs raised the issue again six to eight months later.

Around this time Douglas began to become increasingly detached from WSA matters and started to devote more attention to his insurance company in New York. His board of directors might have been placing pressure on him to return to work, but I also think the glamour of the WSA had simply worn off for him. I also became aware of the widening breach between him and Franz Schneider. As a result, Douglas decreased his presence in Washington to about three days a week, became significantly less effective as an executive, less well informed about what was going on, and less accessible to his subordinates. This might have had little adverse effect if Schneider had continued to be seen as a trusted deputy, but it became apparent to some of us that there were serious disagreements between the two men. Schneider's effectiveness, too, was impaired and the need for Douglas's presence was made all the greater. Partly because there were disagreements, Douglas was not willing to delegate major authority to Schneider, and yet he was not in town enough to exert his own authority directly.

The issue that brought these men to bitter contention was U.S. relations with the British. Douglas worked closely not only with Arthur Salter but with Salter's successors and his colleagues in London as well, taking them into his confidence in ways that left him open to accusations by elements of the U.S. army and navy that he was excessively pro-British. I suspect that somewhat in reaction to this attitude, Schneider increasingly came to take a hard line against the British, feeling we were giving too much away to them over allocation issues. He had little use for the Combined Shipping Allocation Board, regarding it (correctly in my view) as a committee. He preferred dealing with the British mission at arm's length and purely in its capacity as a claimant for shipping space.

Douglas had allowed these substantive differences with Schneider to go unresolved for far too long and paid too little attention to the stresses and strains among key people that were impairing the effectiveness of the organization. It is difficult to relate these deficiencies to qualities of character. They seem to me instead to result, first, from the lack of adequate attention early in the game to problems related to the internal structure of the organization and, second, from his decision in late 1943 to spend more time in New York.

By early 1944 Douglas had left the WSA and been replaced by Granville Conway. Schneider, too, had left. Their departures encouraged Somervell to press his case again for military control of docks and other shipping resources. He sought assistance from the Joint Chiefs, who took up his cause as their own. I got involved in this struggle as the WSA representative to a group called the Joint Military Transportation Committee. The committee included representatives of the army and navy as well, and all of us were good friends. One day I was informed that the committee had received a directive from the Joint Chiefs to prepare a paper to be sent to the president arguing their case for transfer of authority of these docks. My assistance was requested in drafting a reply. I reminded the committee that I was totally opposed to the policy I would be recommending and Marcus Stokes, a senior army member, remarked, "Yes, we know you are, but you can write a better paper than anyone else around here." So I drafted a document that was forwarded to the White House a short time later.

Two days later Conway called me to say he had a communication from Harry Hopkins in the White House. The president had received a memorandum from the Joint Chiefs and needed to reply. I was asked to comment on it. I advised Conway that the thing to do was to write back with a recommendation that the request be turned down. Since he supported my position, I wrote a reply and it was duly sent off to Hopkins. Shortly thereafter, Stokes called me and said, "Well, Dick, it's as you predicted. We lost on that issue." I told him I was very glad to hear that was the case. He then asked if by any chance I had had anything to do with the reply to the Joint Chiefs' memorandum. I answered honestly that yes, I had, and we both laughed. What it amounted to was that I had written the paper from the Joint Chiefs to the president and the president's reply to the Joint Chiefs.

Only days before the Yalta Conference I was notified that I would attend as part of the American delegation. We flew by military air transport from Washington and made our first stop in Malta. The German air force had waged a horrendous war against the island, and when we arrived and surveyed the harbor city, it strained the eye to discern a structure that still retained its roof. We were quartered for four days on a troop ship anchored in the harbor, and during our stay we did a lot of preliminary business with our own military, especially the officers in charge of military transport.

After the delay at Malta we continued on to Yalta, leaving at night in a DC-4 and arriving at an airport on the southwest-facing shore of the Crimea on a dull, gray February day. We waited three hours for automobiles to take us to our final destination, and in the course of the hundred-mile four-hour drive Russian militiamen stationed about every hundred feet saluted us as we passed. I was traveling in a car with British and American military officers who were in uniform and who had to salute back; their arms were very tired by the end of the trip. If Stalin meant that to be a show of strength to impress his Western allies, he certainly achieved his effect.

The American delegation was housed in a pretentious Russian palace that had somehow escaped significant damage even though the Germans had only been driven out of the Crimea about a month before. The building had been cleaned up but was devoid of furnishings; the camp cots that everybody used were provided by the United States. Because people were quartered in accordance with rank, there was one great big room where almost all the admirals and generals were accommodated. I held the assimilated rank of brigadier general, and since there was only one other army brigadier, a General Gross, he and I shared a double room. In Washington we were jurisdictional enemies in almost everything, but we knew each other well, he was a perfectly decent guy, and we got along fine. We slept very well compared with the poor senior officers, who had a much different experience. Numbering about thirty in one communal room, they snored and woke one another up all night and generally had a terrible time. General Gross and I definitely got the better deal with our lower rank and private room.

I enjoyed other perquisites on this trip thanks to my friend Charles Bohlen. Having fairly recently served in the American embassy in Moscow, he was familiar with the Russian delegation, including the cooks and waiters of Moscow's Hotel Metropole, who had been brought to Yalta to serve the visitors. I remember having breakfast with him one morning when he decided caviar would do nicely with our meal. With a few well-placed words and a smile, he had it brought to our table, much to my pleasure. The Russian staff could not be faulted for its efficiency. Maids did not hesitate to walk in and out of bathrooms for cleaning, even if the rooms were in use. Many members of the American delegation found themselves surprised and embarrassed in this way. The Russians meant no harm; they just didn't have a high regard for privacy.

Our work at Yalta was to contribute to planning papers that would outline possible or proposed major operations and to calculate for each operation the dry-cargo shipping that would be required for manpower, munitions, aircraft, vehicles, and other logistic tasks. Our calculations provided a way to compare various combinations of strategic operations in terms of their aggregate demands for merchant shipping.

Yalta has captured the imagination of many as a symbol of what might have been. There are those who believe Roosevelt gave away too much to the Russians. What people don't understand is that you can rarely win at the conference table what you have not won on the battlefield. By the time the Big Three met, Eastern Europe was already occupied by Russian troops. Perhaps Roosevelt and Churchill could have driven a harder bargain, but I think they came away with as much as they thought they could get. Those many miles from the airport with Russian soldiers stationed every hundred feet had made an unforgettable impression. Although I had shaken Churchill's hand and seen Roosevelt from a distance, I left Yalta knowing I would never believe Stalin to be an ally.

By the time of the Potsdam Conference in July and August of 1945, active fighting in and around Berlin had been over for several weeks. There were still trenches and small embankments where some of the last-ditch resistance had occurred, but weapons and bodies had all been removed. Perhaps the most depressing reminders of the war were the unending streams of German refugees straggling westward. There were some men but more women and children, thin files of homeless, hopeless people; they were silent, usually walking rather slowly, carrying a few belongings. I remember often wondering where these poor people were going and where they would settle. You could harden your heart and say the Germans brought it on themselves, but you couldn't appreciate the atmosphere of that conference without some reference to their terrible plight. All of us attending the conference—Russians, British, and Americans—lived in the comfortable, virtually undamaged suburbs on the west and southwest edge of Berlin. We were, of course, well fed and provided for. The contrast with the vanquished was striking.

It was at this time that I became aware of frictions between the United States and Russia that indicated the likelihood of what was to evolve as the cold war. The attitude of the Russians toward German recovery provided particular evidence. They advocated removing machinery from Germany and taking it back to Russia as reparations, while the Americans were trying to pour resources into Germany and get it functioning again.

A more amusing example of growing American-Soviet tension occurred when I was nearly arrested by the Russians. My opposite number in the British Ministry of War Transport was Max Nicholson. As was usual at the conferences, we had a certain amount of leisure time. Nicholson was a notable and sophisticated bird-watcher, and one afternoon when we were both free we started off on a walk in the woods. Apparently we strayed over the boundary of the Russian sector, because we found ourselves apprehended by a uniformed Russian militiaman. We were not, of course, able to communicate with him, nor was he with us, and our various identification badges elicited no reaction. We were taken to his local command post, where a Russian officer, though unable to speak English, recognized the badges that authorized our presence at the conference and promptly led us back to the zone border.

My attendance at the Quebec, Yalta, and Potsdam conferences made it clear that the Anglo-American alliance had been running the war and doing so in a good deal of the world. It also gave me an exposure to frictions, especially the U.S. military's feeling that Roosevelt had given away too much to Britain. I think this wartime experience made me unconsciously assess the power of the British much more highly than the facts warranted, but I did not have any sense that Britain was close to collapse, that it would have to pull out of Greece, for instance, or that it would have a major continuing economic crisis after the war.

By late autumn 1945 the War Shipping Administration was winding down. My work there had turned out to be a much more intense, demanding, and important assignment than I had expected. It was dealing with the real world as distinct from economic model building, which was my first love. It provided me with experience in two important respects: first, I had learned about the flow of commodities in international trade (which is what Salter had originally asked me about) and, second, I had gained self-confidence. There was a lot of wheeling and dealing to be done, mainly with our customers—that is, the competing claimants for shipping space. Being involved in negotiation and management and having to make decisions that had visible consequences in the real world could not have given me a more valuable education.

One of the main reasons I found my niche during those years in the War Shipping Administration was that the U.S. shipping industry was staffed, pretty much up to the top levels, with tough, narrowly focused operating people. There weren't many who had experience in political affairs or the making of broad economic decisions or who even had competence as civil servants working in the shipping business. I was soon able to write policy papers, present and argue the administration's case in committees, and generally make myself useful to a boss whose inherited staff was short of these skills. As I acquired more experience (along with some of the factual background that Salter had been seeking), I developed rather unsophisticated but effective forecasting procedures that were of great assistance in the allocation of shipping. I came to be recognized as the government's preeminent analyst of dry-cargo shipping supply and demand. That was a heady experience for me.

A new organization, the United Maritime Authority, took the place of the WSA and of the Combined Shipping Adjustment Board (always largely fictional). The WSA continued as the operating entity, and its officers were chairmen of various committees of the new authority. I became secretary of the Shipping Employment Policy Committee in early 1945. My work continued as before, with two notable changes: there were now quite a number of governments, in addition to the British, that had to be gradually brought into the decision-making process, and the sense of wartime urgency was evaporating despite the parlous state of the world and the desperate need for reconstruction. I was quite ready to make a change, and an opportunity soon presented itself at the Office of War Mobilization and Reconversion (OWMR).

The office had been created by Roosevelt in May 1943 and given wide statutory authority by Congress to deal with the bureaucratic gridlock that Roosevelt's own leadership had helped to perpetuate in Washington during the first years of the war. After V-E Day, its responsibilities expanded to include reconversion. By October 1944, the war had progressed to the point where it was essential to begin planning for the transition from a wartime economy to peacetime expansion; it was at this time that Congress renamed the agency the Office of War Mobilization and Reconversion. The OWMR was responsible for all aspects of the domestic war effort, just as the War Production Board had been earlier. Its small (twenty- or thirty-person) but potentially powerful staff was headed by John Snyder, a good friend of President Truman's who left about a year later to become secretary of the Treasury.

The OWMR had a senior economist, Robert Nathan, who was experienced in public affairs and politically slightly to the left of center. In contrast, Snyder and his deputy were quite conservative. Late in 1944 Nathan decided to leave the government and found his own firm. A friend and neighbor of mine, Hans Klagsbrun, became the deputy director of the OWMR and asked if I would join the staff as chief economist. It was obviously an opportunity to be at the center of things and to watch from an inside seat the definition and resolution of major issues arising in the immediate postwar years. I accepted with little hesitation. As it turned out, Klagsbrun, too, became increasingly dissatisfied with Snyder's policies and resigned about two months later, at which time Snyder promoted me to the position of deputy.

Senior officers of the OWMR were allowed (or required) to be not only intimate observers but participants, especially in the bureaucratic battles of the early postwar period. Price controls were still in effect, although wage controls had been given up and the Office of Economic Stabilization, headed by Chester Bowles, was struggling through the Office of Price Administration to prevent the cost of living from going up too fast. The War Production Board was also still in existence, though many of the really able senior people had left its ranks to return to their increasingly liberated and competitive businesses. The OWMR and the War Production Board were intent on speeding up the recovery of civilian production, an objective with which Bowles had no disagreement. Increasingly, however, Bowles realized that the attempt to keep prices down to their wartime level was an objective in direct conflict with reconversion. A continuing conflict between the agencies was unavoidable.

The confusing system of wartime administration had yet to be dismantled. Along with the beginnings of much freer markets, there was considerable transitional unemployment, and domestic economic affairs focused on inflation, production bottlenecks, and jobs for returning soldiers. The entire country was concerned about the economy because nobody had seen even reasonably full employment for over fifteen years—except in wartime. There was, as a result, a good deal of worry as to whether stagnation or even depression would reappear.

The solution was to adopt a government policy for stimulating the expansion of production. Not only would the supply of consumer goods increase but the slack of unemployment would be taken up. This, however, was not as simple as it sounded. There were individuals on the War Production Board who wanted to stimulate the output of civilian goods; there were also individuals in the Office of Price Administration who were trying to maintain direct control over prices and who rightly feared a cost-push inflation. To complicate matters further, wages had been decontrolled. While that may have been politically necessary, it was a grave mistake as long as prices were still controlled.

Throughout American industry, inconsistent government policies created conflicts. An industry's union would ask its employees for a wage increase. The industry leaders would then come to Washington and request a 10 percent price hike to pay the higher wage rates. The Office of Price Administration would refuse the price increase because it wanted to control inflation. Thereupon the industry leaders would refuse the wage increase, which of course caused the unions to call a strike. Thus, every major wage negotiation threatened in effect to pit the production stimulators, chiefly on the War Production Board, against the price controllers in the Office of Price Administration and the Office of Economic Stabilization. There were not only these conflicting policy objectives of accelerating production and fighting inflation but vigorous personality conflicts as well. World War II may have ended, but the battle of Washington wore on.

I was allied with John Snyder. He and I had a pretty good relationship and I later came to like him very much, but the truth is that he was hampered by a somewhat old-fashioned and unintellectual conservatism. He was suspicious of people like Bob Nathan, for instance, whom he had inherited, and he even suspected some of my philosophic moves. Activism by the government was not something he much believed in. He did not like making decisions, particularly because the OWMR had really become part of the White House and was located in a wing of it. I, on the other hand, was quite willing to make decisions and very often did. I don't think I ever took an important action in national terms without checking with Snyder and other senior people, but that did not prevent him from getting mad at me a number of times.

The steel industry was one battleground in the conflict between accelerating production and controlling prices. When a major steel strike broke out in early 1946, the inconsistencies in these policies came to a head. The steel unions demanded a wage increase but, not surprisingly, the companies refused, protesting that a wage increase could not be given without the government's granting the industry a price increase. While Snyder was willing to agree, Bowles would not. Snyder was eventually victorious, but Truman complicated the situation by splitting the Office of Economic Stabilization off from the OWMR and making Bowles head of the new agency. This, of course, made it appear that Snyder had been rebuffed even though he won the policy fight, and it caused their already cool relationship to deteriorate.[4]

Chester Bowles was an old friend whom I had originally known through my brother, Bill, and I remember his saying, "I can administer what we've had in the war—that's a price freeze. I cannot administer a moving price level." What he meant was that if you had fifty firms in the steel business, each of them with an application for a price increase, the sheer bureaucratic load of administering constantly changing prices was beyond the ability of government to carry. To justify a request for a price increase the seller had to supply evidence of cost increase to support its case, placing a great administrative burden on companies, which had to do a great deal of analysis and auditing of cost increases. In essence this is why any centrally planned economy like the Soviet Union must ultimately fail. It's too much of a burden for a company or an economy to bear in the long run.

When Bowles became director of the Office of Economic Stabilization, he asked me if I would join his staff. I had been working for Snyder only a short time, and the OWMR had an opportunity to make some important contributions that I wanted to be involved in. Moving didn't seem a wise idea.

"Look," Bowles said, "you go on being John Snyder's deputy and come and be one of my deputies as well." I told him I would talk to Snyder about it and see what he thought. Much to my surprise, Snyder said, "I think that might be a pretty good idea. Maybe you can drum some sense into his skull."

So I was soon working part-time as Snyder's deputy and part-time as Bowles's, which made me a kind of personal interlocking directorate. I would come to Snyder and say, "This is what Bowles wants." He would boil over and say, "Goddamn it, go back and see if you can't get him to do something more sensible." Then I'd approach Bowles and he'd say, "Well, of course, I knew John wouldn't go for that. Can't you possibly bring him around?" It was not exactly a comfortable position, but for someone who wanted to learn something about how government and big organizations operate, there was no better education.

Unfortunately, although I helped reduce the conflicts between Bowles and Snyder, they continued to be very much at odds with each other—so much so that Truman finally called all of us in to the White House to resolve the matter. We gathered in the Cabinet Room and the president told Bowles and Snyder that he wanted them to start working together to promote a healthy and rapid reconversion. There wasn't a lot of discussion. There weren't any arguments. Truman made the statement that he wanted all this internecine squabbling to cease. Then, in what I considered an unexpected dramatic gesture, he went around the whole group and shook everyone's hand.

My education in Washington bureaucracy was one aspect of the war years. Those years also saw changes in my personal life. In July 1941 my father died, and soon after, my mother moved to Washington to direct the volunteer operations of the Red Cross. Ann and I had begun our family with Richard Mervin III, born in 1942, and Ann Harriet had followed in 1944. We lived in a rented house on Q Street in Georgetown (we never bought a house in all the years I worked in Washington because I expected to return eventually to teaching). The rented house was finished shortly before Pearl Harbor, and we were its first tenants. It was cramped but nice, considering what was available. Even with two children, we were happy to have it and stayed there all through the war.

Ann has always claimed that I was "incredible," compared with our friends' husbands, in sharing child care with her during the war. That's an exaggeration, but I did try to be helpful when I could. She appreciated the fact that I could deal more effectively with the unpleasantries of infants, and so I was assigned that task quite often. (Ann claims to have been blessed with an acute sense of smell, inherited from her mother—I've always considered it a curse.) We both walked the floor many nights with sick children. At one point, an epidemic of

German measles had been going around Washington and our children were infected. I attended a meeting with President Truman in his office and was appalled to find the next day that I was covered with a rash from head to foot. I said, "I'm going to the office." Ann said, "Oh no you're not," and summoned the doctor, who confined me to the house for several days. We didn't have the courage to notify the White House that the president might also have been exposed, but Ann and I watched the newspapers quite carefully, hoping not to read a headline that the president had been stricken. It turned out he escaped. I reported to my office that I was "indisposed" and would not be into work for a couple of days. It was somewhat embarrassing to have to admit to contracting measles at my age.

We had many close friends in Washington during our years there: Stewart and Tish Alsop, Joe Alsop, Frank and Polly Wisner, the Brackley Shaws, the Andrew Kecks, Charlie and Freddie Child, Paul and Julia Child (who were always in and out of town), the Charles Seymours, Walt and Elspeth Rostow, Max and Jean Millikan, Sherman and Bessie Kent. Ann and I came to enjoy Washington very much, but in 1946 I decided that if I was to return to an academic career, it would have to be that year. I took a three- or four-week vacation that summer, and when I returned it was obvious that my intended departure from OWMR was generally known and I could no longer be effective. Accordingly, I resigned in September and moved to Cambridge and to MIT (where I was on leave as professor of economics), having threatened to do so for at least two years. A year later, however, another opportunity related to postwar recovery was offered to me. The challenge and stimulation I knew I would experience convinced me to postpone academia and accept. What followed were perhaps the most worthwhile years of my career.

CHAPTER THREE

The Marshall Plan

It is tempting to turn a commentary on the Marshall Plan into a historical note on the success of the most dramatic and, for its duration, the largest program of foreign aid in our nation's history. Nevertheless, to describe the Marshall Plan as a foreign-aid program, even a bold one, would be a misleading oversimplification. The word *recovery* in its official name, the European Recovery Program, describes its purpose correctly. Its accomplishment within the originally established time limit of four years was to restore Europe to its prewar position as a wealthy and highly developed economic area. That this could be done so quickly was due primarily to the fact, not always properly emphasized, that Western Europe, though in political and economic crisis after the end of the war, still possessed the infrastructure of a modern industrial economy in the form of established political and economic institutions with trained personnel and access to substantial resources of managerial and technical competence. The skills, habits, motivations, customs, and procedures required for the operation of a modern economy were available. By as early as 1947 much of the physical damage of the war had been made good (except in Germany). In short, most of the elements—human, organizational, and physical—of a productive economy were present.

The reason that Europe was nevertheless in crisis was the disorganization of its economic life and the breakdown of the market mechanism. The most pervasive form these took was the loss of value of most Western European currencies. Inflation was endemic and government budgets were far from being under control. Widespread price controls typically held prices down to levels at which demand far exceeded supply, so official or random rationing was in effect. Mistrust of both the internal and external values of currencies made individuals reluctant to hold them; there was and could be little incentive to save except by the hoarding of goods. Incentives to work were also undermined in a situation in which real income was largely determined by rations and there were few goods to be bought with increased money income. Trade within Europe was tightly regulated by exchange controls and quotas. In the absence of convertibility of European currencies into one another, let alone into dollars, there was inexorable pressure on governments to achieve bilateral balancing of trade, efforts that were profoundly disrupting to the formerly interdependent economies of the area. Thus, what had to be accomplished was not so much the physical rebuilding of Europe (what the Marshall Plan is remembered for in the popular mind) as the restoration of functioning market economies within and among the participating countries. This was the key purpose and achievement of the Marshall Plan.

Of greater contemporary relevance than the economic processes is the experience gained in the relationship between the provider and the recipient of aid, in the organization of a collaborative international program of economic development, and generally in the way governments can work together in a field in which delicate questions of sovereignty are always present. But even in these areas, the relevance of the Marshall Plan is limited. It cannot be overemphasized that Europe, even when prostrated, possessed the resource that is lacking in underdeveloped nations and that requires the longest time to develop: skilled and motivated people existing in a framework of established institutions.

The Marshall Plan as an act of United States foreign policy was intended to accomplish much more than a series of measurable increases in European production and consumption. It was one of the major programs undertaken to build a world order within which the United States and other friendly nations could live in security, prosper, and evolve in peace. A specific expectation was that the revival of the economy of Western Europe would stabilize the societies, strengthen the democratic institutions, and thereby restore the effectiveness of a group of increasingly strong partners who would share the responsibilities and benefits of that world order.

The Marshall Plan was only one of the major efforts through which U.S. policy objectives were pursued, and it cannot be discussed in isolation from both political and military activities. The signing of the North Atlantic Treaty Organization pact in 1949 followed close behind initiation of the Marshall Plan, and there is little doubt that the emergence of NATO had a direct influence on the procedures and organizational apparatus of the Marshall Plan. Moreover, the course of European economic recovery was modified by the outbreak of the Korean War, whose inflationary impact on commodity prices involved a deterioration in Europe's terms of trade. By the end of 1951, the rearmament of the NATO nations began to have a significant economic effect. Thereafter, the economic problems of Europe involved not so much reviving the economy as financing a growing military establishment while keeping the international accounts in balance.

After 1950 concern with the Korean War and with the rearmament of the West European countries gave added importance to military plans and arrangements as elements of a world order. To begin with, the expanded NATO organization was explicitly an Atlantic instrumentality, as the Marshall Plan instrumentality—the Organization for European Economic Cooperation—was not. This new focal point of collaborative international efforts thus symbolized an apparently deepening unity in the Atlantic community. It also symbolized the sharpening of the division between the Atlantic and Communist worlds provoked by the Korean War. In practical terms, the new collaborative enterprise made the military representatives of the member countries close working colleagues, as the Marshall Plan had made the financial and economic officials of the several governments.

The initial success of NATO presumably encouraged the United States to promote additional regional military alliances. CENTO was established as a formalization and expansion of the Baghdad Pact; partly in response to the French defeat in Indochina, SEATO was created. These two international organizations, together with the OAS and NATO, included virtually all the nations of the non-Communist world other than the sophisticated European neutrals (Switzerland, Austria, Sweden), Japan (disarmed by treaty), and the newly independent neutralist nations of Asia and Africa (notably India, Indonesia, and Egypt). Thus, as the structure of alliances was extended, there was a reason to look forward to a restored world order that would be centered in Washington but more broadly based on and dominated by the partnership between the United States, Canada, and the nations of Western Europe.

By the midfifties, when this vision seemed almost within our grasp, European recovery was already well advanced. It was generally recognized that were it not for the rapidly growing social cohesiveness, wealth, and military strength of this area, a rather different kind of world would have been in prospect. This grand design, though describable mainly in military and political terms, was in effect an elaboration of the purpose with which the Marshall Plan had been launched: to bring into being a revived and vigorous Western Europe that could play an essential role in making the world a tolerable environment for all the Western powers.

Credit must also be given to the people involved in the Marshall Plan. I have always been a great admirer of Harry Truman's, primarily for his practice of selecting senior subordinates, delegating to them, and backing them up to the hilt. His most important selections turned out to have been superb. I would find it difficult to name four men as able, distinguished, and well-suited to the tasks he gave them as George Marshall, Dean Acheson, Averell Harriman, and Robert Lovett.

In 1947 the European situation looked bleak, with industrial production levels averaging 10 to 15 percent below those of 1938. Germany, however, represented the gravest concern, as its industrial production was only 35 percent of its prewar level. The problem was exacerbated by an increase in population of over 15 million people despite the ravages of war and the hard winter of 1946–47. Expected fuel shortages and depleted food stocks due to widespread crop failures made the danger of famine very real.[1]

The task was not to reopen rail lines, rebuild docks, or get power stations working at capacity but to provide coal and oil to operate the railroads, fuel steamships, and run power stations and have enough raw materials to permit factories to produce goods. Purchasing these materials and food required money. In short, it was clear by 1947 that the greatest single impediment to the rapid expansion of production in postwar Western Europe was a desperate shortage of working capital. Injecting billions of dollars into Europe through the Marshall Plan would make it possible for the Europeans to import on a large scale and to rebuild their working capital in real terms of inventories of raw materials, semifinished goods, and everything else necessary for smooth production.

In June 1947 Secretary of State George Marshall gave a commencement address at Harvard that outlined the concepts and goals that not only defined what became the Marshall Plan but provided the values that imbued the agencies and personnel called to serve the cause of European reconstruction. Those values and beliefs were the means that would enable Europe to deal with its crisis through a multilateral process that would encourage integration, promote free trade, and result in stability. Although the ideas contained in this speech were anticipated by an address Dean Acheson delivered several weeks earlier, they nevertheless became a defining moment in postwar foreign policy.[2]

Marshall's speech reveals the extent to which the plan began as a concept for the reconstruction of Europe; America's policy, Marshall said, "is directed not against any country or doctrine, but against hunger, poverty, desperation, and chaos. Its purpose should be the revival of a working economy in the world so as to permit the emergence of political and social conditions in which free institutions can exist." The fact that the United States's $3.75 billion loan to Great Britain to support the convertibility of the pound was depleted in no more than a few weeks had taught Marshall that "any assistance that this government must render should provide a cure rather than a mere palliative." While Marshall felt strongly that the United States must take dramatic steps to stabilize Europe's declining economic and political situation, he also believed that any solution imposed on Europe by Washington would invite failure. He told his audience at Harvard that "it would be neither fitting nor efficacious for the government to undertake to draw up unilaterally a program designed to place Europe on its feet economically. This is the business of the Europeans." He did not mean European statesmen dealing unilaterally with the United States to solve the problems of individual nation-states but the statesmen of a region working together to solve through cooperative effort a region's difficulties.[3]

Fortunately, Marshall commanded vast respect. His deputy Bob Lovett, whose temperament and experience were assets in coping with a rapidly intensifying economic crisis, and his assistant Paul Nitze helped him generate the concept of a major foreign-aid program and write the Harvard speech. By early summer 1947 the British took the initiative, organizing a meeting of what later came to be called the participating countries and bringing a delegation, headed by Oliver Franks, to Washington to present their proposals for a recovery program. In the period of debate and discussion that followed, the State Department, and particularly Lovett and Nitze, took the lead on the U.S. side.

At this point Arthur Vandenberg, chairman of the Senate Foreign Relations Committee and a very eminent Republican, urged that a small advisory committee of distinguished Americans outside of the government be formed to review the Europeans' proposal formally and make recommendations to the government. The uncontested prestige of such a group would lend crucial weight to the views brought before Congress, which was unsympathetic to the notion of a large, costly new program for the benefit of foreigners. Truman named his secretary of commerce, Averell Harriman, to head this review committee, called the President's Committee on Foreign Aid. Harriman was the only member who held a position in the executive branch; the rest of the participants were businessmen, labor leaders, academicians, and other representative citizens with experience and reputations. The President's Committee on Foreign Aid (or the Harriman Committee, as it would be more popularly known) was charged with a number of responsibilities, including evaluation of any problems that might develop in the European situation and review of methods of analysis and potential programs.[4]

Marshall agreed with the decision and felt, as did Lovett (and, I assume, Harriman), that the program needed to be conducted as an independent organization that would be trusted by Congress and the public. Government "bureaucracy" was viewed with suspicion at the time, and rightly or wrongly, the State Department was in especially low repute with Congress. The backers of the Marshall Plan wanted a visible and symbolic independence. They did not want anyone from the State Department put in charge of it, lest it be said that the plan was under the department's control.

My involvement on the Harriman Committee began with a telephone call from Harriman in late July 1947 asking me to serve as its executive secretary. I had known Harriman during my War Shipping Administration days, when he was head of all war agency and economic activities at the London embassy, and he was eager to have me serve. The job required that I initiate, develop, and direct the reporting and editorial work that would go into the committee's final report to the president.

I did not arrive in Washington until the beginning of September because of a prior commitment to a cruise on the Maine coast, but once on the scene I made it my first priority to put together a small staff, mostly of men whom I had worked with in the past and whose competence and loyalty were proven. We immediately found ourselves engulfed in committee meetings and report writing. We met with representatives of the European contingent and spent a certain amount of time making our own estimates (cruder than theirs) of how much money the program would need. I started in September, and our report was due out in late November, which didn't allow much time. Senator Vandenberg was insistent that there be such a report, and he had already stated publicly that he would not proceed with any hearings on enabling legislation until it was available. We worked, therefore, under considerable pressure, producing, however, a document that became one of the major reports in support of the plan.

Harriman was an effective chairman and an authoritative figure. He avoided instructing the members of the committee on where they were headed or what their views should be. This was fortunate, since a number of the members were sufficiently strong-minded to prevent Harriman from dictating a set of positions had he chosen to do so. He did conduct a certain amount of conversation with individual members, however, especially those whose views he was somewhat worried about.

Many expected the committee's work to serve as an endorsement for policy decisions that had already been made, but the committee performed a very real function. Although its members were a rather conservative group of men representing major economic interests of the country, they spent a number of months debating and discussing the concept of a costly interventionist foreign policy. The sessions were quite lively. Certain individuals were unsympathetic to one or another of the conclusions in the report, but the momentum was sufficient that nobody felt strongly enough to dissent from any part of the finished product. The labor members had a few differences, but not very many. Although George Meany, secretary-treasurer of the American Federation of Labor, could be cantankerous, he never attended meetings and therefore did not contribute to the cacophony. W. Randolph Burgess, vice chairman of National City Bank, was one of the more troublesome members; he was unhappy about the way in which monetary policy and arrangements were being handled in discussions. Red Deupree, president of Proctor & Gamble, was very conservative and plainly dissatisfied with the committee's direction. We expected him to abstain when the report was completed. Robert Collyer, president of B. F. Goodrich, strongly supported the committee's conclusions and the notion of foreign aid, as did Robert Koenig, president of Ayrshire Collieries Company. One of the most active and hard-working members was Robert La Follette, a converted isolationist who was realistic, accomplished at debate, and highly effective.

Another important committee member was Paul Hoffman, president of the Studebaker Corporation and a Republican. I had known Hoffman at Yale, where I had served on several panels of the Committee for Economic Development, in which he was active. We had some dealings early in the war, but our contact was renewed soon after the war ended. Hoffman was one of the committee members who wanted me as executive secretary and he exerted the most influence on the report as a written document. During one of the final committee meetings he made a moving statement that elicited spontaneous applause from the other members. We got him to dictate that statement and it was used almost word for word as part of the opening remarks of the report.

Overall, the committee members made constructive contributions in the best spirit of civic-mindedness. Their extremely enlightened attitudes toward public policy generally resulted from their almost all having had experience in governmental policy during the war. That experience, coupled with a sense of duty and statesmanship, made it possible to come up with a serious report in a short time. Furthermore, the wartime tradition of creating a special agency to do a particular job and disbanding it on completion appealed to them. It would have been impossible to bring together any group like the Harriman Committee if not for the war. Not only the conclusions reached but the whole tenor of the discussion would have been far different.

Although the committee had been formed in July, it began its work in earnest in late August and held its last meeting in early November. The final report was written as a staff project, with the assistance of, among others, my two old friends from Yale Max Millikan and Fritz Liebert. Bob La Follette was a leading contributor in the final drafting process. Working through the night in our offices in the Department of Commerce, we finished writing at 4:00 a.m. on November 7, sent a copy to the White House, and released the report to the press at 10:00 a.m. The date had been fixed in accordance with Vandenberg's wish to have the report ready in time for Congress's consideration of the Marshall Plan. We could only hope that the report would be well received, especially since the names of the entire committee were appended. Fortunately, the report, entitled *European Recovery and American Aid*, received magnificent press. There was an outburst of news items across the land the next morning, almost all of them supporting the report's affirmative conclusion that the United States could not afford the political and other consequences of failing to back an effective economic program. This positive outcome was extremely important; without it, a couple of committee members might have spoken out to reveal that they had not seen the report in advance, had had no opportunity to voice their dissent, and therefore could not endorse it. As things evolved, the report received such a favorable reception around the country that no member of the committee stood up to take exception to it. The fact that La Follette was the only committee member who reviewed the document before its release was an unavoidable consequence of the tight deadline.

In some ways the excellent press overshadowed much of the fine preparatory work that the State Department had done. The strain that later developed between the department and the Economic Cooperation Administration may have had its roots during this period. Paul Nitze, who was working for the State Department, recalls: "There was a certain amount of tension between me and the whole Harriman effort. I didn't think they had a clue as to what was necessary and how it was going on. . . . We had done a hell of a lot more work than anybody working for Harriman, but they were getting a hell of a lot more publicity."[5]

While that is true, it is important to remember that a key objective of the process was to prepare the American people for a foreign-aid program on a scale never before attempted in American history. The report's impact was crucial. It was part of an orchestrated effort to develop bipartisan backing for the European Recovery Program, and as it turned out, the report proved quite persuasive with moderate Republicans in Congress.

Vandenberg was able to begin the congressional hearings as soon as the report was published. The foundation of a program and a framework of analysis had been provided by the Harriman Committee, but the State Department was still embroiled in debate over organizational issues, financing, and ways to gain rapid congressional approval and enactment. Marshall's lieutenants in the department considered the desirability of including requests for funds for military aid to Greece and Turkey in one omnibus bill. John Hickerson, director of the Office of European Affairs, strongly argued against this plan in a well-balanced memorandum to Undersecretary Lovett. He explained that connecting the European Recovery Program to military aid would "inevitably link ERP to potential military action against the Soviet Union or its agents. This would change the whole emphasis of ERP from a program to promote European recovery positively to a program of defense against Soviet aggression."[6] Although the ERP was ostensibly designed as a plan for peace, it was well understood by U.S. officials that a strengthened Western Europe would better serve the United States not only as a trading partner but also as a military ally.

Marshall met with the House Committee on Foreign Affairs and described the kind of agency he envisioned. When questioned by Congressman James Richards as to why existing government agencies were incapable of promoting European recovery themselves, Marshall explained that the rapidly deteriorating situation in Europe required a very different kind of agency, one with highly concentrated authority and the ability to adopt new tactics swiftly. The agency Marshall described would become the Economic Cooperation Administration (ECA).[7]

Vandenberg took Marshall's concept of how the ECA would work one step further. Marshall supported an administration bill in which the ECA administrator would act under the "direction and control" of the secretary of state.

With Vandenberg's guidance, the ECA administrator was elevated to cabinet status, a change that prevented the secretary of state from controlling the ECA and required that the president settle any dispute between the secretary and the ECA administrator. This alteration would prove to be an important factor in the success of the ECA, especially when progress toward European economic integration stalled in 1949 and Paul Hoffman came to realize the extent in which he could act independently of the State Department.[8] The organizational framework also ensured that the ECA administrator's special representative in Paris was given ambassadorial rank and prerogative, and the ECA mission chiefs in each country communicated with and reported directly to the administrator with only a minimum requirement of coordination with the assigned U.S. ambassador.

This setup could not help but create tension between an independent ECA and a cautious State Department, which was increasingly defensive about perceived infringements of its foreign-policy prerogatives. The natural frictions were reinforced by what, in my view, was the greater stature of the ECA mission chiefs compared with that of their ambassadorial counterparts. As is apt to be true in the early days of an exciting new undertaking, it was possible to recruit outstanding people; the ECA attracted Barry Bingham, David Zellerbach, Thomas Finletter, and David Bruce. Their evident competence and prestige and the fact that they represented an independent agency all served to enhance their authority.

The Economic Cooperation Act of 1948 passed both houses of Congress and became law of April 3, 1948. It noted that assistance was stipulated on "the multilateral pledges of participating countries to use all their efforts to accomplish a joint recovery program based on self-help and mutual cooperation." It also required that to receive assistance each participating country conclude a bilateral agreement with the United States and become part of the Organization for European Economic Cooperation (OEEC).[9]

Just days after its passage, Undersecretary of State Lovett outlined some thoughts on the appropriate organizational structure for implementing the goals of the ECA. These ideas were the product of discussions that included Paul Nitze and the newly appointed ECA administrator, Paul Hoffman. Lovett observed that, although the basic responsibility for designing and allocating U.S. aid was with the ECA administrator in Washington, a decentralized organization structure would best serve the ECA's objectives; it would have the benefit not only of encouraging the administrator to rely on his representatives abroad but also of avoiding a concentration of ECA operations in Washington. Lovett feared that if there were such a concentration the participating European countries would send their high-caliber officials to Washington to deal bilaterally with Hoffman instead of working multilaterally through the OEEC in Europe.[10] Although the structure that Lovett advocated may have helped promote the OEEC as an organization and bolster European integration, it also created an entity with inherent conflicts. One example was its dual headquarters in Washington and Paris. Fortunately, all the problems that arose early in the Marshall Plan proved short-lived.

As the U.S. government created the organizational structure to promote its objective of strengthening Western Europe through political and economic integration, the leaders of the American-led effort realized that they had only a limited chance to change Europe from a region dominated by nation-states to one characterized by supranational cooperation. The economic position of the United States in relation to Europe presented what Lovett termed "an opportunity for achieving objectives which may not occur again."[11]

My own involvement in the ECA came about unexpectedly. Two days after legislative authorization of the Marshall Plan, I received a call from Hoffman summoning me to Washington. Because I was teaching at MIT, I told him I could be there at the end of the week. He insisted that I take the next train out of Boston. When I replied that it would be impossible for me to obtain a hotel room at such short notice, he said there was an extra bed in his room and I could sleep there. Sensing his urgency, I went home, packed enough essentials for a few days' stay, and boarded a train two hours later. I arrived in Washington on a Wednesday, about midnight, and went directly to Hoffman's room. He greeted me with the unwelcome news that the first business meeting of the ECA would be in his room at 7:00 a.m. and would include most of the staff, which numbered less than ten people. Everything went according to plan over the next few days except that Hoffman would not hear of my returning home, even though I had commitments at MIT and my assistance to him was meant to be brief. Because I had had much more recent contact with the workings of government than the other early arrivals had, he depended on me to run the shop while he was busy recruiting people.

It was a helter-skelter beginning. On Friday morning, my second full day in office, Nitze came over with a plea from the State Department that we get the disbursements of funds moving. Several of the participating countries were about to run out of dollar exchange and were going to have to stop signing purchasing contracts for various essential imports. Having assembled about fifty or sixty procurement authorizations for specific import transactions by the participating countries, he turned them over to me. In the chaos that prevailed in the fledgling ECA, no responsibility had yet been delegated for taking this kind of serious action. Hoffman himself was too desperately busy to turn his attention to the matter.

I had the pile of procurement authorizations brought into my office by midday and gave them to my able assistant, Samuel Van Hyning, for review and elimination of any that seemed of doubtful validity, that were politically sensitive (such as for luxury imports), or that might have an adverse effect on public relations. Van Hyning had worked with me in the War Shipping Administration and I had borrowed his services from some other agency the day before. He returned that afternoon, having weeded out close to twenty problematic requests.

After deciding on the merit of the remaining vouchers, I signed off on them and thereby obligated the first $35 million of Marshall Plan funds to be transferred before the close of that day. They moved through the system without any complications. The following day, Saturday, another batch of requests were received and dealt with in exactly the same fashion. This, indeed, became the accepted procedure. I believe that about 80 percent of the first appropriation, which was in the neighborhood of a few billion dollars, was released over my signature. Thereafter, the volume became so burdensome that signatures were handled by an immediate subordinate of mine, but I still retained effective control over spending transactions.

It became apparent after a couple of weeks, especially with Hoffman's insistence, that I would stay with the ECA for at least a year. Certain that this was going to be a challenging, exciting, and worthwhile project, I requested another leave of absence from MIT, moved my family back to Washington, and plunged into what would become the project of which I am most proud. I had packed for a five-day assignment, but in the event, I never returned to live in Cambridge.

Hoffman's preoccupation during the first weeks of the ECA was with establishing and staffing the organizational structure, especially in Europe. As things settled down, however, he became active in policy making. He was the sort of executive who expects his staff to define issues and propose positions so that he can then consider, discuss, and examine them in detail before arriving at decisions. Only infrequently did he receive opposing views from different parts of his staff. By the time I had the title of assistant deputy administrator, I was developing most of the substantive issues and reconciling differences at lower levels.

Although he had an extremely busy schedule, he was an accessible manager and easy to work with. I liked his style and learned a good deal about management from him. Because we were basically in agreement on the mission of the ECA, he gave me a lot of latitude and was willing to delegate a large degree of authority to me. He was a good assessor of people, which in some ways is the ultimate skill in management; he was also receptive to ideas. He did not know enough about economics to be the originator of policies, but he could recognize clear thinking in other people's initiatives and was able to take an initiative, explain it, publicize it, gain support for it, and back it up. For that reason I respected him tremendously.

There were four principal divisions under my jurisdiction. These would bear the primary responsibility for analyzing Europe's economic situation and creating appropriate programs to restore its economic health for the next four years. The Industry Division and the Food and Agriculture Division examined specific commodity requirements and production problems and assessed the availability of supplies. They were largely responsible for the formulation of our policy on pricing and similar matters, and in a certain sense they were operating divisions because they originated the financial documents and procurement authorizations we used. The third division was concerned with fiscal and trade matters, especially relating to our policy on exchange rates, the financial policy of the European governments, and the management of local currency counterpart funds. The fourth, the Program Coordination Division, was divided up by country and staffed by specialists who dealt with the general economic problems of each one.

My staff calculated estimates of annual foreign aid based on our projection of the current account balance of payments for the various countries. What this really entailed was an income and expenditure statement that showed each country's probable expenditures of foreign exchange for imports, as well as its earnings of foreign exchange from exports. The difference between the two is either a surplus (if a country exports more than it imports) or a deficit (if a country imports more than it exports). Many of the countries participating in the Marshall Plan had deficits. Our projection of a country's deficit was the basis on which we calculated the amount of aid that country would require.[12] During this period, many deficit nations were running out of foreign exchange.

U.S. aid would allow them to import the food and essential materials their economies needed.

After evaluating the probable outlays of dollars and other foreign exchange by these countries, we would produce an appraisal based on recent experience of their earnings of foreign exchange. On the whole, the latter was a more difficult function to perform than the former. It involved a forecast of their exports, especially exports to hard-currency areas. Early on it became clear that Europe could only become self-supporting by successfully expanding its exports since its imports, of which raw industrial materials and foodstuffs were the predominant portion, were not a highly elastic number. Therefore an important part of European recovery would depend on demand in the United States and other non-European countries.

At the beginning of the Marshall Plan the quality of government-collected economic data and of national-accounts analysis and concepts was appalling, especially on the Continent. The success of the program, predicated as it was on economic data in which everyone had a reasonable level of confidence, was clearly jeopardized. I remember, for instance, that the Frenchman who was responsible for his country's accounts called together a sizable group of statisticians and retired with them over a weekend to make up, retroactively, national accounts going back four or five years. A gentleman named Stone for the British (who was very up to date on national-accounts concepts) and someone from the French Ministry of Finance served on an OEEC-established panel funded by the ECA to establish standards for national accounts and encourage participating members to bring theirs into conformity with those standards. The hope was to obtain from different countries comparable figures that could be added together to produce a meaningful result.

Although the basic case of the Harriman report had been presented to Congress in national-accounts terminology and proved to be pretty accurate, these numbers were largely pulled out of the air because they were not available in actual terms from the European countries. One of the unstated benefits of the Marshall Plan was that the formulation and maintenance of national accounts during those three or four years were enormously advanced. The OEEC contributed a great deal by improving the consistency and quality of economic statistics.

Once the estimates were calculated, it was possible to determine the cost of the program and the amount to be requested from Congress. In an innovative move that would make the funds perform double duty, it was proposed that each recipient country contribute to the foreign-aid effort by depositing an amount equal to the U.S. contribution in its central bank. A bilateral agreement between the country and the United States allowed these funds to be used jointly. The bulk of the currency funds (95 percent) remained the legal property of the country's government while 5 percent of the funds became, upon deposit, the property of the United States government. These monies could be used to cover administrative costs of the ERP program in the participating country, to acquire strategic materials required by the Pentagon, or even to pay for covert operations.

Such a structure ensured that goods imported into the European countries and financed with Marshall Plan aid were not provided freely as gifts to the participating countries. This was important because Congress would never have approved the program without an assurance that taxpayer dollars would be well spent. Purchases using counterpart funds could only begin when a program based on mutually agreed-on goals had been developed; these purchases were generally imported through ordinary commercial channels and sold at retail prices that were determined in the usual fashion. Proceeds from the sale of these goods were then available to replenish a nation's counterpart-fund account.

As Marshall Plan funds were received by participating countries, they found their way into the hands of European importers (whether state organizations, state-owned industries, or private traders) in exchange for payments of the local currency. A French would-be importer who wanted dollars had to pay for the dollars in francs. The result, obviously, was an accumulation of francs (or other European currencies) in central banks or governments that was of the same magnitude as the inflow of Marshall Plan dollars on a grant or loan basis. This flow of local currency into European central banks and governments was designated as counterpart funds—the counterpart of the dollar funds that had been provided. From the very beginning certain restrictions and procedures were imposed that determined the way in which those counterpart funds of European currencies could be used by their own governments.

I was the principal spokesman before Congress for the ECA. Lincoln Gordon, who worked with Harriman in Paris, remembers my saying frequently that the year was divided into two more or less equal parts—the part when Congress was in session and the part when we could think.[13] Testifying before the House Appropriations Committee was one of the toughest assignments I faced during my first year at the ECA. The hearings, which began in early 1949, were held morning and afternoon for three-weeks. Paul Hoffman would appear occasionally to respond to special inquiries.[14] I would talk at length, perhaps six hours of continuous presentation; it was the hardest work I have ever done. The transcript produced a book many inches thick.

When I resigned from the government in 1952, Vaughan Gary, a Virginia Congressman and anything but an effusive man, sent me a fulsome letter, of which I am very proud, testifying to my success. He wrote: "I wish to take this opportunity to say to you that your presentation each year of the ECA program was the clearest, most illuminating, and most comprehensive of any witness that has testified before any of my committees during my entire stay in Washington."[15]

I was always accompanied to the hearings by Dennis Fitzgerald of the Food and Agriculture Division, Jim McCullough of Fiscal and Trade Policy, and a representative of the Industry Division; I would usually, however, field most questions myself. The chairman of the subcommittee was John Tabor, a fairly elderly gentleman, deeply conservative, honest, honorable, and quite intelligent. Tabor was a difficult opponent. He didn't like foreign aid and he didn't like the Marshall Plan. When the hearings began, he stated frankly that he was going to vote against it, and he kept his word. His opening statements went something like this: "Now, Mr. Bissell, we'll start with Austria because it begins with an *A*, and in Austria we will start with bread grains because that is the first commodity you list in your tables that they are going to need. We'll go over all the commodities for Austria and then we'll move to Belgium because it's the next alphabetically, and you'll do the same for Belgium. And of course, we'll want you to give a statement at some point on each country about their monetary policy, trade policy, fiscal policy."

There were roughly twenty-six commodity categories, and we were expected to explain why each of the seventeen participating countries needed imports of the quantities estimated. I remember that of the Netherlands Tabor noted that we had them importing large amounts of oilseed and at the same time exporting a great deal of butter—could I explain how that could be? Fortunately, Dennis Fitzgerald handled the question. He had known Tabor from the days of Hoover's famine-relief mission in Europe after World War I, and Tabor had a thorough respect for him. Fitzgerald explained that historically the Netherlands had always imported large amounts of oilseed. Their main domestic consumption was margarine rather than butter, and that's what they needed the oilseed for. They used butter as an export to earn foreign exchange. Tabor replied in effect, "Well, all right."

I once asked Tyler Wood, our congressional liaison officer, who knew all the congressional figures quite well, why we had to go through this kind of ordeal, especially since Tabor was going to vote against the plan anyway. Wood gave me the perfect answer. He said, "I know they're going to vote against it. I know there is nothing you can say or do to persuade them otherwise, but there is all the difference in the world between casting their individual votes against us and fighting us. John Tabor does not fight us, and the reason he doesn't is that we're honest."

I remember a low-key dinner Paul Hoffman hosted for a number of members of Congress to discuss the legislative process. Wood told me afterward that Tabor had spoken to Hoffman and had told him to be careful. Hoffman was one of the few people left in Washington who told the truth, Tabor said, and therefore the only one Congress could trust. Tabor did not mean just Hoffman individually; he meant the delegation as a whole. I believe we merited that praise from Tabor, and I think it made a big difference.

The experience of testifying before Congress was almost like being on trial. One had to justify all the imports and exports and national accounts of seventeen countries. It was ridiculous. On the other hand, I had a healthy regard for the audience and I was there solely to get an appropriation for foreign aid and not to antagonize. We had to use whatever evidence there was, and there was no doubt that indices of production were a persuasive form, more so than indices of price stability, for instance. Although some may argue we should also have focused on price stability, I don't think that Congress was very much interested in it. As a result, inflation did not receive the emphasis it should have, even though at the ECA we regarded it as a major cause of the economic dislocation we were trying to overcome.

My presentations to Congress became increasingly difficult after NATO's inception. Then one had to find some way of explaining in an understandable fashion how the process of European rearmament affected the international accounts of a particular country and of the region. That was an exercise I would not recommend to anyone, and an anecdote may explain why. At a time when European military expenditures were increasing rapidly, Tyler Wood, Paul Hoffman, and I thought that before the congressional hearings started we had better try out on Senator Vandenberg the logic we would use to make our case for European aid. I explained that with an increasing burden of rearmament European defense-related imports would rise, as would each nation's level of economic activity. There would be competing domestic demands for output that would squeeze out those goods normally produced for exports. As a result, exports and foreign-exchange earnings would probably fall. Each European country would therefore need a certain amount of economic aid to enable it to carry the burden of so many dollars in rearmament expenditure and to import the goods it required without too much economic disruption. I got through this elaborate explanation and thought I had done pretty well. Vandenberg looked up and said bluntly, "It won't sell. You simply won't get an appropriation on that basis, period." So we went back to the drawing board and ended up with no recourse except to continue with essentially a national-accounts justification. Our meeting with Vandenberg was the clearest single test before a highly friendly and fairly sophisticated member of Congress of how a more complex analysis would fare.

The Marshall Plan was a joint enterprise undertaken by a group of nations with a common cultural heritage, a common opposition to Communism, and a strong community of interest in the specific goals of the program. The character of this partnership was formalized by empowering an international organization to carry it forward, namely, the Organization for European Economic Cooperation. This entity grew out of a committee formed in Paris in summer 1947 to prepare a European proposal in response to General Marshall's invitation. In its early years the OEEC existed solely to carry out the European Recovery Program.

The OEEC consisted of a council on which the European governments were represented at the ministerial level and which met about four times a year. A permanent council remained in Paris and comprised the resident representatives of the member governments (who were senior officials) and a secretariat headed by a secretary-general. The U.S. representative, Averell Harriman, directed a large office.[16] In the aggregate, these organizations were made up of a sizable number of carefully chosen senior civil servants whose daily contacts encouraged the evolution of a generally shared philosophy. The result was an extraordinarily able group within which the continuity of contact and community of interest promoted highly effective communication. Quite aside from their common vocabulary and concepts, the members of this group became informed on the economic and social problems not just of their own countries but of all the countries of Europe. Within a year or two they became in spirit less an assemblage of national representatives than a group of Europeans.

The role of the OEEC in achieving such visible results as expanding production, ending inflation, and reviving exports requires explanation. As happens in most other international organizations, the position of each government was hammered out at home and brought to the international forum for debate and negotiation. A great deal of policy making (at least among the civil servants) went on within the OEEC in Paris, and a collaborative consensus often developed among the members even when their governments differed. The delegations from each country not only conveyed the views of their governments to the forum but conveyed the views of the group in Paris back again. It is difficult to measure the impact of an intangible development of this sort, but I believe the ascendancy, or at least the unusual influence, of the taskmaster (the United States) had a lot to do with the behavior of the governments and with the success of the whole effort.

From the very start the United States imposed on the OEEC the role of recommending on an annual basis the amount of aid Europe required and how such aid should be divided among the participants. Supported by the ECA, decisions of great national importance to the various participating countries were thrust on a new organization that could act formally only by unanimous consent. On at least one occasion partway through the year, the OEEC was forced by the pressure of circumstances to agree on a modification of aid quotas to increase the share of the United Kingdom at the expense of others. The United States took part in the protracted debates but never insisted on a solution. This role largely shaped the character of the organization for the duration of the recovery program. As a result, the United States and the governments of the participating Marshall Plan countries came to regard the OEEC as a respected partner in the process by which aid quotas were developed. At a later stage, too, it played a crucial part in negotiating the removal of direct controls over trade and in the formation of the European Payments Union. The ECA's policy regarding the OEEC was by no means universally popular in Europe, but no European statesman could afford to stand up and argue against it.

This mode of operation accomplished several things. First, what went on at the OEEC was of great importance to governments and acquired immense prestige. Since the organization was concerned with matters of domestic and international economic policy, the European and American senior civil servants who staffed the secretariat and the delegations were experienced in economic and monetary affairs and were technocrats in the best sense. Second, the OEEC compelled a group of seventeen formerly rival nations to find some way of arriving at agreement. Third, the fact that this vital set of decisions was made each year in the OEEC acted as a sanction that induced the members to work seriously in other collective enterprises (such as the setting up of the European Payments Union) and to take seriously the mutual obligations they accepted.

As the grantor of aid, the United States was in a position to exert leverage on the OEEC. It could, and did try to, facilitate and induce the adoption of policies and arrangements that were almost as essential for recovery as the flow of real resources were. The United States made no effort to impose behavior that was not in accordance with the perceptions and objectives of European governments but rather endeavored to support those governments as they took difficult and sometimes domestically unpopular actions.

From the standpoint of the United States and thus of the ECA, the OEEC played an important role in this process. It became the instrumentality for generating pressure on national governments to pursue sensible policies. This pressure could be powerful indeed, in part because the consensus arrived at in Paris (if supported by the United States, as it always was) greatly influenced the amount of aid to be provided. In part, too, the pressure derived from the fact that the governments negotiating in Paris confronted the judgments of one another. If no consensus on an issue could be arrived at, then clearly no pressures were exerted. But if one government attempted to hold out against the others or to pursue what were plainly not sensible policies, it could hardly ignore the majority view—and rarely did. In the process of exerting pressure, the OEEC (and the United States in association with it) made some actions easier for governments by being an obvious scapegoat. Today, the International Monetary Fund can ask national governments to accept constraints on their fiscal and monetary policies that their ministers probably regard as desirable but would rather not have to originate themselves; at the time, the OEEC and the United States together took the blame for unpopular actions. The whole can be more effective than the sum of its parts, in that policies reviewed and endorsed in an international forum can carry greater weight within a country than those that emanate exclusively from the country's government.

The men gathered in and around the OEEC were able and informed, and when they spoke to their governments they reflected the views and attitudes of a wide circle of people in Europe and the United States. In particular, these men could convey to their governments the views of the United States at a time when our nation's real power and prestige were at a peak. The men of Paris, therefore, although senior officials rather than ministers, spoke with authority in their own countries and exerted influence in this way.

These views of the OEEC are mine, and they were not completely shared by Averell Harriman. One reason was that Harriman was something of a snob about the civil service. He felt that in parliamentary governments, particularly the British government, there was a definite step-down in prestige and authority from the ministerial rank to the civil service. He wanted to deal only with ministers and felt that if he, an ambassador and the senior representative of the Marshall Plan, worked below that level it would lessen the influence of the United States in almost all its relations with the Europeans. In his countless high-level positions, including secretary of commerce and ambassador to Russia, he was frustrated at what he perceived to be the low level (in terms of government rank, not personality) of the dignitaries with whom he was forced to work. For instance, he had a poor opinion of Edmund Hall-Patch, the representative from Great Britain, who was a rather old-fashioned senior civil servant and who regarded himself as coequal to Harriman. If Harriman had been allowed to draw the organization chart, he would have shown Hall-Patch as corresponding to his deputy rather than to him.

Harriman was absolutely right in assessing the distinction between civil servants and ministers in European parliamentary governments as much sharper than it has ever been in our own government. He felt that in seniority and authority he was fully the equal of the British chancellor, who was the minister with whom he dealt. Aside from Harriman, Hoffman, and possibly William Foster (Harriman's deputy in Paris), however, there was nobody of legitimate ministerial rank in the upper levels of the ECA. Harriman had, I think, a valid point and was not just vain in attaching importance to the distinction he made. He felt that he ought to be dealing with men who, especially in the case of the British, were members of Parliament in their own right and who headed important departments. He may have overemphasized this point, but that doesn't mean his position was wholly without merit.

In any event, he handled himself rather undiplomatically. He was extremely eager to build up the authority of the OEEC and in effect wanted some shift in power from the national representatives to the OEEC itself—and that meant partly to the secretariat. I doubt if things would have moved ahead any faster if Hall-Patch had been replaced by someone of higher standing, because he fairly faithfully reflected the views of the British cabinet and those views would have prevailed in British policy. I think it was Hall-Patch's misfortune to be the messenger conveying policy positions that were unwelcome not just to Harriman but to the United States more generally.

Harriman ultimately came to terms with the realities of life at the Paris office and with his dissatisfaction about the OEEC. He even overcame his slight discouragement at not being selected as head of the ECA, a position he felt should have been his. To create bipartisan support for the Marshall Plan, Truman had found it necessary, however, to appoint a Republican. Harriman and Hoffman eventually developed a highly effective partnership, but human factors such as these, combined with the dual headquarters structure of the ECA, made the potential for conflict high.

Tensions were especially evident during the first two winters when the ECA was going back to Congress for renewal of its appropriations. Everyone in Washington was a bit suspicious of judgments from the Office of the Special Representative (OSR) in Paris, probably in large part because of an underlying power struggle. OSR proponents felt that the Paris office should be the prime creator of policy and programs. Conversely, they believed that the ECA in Washington should concern itself primarily with processing paperwork and preparing and making the annual congressional presentation. These advocates (who, not surprisingly, included Harriman and one of his deputies, Milton Katz) also felt that the ECA country missions were subordinate to Paris and should report all matters of importance to Paris for review and advisement. In this view of the world, Washington headquarters would have had to go through the OSR to obtain information from the country missions or give them instructions.

I have always felt that Katz was the individual who was most protective of the office's jurisdictional rights, although he could not have been so vocal without Harriman's backing. Nevertheless, neither gentleman's activities influenced my working relationship with others in the office. On my frequent trips to Paris I always spent enjoyable and productive time with Lincoln Gordon and the staff in the OSR's Program Division. Furthermore, Washington's working relations with them were very good.

I was a strong advocate for Washington's leadership and prerogatives and felt that Paris was both a coordinator and our embassy for the OEEC. I kept lines of communications to the ECA missions open, and—by sending cables directly to them, with copies to Paris, and instructing them to respond directly to Washington, also with copies to Paris—I prevented the OSR from filtering information. We wanted feedback from the countries to go straight to our Program Division, especially in the period when the congressional presentation was being made. We were fairly cautious about issuing instructions to a country mission without having discussions with Paris, but we were not usually challenged on matters of substance. This method of keeping all sides informed, without ceding any authority to the OSR, allowed us to meet our objectives and still avoid forcing the OSR into an open bureaucratic battle.

I am inclined to view tensions between Washington and the OSR as a function of inherent organizational conflicts, exacerbated by certain worries and personalities. No member, however, ever put personal ambition above the attainment of goals. Harriman could have used his close relationship with Truman to Hoffman's disadvantage, yet he was extremely loyal to Hoffman. They were honest with each other and treated each other with great courtesy. Harriman was sensitive to Hoffman's position and never tried to circumvent him. All in all, tensions greatly dissipated over the course of time.

Organizational conflicts aside, though, the philosophical differences that separated Hoffman and Harriman remained significant. Harriman's strong support of NATO and European rearmament was intelligently framed and diplomatically evoked. He used to say, correctly, "There will never be a solid recovery unless the Europeans feel physically secure. They are not going to make long-term contracts and investments and we are not going to have a normally functioning society and economy. Therefore, the purpose being served by NATO is absolutely essential to economic recovery, and vice versa." I don't think Hoffman would have been willing to endorse that view fully. He was impressed by the fact that rearmament was competitive with other uses of resources in Europe. Primarily, he was uncomfortable with military matters and always wished to keep the ECA strictly an economic operation.

When I began working on the Marshall Plan I felt strongly (perhaps even more so than Hoffman) that it had both a political and an altruistic purpose. Hoffman was concerned, wisely, I think, that it be run domestically in the United States in a wholly nonpolitical fashion but also with minimal emphasis on ideology and maximum emphasis on the hard business of economic recovery. He had a fairly strong streak of pacifism in his views about public affairs, and he felt it was extremely important that the task of economic rebuilding and recovery be approached in what today would be called a technocratic fashion—that is, with a strict stress on what needed to be done country by country to achieve measurable results and without any particular concern as to who did it.

Although I started out siding with his view, I came to recognize the validity of Harriman's broad position.

Harriman was an inspiring leader, and working with him was a satisfying and thoroughly pleasant experience. We had disagreements on occasion, but they were not serious. We always agreed on substantive matters. Harriman would develop strong views from time to time, and it was hard indeed to argue him out of them. Generally speaking, however, he was eager to be advised and receptive to what his assistants told him. He believed in delegating but always kept the final decision in his own hands. He was a good administrator in the fundamental sense. Paul Hoffman was less subtle and less sophisticated in the ways of diplomacy; Harriman had a superior understanding of the balance of power and the power structure within each of the European countries. What Hoffman possessed was a core set of beliefs that made him an inspiring leader most suitable to head the ECA.

The organization of the ECA was a good deal less than ideal, but it wasn't clear, at least at the time, how it could have been different. The Program Division, organized on a country-by-country basis, was where the country programs were dealt with at the Washington end, and it was the most important part of the organization. The Food and Agriculture Division, in turn, was more important than the Industry Division. My recollection is that we had a high regard for the ECA mission to France (not to be confused with the OSR in Paris). We also tended to give weight to the views of the Italian mission. Our London mission was headed by a succession of able people, but it was difficult not to believe that it had been taken pretty much into camp by the British, who, in addition to being articulate, were more skillful and professional in economic management than anyone else, by a wide margin. We were suspicious that the mission reflected the view of the British government.

Eventually the ECA's organizational problems in Paris were ironed out, and when, by September 1948, France had experienced a rapid deterioration of fiscal and monetary stability, the French became the focus of its efforts. David Bruce, the chief of the ECA mission in France, sent a secret and urgent telegram to Hoffman in Washington: "Financial situation France heading for tragic climax unless immediate steps taken to cure present distemper. Prices still rising; uneasiness in rank non-Communist labor has made hold-the-line attitude of leaders nearly untenable in face of threatened strikes. . . . Unless checked soon, inflation will destroy gains painfully achieved during first six months 1948.[17]

The French crisis and the ECA's efforts to deal with it are important to note because they underscore the degree to which the Marshall Plan was concerned with issues forgotten by those who call for a similar program today. People remember that U.S. emergency aid kept Europe from starving during that first hard winter; they also remember that Marshall Plan aid helped increase industrial production. Hoffman declared during his nomination hearings before the Senate Foreign Relations Committee in spring 1948 that he would focus all his energies on "one goal . . . increased production." He added, however, "At the same time I want to be sure that the [European] economies are sound from a fiscal monetary standpoint."[18]

At the heart of the French crisis was an explosive situation created by monetary and fiscal irresponsibility. In October, a secret State Department memorandum entitled "The French Crisis," issued by Henry Labouisse, the coordinator of foreign aid and assistance, described France as "the major current problem of European recovery." The memorandum explained that the success of the European Recovery Program was "jeopardized" by the French situation.[19]

We in the ECA felt that to allow the French economic situation to deteriorate further would not only hurt our efforts in other countries but create a fertile political environment for Communist incursions. In December 1948, using the independence of authority granted by Congress, the ECA moved to counter the French situation with the only means at its disposal—threatening to cut off counterpart funds. David Bruce, in a speech delivered to the French Association of Woolen Manufacturers, announced that "the Congress of the United States will convene in a few weeks, and shortly thereafter will begin consideration of the question of a continued contribution by American taxpayers to the recovery of the French economy. These are fateful days. The measures which the French people now take . . . may well be a decisive factor in preserving [the] civilization in whose formation and preservation France has always played such a glorious part."[20] While straining American-French relations, Bruce's speech helped achieve the ECA's goal of getting France to adopt an austerity program to fight inflation and stabilize the economy. His actions may have been considered undiplomatic, but they were the logical consequence of objectives combined with the institutional authority to see them reached.

Bruce was a superb person in all his various roles. He could be tough; he could be decisive. He was extremely skillful as a diplomat in a general sense—that is, in dealing with people and putting them at ease yet sometimes expressing difficult and unwelcome views. There is little doubt that the threat to withhold the use of counterpart funds in France was an interference, but in my view it was a well-justified one.

Late in the course of the Marshall Plan, the ECA in Washington exerted pressure to have counterpart funds directed toward ventures that enhanced the idea of European unity, particularly economic unity in Western Europe. Harriman was particularly interested in promoting an ultimate political European entity, and most of the senior people working on the U.S. side shared his interest. Some Europeans, on the other hand, were not as enthusiastic about the idea. There was a strong tradition of the nation-state in Western Europe, involving differences of culture, language, history, and so forth, and it was not surprising that the Europeans wanted to move toward political union slowly.

The use of counterpart funds provided the ECA with leverage. As my special assistant Theodore Geiger recalls: "We exercised enormous pressure behind the scenes, both to get things done that we wanted to have done and to prevent things from being done that we thought would be harmful for the Europeans and also sometimes harmful for the United States."[21] European political leaders were invited to private dinners and clubs to discuss what goals would be acceptable to the United States. These meetings were always very discreet so that the leaders were able to accept the strong measures recommended, confident that their actions would be supported by ECA financing without their seeming to have been unduly influenced by the United States. I believe one of the reasons the Marshall Plan was so successful was that this method of bringing pressure to bear was applied in private. In Italy we were trying to induce the government to have a more expansionist fiscal and monetary policy; our goal with the French was to influence them to pursue a tighter anti-inflation policy; we wanted the Belgians to grant more credit to the other trading nations of Europe.

The notable exception was the United Kingdom, which relied on its special relationship with the United States. It retained the prestige of having been a partner in the war rather than a territory fought over and ultimately liberated, and the map of the world, of course, showed that quite a lot of the British Empire still had a political relationship with Britain. For these and other reasons, the British were determined to make their own fiscal policy and were resistant to anything the United States could bring to bear. The philosophy of the British government was to maintain a degree of inflationary pressure domestically and to contain the resulting pressure on exchange rates through direct trade and exchange controls. This was a means of securing full employment or overemployment domestically and preventing it from giving rise to a disastrous loss of reserves and imbalance in trade. In most of the rest of Europe, the trend was much more toward the liberal solution of trying to curb domestic inflation so that it wouldn't be necessary to use direct controls over trade and payments.

Britain's difficult behavior arose not only from its failure to come to terms with its loss of empire but from our own indecision. I outlined the problem in a memorandum in fall 1948:

> I believe we have been guilty, at times, of a major inconsistency in our attitude toward the U.K. We have suspected them of wishing to circumvent the OEEC and of wishing to establish for themselves a special privileged status as senior partners in the enterprise and have been on guard against any attempt on their part to do these things. Consequently, we have not consulted with them and taken them into our confidence as fully as they might have desired. Yet, at the same time, we have complained of a lack of cooperativeness on their part and of their willingness to assume effective leadership. I believe it is essential that we decide exactly what we think the status of the U.K. should be.[22]

Britain's economic policy seemed an impediment to success, but although it may have delayed the formation of the European Payments Union by at least a year, it was not too serious. Consideration also had to be given to factors like the onset of the Korean War, which disrupted trade patterns significantly and helped cause an inflation of commodity prices. The terms of trade worsened for most European countries in their dealings with areas of the world that produced raw materials and food. The pound, in particular, was plunged into deep difficulty, and there had to be a special rescheduling of Marshall Plan aid to provide a larger grant to the United Kingdom to offset the problem. On the whole, I think that the twists and turns of British policy were reasonably understandable. I am uncertain, though, whether the issue of British status was resolved during the Marshall Plan days. Perhaps, instead, the defining moment in the United Kingdom's coming to terms with its changed role in the world occurred with Eisenhower's forceful actions during the Suez crisis. That, however, is another story.

One of the principal and most clearly recognized objectives of the European Recovery Program (and therefore of the ECA as an agency) was the restoration of intra-European trade. The traditional prewar trading patterns of Europe had become choked in the early postwar period by exchange controls, bilateral trade agreements, and barter arrangements. This led to the institution of successive arrangements designed to make the European currencies more freely convertible into one another (while maintaining tight exchange controls on transactions in the dollar area) and to dismantle direct controls of intra-European trade. In these efforts, which culminated in the creation of the European Payments Union (EPU) in 1950, the ECA was obviously deeply involved in policy making with respect both to currency arrangements and to trade practices. It is not surprising, therefore, that we designed a European solution that by its very definition would be regional.

In my view, the EPU was the greatest achievement of the Marshall Plan since once and for all intra-European trade and payments were freed up from quantitative controls. Robert Marjolin, who served as secretary-general of the OEEC during the early Marshall Plan years, wrote in 1953 that the establishment of the EPU "created powerful ties and a habit of working together which may perhaps be regarded as the most important political success of the Marshall Plan . . . and as the prelude of an even closer cooperation."[23]

The easiest way to explain the EPU is by reference to earlier payments plans. At the beginning of the Marshall Plan, trade among the participating countries was being strangled by trade restrictions. This was not a new phenomenon but a continuation of a state of affairs that developed in the 1930s and increased in the prewar years. The cause of these trade restrictions in the early postwar era was a general shortage of foreign exchange, particularly dollars. Such a condition arises when a country's earnings from exports are less than the foreign exchange the country requires for its imports. Many European countries began to look for ways to conserve their supplies of foreign exchange, especially dollars, and it was only natural that they would turn toward solutions that led to trade restrictions. For the most part, these solutions gave rise to bilateral trade agreements that sought to protect countries from running up trade deficits with their trading partners. Since currency shortages ultimately arose from trade deficits, countries quite naturally wished to reduce their trade deficits with the "offending" countries. What was needed was a way for trading partners to cut down imports from those countries with whom they were running deficits.

A whole complex of bilateral trade and payments agreements arose between pairs of countries. The agreements typically listed commodities that the two countries expected to trade with each other so as to achieve bilateral balance that would prevent either country from having to settle a deficit through gold payments. Usually the payments agreement that accompanied the trade agreement specified the dates on which surpluses and deficits would be settled and the currencies in which they would be paid.

Immediately after the war these bilateral agreements almost always provided for some extension of credit by each country to the other. In other words, the creditor country (the country running the surplus) would provide credit to the debtor country (the country running the deficit). Within a year or two, those credit margins were pretty well used up, so that there was no longer any trading flexibility within the constraints of the agreements.[24] To make matters worse, the system gave rise to a large structure of short-term indebtedness between countries, with the result that trade began to strangle. In November 1947, France, Italy, and the Benelux countries signed an agreement that attempted to address the situation, but lack of cooperation doomed this first effort.[25]

Given the situation, it seemed urgent to us at the ECA that we find ways to free trade in Europe or at least relax the restrictions. The first, and administratively the easiest, method was simply to permit each country to use some of its ECA aid to make dollar purchases in other participating countries. In that way ECA aid could be used by any participating country to finance imports either from other European countries or from elsewhere in the Western Hemisphere.

In the early months of the ERP this system served to free European trade from restrictions because countries that had been compelled to restrict imports now had a new source of funds with which to finance their trade deficits. While this was progress, the system had important defects; namely, such a system meant that a large volume of the transactions between commercial buyers and sellers would have to be made in dollars. Governments and private sellers both began to insist more widely on receiving payments in dollars, and it was apparent that if the system continued the number of dollar transactions would increase and the problem would begin to be aggravated rather than cured.

It was in response to this situation that the EPU's forerunner, the Intra-European Payments Plan, was created in 1948. Its purpose was to accomplish exactly what had been achieved by letting France use ECA dollars to buy in Belgium, but it sought to avoid the defects of our early attempts at trade liberalization—that is, to avoid the dollarization of a nation's economy. A program had to be devised that encouraged countries to rely less on the dollar and more on other European currencies. Since the basic source of the problem was trade imbalances, a mechanism had to be created that would "recirculate" back to the deficit nations the currencies accumulated by the surplus nations. This type of behavior among trading nations was not something one could expect to occur without some form of encouragement.

It was decided, therefore, that, in addition to the traditional foreign assistance associated with the Marshall Plan, the ECA would provide the trade-surplus countries with something we called conditional aid. The amount of conditional aid given to a country was determined by the size of its trade surplus with its European trading partners. The recipients of such aid—countries like Belgium, which ran large trade surpluses with its European neighbors—were then obligated to provide credit denominated in their own currency to their trading partners. What this effectively meant is that we financed the largesse of European creditor nations.

An example will serve to illuminate the process. Since Belgium was a creditor with most of its European neighbors (it exported more than it imported), in certain years virtually all our assistance to Belgium was in conditional aid: for every dollar of conditional aid from the United States to Belgium, Belgium made a corresponding grant-in-aid to France, Germany, and the United Kingdom. This aid was denominated in Belgian francs because France, Germany, and the United Kingdom, by running trade deficits with Belgium (buying more from Belgium than they sold to Belgium), had in effect been unable to earn any Belgian francs. Since these countries needed Belgian francs to buy Belgian products, they were frozen out of the Belgian market unless a mechanism for providing them with Belgian currency could be found.

On a broader level, the goal was to encourage intra-European trade that was denominated in local currency terms and not dollars, which meant that it was necessary to find a mechanism that would provide countries running trade deficits with a basket of European currencies to fulfill their import requirements. By granting conditional aid to creditor countries, we required each to extend aid in its own currency to the countries with which that creditor had a trade surplus. By that device, each debtor country was given, in addition to its ECA dollars to be spent in trade with the United States, some Belgian francs or some pounds sterling to finance a trade deficit with Belgium or with Britain. The package of European currencies given to a debtor nation was called drawing rights.

By late 1949 we felt that the time had come to go beyond this scheme. The plan had contributed a great deal to the revival of trade among the European countries, but it still had two serious limitations. First, it did nothing to break down bilateral trading patterns. While it is true that the Intra-European Payments Plan avoided the dangers of dollarization inherent in allowing ECA aid to be used for offshore procurement, the use of conditional aid did not build flexibility into the system, and as a result many of the benefits of a true trade liberalization were lost. Let us suppose, for example, that a debtor country in this system receives a package of Belgian francs, British pounds, and French francs, all financed by conditional aid from ECA. Let us also suppose that the country wants to buy steel. As the country shops around among Belgium, France, and Britain for the best deal, it is very much limited and very directly restricted by the amounts of each currency (drawing rights) it holds.

The defect inherent in this arrangement was reinforced by another mechanical problem. The payments plan depended on forward estimates, which meant that before we could determine how large a debtor nation's currency basket would be and what currencies it would contain, we had to estimate which countries that nation would have a trade deficit with and how large those deficits would be. Whenever those estimates were wrong, a country found itself running out of currency to trade with a particular country. This system could then produce harmful distortions in trading patterns. If a country found itself running out of German marks but still had a lot of Belgian francs available, for a few months that country had every incentive to satisfy its import needs exclusively by making purchases in Belgium and, correspondingly, to restrict purchases in Germany. Clearly, this caused trade inefficiencies.

During the first year, the system worked fairly well, but its success was ephemeral. The technicians and economists who developed the blueprints for conditional aid guessed accurately the currency needs that European trading patterns would create. By the fall of 1949, however, our luck ran out. Currency devaluations altered trading patterns, and consequently, aid packages based on prior currency relationships proved to be off the mark.

Until this time, France had been a prime example of a debtor country. In the months after devaluation, France brought its trade within Europe completely in balance. Germany, which had been running trade surpluses in summer 1949, was running a deficit by 1950 and was thus a currency debtor. Britain, which, like France, had been running heavy deficits, was running a surplus within months of its devaluations. France and Britain now had large drawing rights on a lot of countries in Europe, but there was no use for those rights. It would be an unfortunate system indeed that created a situation in which a country had an incentive to build up imports deliberately and buy goods simply to use up its drawing rights.

A change was needed. Apart from its tendency to distort trade, the Intra-European Payments Plan (and, before it, the system of offshore purchases) did little to cure the disease; that is, there was nothing about it that provided any incentive to creditor or debtor countries to try to bring their trade into reasonable or close balance within Europe. It was felt, therefore, that it would be desirable to create a different kind of payments arrangement in Europe, one that would be completely multilateral and would begin to apply some pressure on the participating countries, preferably in an automatic manner, to bring their trade more nearly in balance with one another's.[26] The shaping of ideas that would lead to these proposals fell under my jurisdiction, and I spent long hours working closely with the good group of young professionals in the Program Division to design a new mechanism. We developed an effective pattern of teamwork based largely on an atmosphere of free debate. The European Payments Union was very much a product of this internal debate. It may be difficult for anyone in the 1990s to comprehend totally, but at the time the carnage of World War II was still a reality in people's minds, and the memory of the Hawley-Smoot tariff and its consequences remained vivid. A memorandum written by Theodore Geiger and Harold Van B. Cleveland in October 1949 illustrates how strongly some of my staff felt about the power of trade liberalization and European economic integration for promoting peace. "What solution is there to the German problem outside of membership in a Western European union?" they wrote. "Membership in a union might well be the one method for making Europeans out of the Germans." They felt a European union would provide the best "hope for a regeneration of Western European civilization and for a new period of stability and growth." They also believed we had a brief historic moment to create it. "The participating countries possess their greatest post-war ability to withstand the necessary economic adjustment and ECA is now best equipped to assist them."[27]

I have to admit that I did not have as strong a sense of the tide of history as these two men did. Nevertheless, I was convinced of the power of freer trade and markets. Ted Geiger, who worked closely with me on trade and financial matters and played an important role in the development of the EPU, recalls my excitement when staff members came to me with an idea; I didn't want yes-men around, he says. I established an ECA policy series of memoranda to which anyone could contribute, and they were circulated to everybody of policy-making level, "just to create a firmament of ideas," as Geiger puts it. Many initiatives in various fields arose out of these memoranda. The EPU was just one of them.[28]

In addition to Ted Geiger and Van Cleveland, John Hully, Milton Katz, Lincoln Gordon, Henry Tasca, and Robert Triffin (some of whom were stationed in Europe) all enjoyed, profited from, and contributed to the open environment. Katz had less to do with the EPU in the early stages, but he nevertheless became a stalwart supporter. Tasca and Triffin, while staff members of government agencies, played an important role in the dialogue. They were both fascinated with the task of putting the EPU together.

The key problem our group had to come to terms with in the fall of 1948 was liberalizing European trade. The ideas that had been argued back and forth began to take shape, and by the fall of 1949 we were able to crystallize these concepts in a memorandum that has since been called by some historians the Bissell Proposal. Ted Geiger says: "We were students and Dick was the professor. And we were writing a paper for the professor and he went over it very carefully. . . . He did exactly what a professor would do with a couple of graduate students who had written a brilliant paper but didn't have his experience and insights. . . . So he raised the intellectual level of what we did.[29]

We had devoted our efforts almost exclusively to trade issues, but Paul Hoffman was concerned that unless the Europeans worked harder toward achieving freer trade, the success of the Marshall Plan would be threatened. From his perch in Washington during this period, European progress toward integration appeared stalled and leaning precariously toward failure. He felt enough urgency to fly to Paris to address the OEEC personally. Along with other members of the ECA staff, I assisted him in drafting his speech, and then I accompanied him to Paris. The draft was cabled back to Washington soon after its completion. A few hours later, a return cable from the State Department informed us that they did not approve of this line of policy by a senior representative of the United States. We were all quite angry at the State Department for trying to second-guess us from Washington, although that is probably an unfair characterization of what they thought they were doing. After discussion, Averell Harriman said that, since the speech was a statement of Hoffman's views and Hoffman had authority as a cabinet-level official, he should go ahead with it. Katz, Gordon, Tasca, Triffin, and Thomas Tomlinson shared his view and conveyed their support of the policy. Cheered on by quite an influential group of people, Hoffman courageously gave the speech pretty much as it had been cabled to Washington. We were very pleased with him.

Fifteen times in the speech he used the work *integration*. He noted perceptively that, with a population of 270 million people, the countries participating in the Marshall Plan had the potential to develop the kind of mass market that promoted economies of scale and thus industrial efficiency.[30] He gave the OEEC members ten weeks to devise a plan to deal with the trade problem and integrate their economies into a single common market. Following the speech, he continued to put pressure on the Europeans to make progress. With his prompting, newspaper articles appeared stating that Congress could not be expected to renew ECA appropriations for the next year unless significant efforts toward economic integration were made.[31]

Pressure also had to be maintained on Congress to support our programs. The EPU required working capital, and that meant that Hoffman and I had to go before Congress to explain why United States taxpayers should support the new concept. We went to Capitol Hill in February 1950 to testify before the House Committee on Appropriations once again. Hoffman made a strong case that the EPU had ramifications that went beyond currency and trade issues and that it could affect such fundamentally important issues as peace and war. "You would not have had World War II," he explained, "if it had not been for the thick and high trade walls behind which Hitler built up completely uneconomic industries." He added that the best way the ECA could help improve the standard of living for Europeans was to bring down the cost of the consumer goods they purchased. As the former president of the Studebaker Corporation, he understood the economies and efficiencies needed to achieve such cost savings, and his highly credible testimony played an important part in gaining much-needed congressional support. "There are various factors involved in costs' coming down," he said. "The underlying factor is the large market you must have, a market large enough so that you can afford to make the investments in large-scale manufacturing. That is why we are putting such emphasis on this matter of bringing down barriers."[32] Congress funded the EPU and we were on our way.

The new payments system successfully liberalized trade in Western Europe. Not only did the members of the OEEC participate, but all present and former colonies or territories that were linked to a particular European currency profited indirectly. As a result, most African nations and a great part of Asia and Latin America became beneficiaries of the EPU.

Under the direction of a managing board, the EPU created a clearing mechanism for payments made in any European currency. With all European currencies readily transferable, the barriers of bilateral trade arrangements were broken. Countries that had once worried about particular bilateral balances now could focus their trade policies on rectifying imbalances with the EPU system. This simplified matters greatly.[33] I have always felt the EPU was in some ways the supreme organizational achievement of the Marshall Plan, and although it didn't last very long, it worked very well.

Its creation, though, brought the ECA into conflict with the Department of the Treasury and the State Department's Bureau of Economic Affairs more than once. The intransigence the British exhibited toward the EPU was equaled, if not exceeded, by the inflexibility of our own Department of the Treasury, but for very different reasons. The Treasury, almost always in alliance with the Bureau of Economic Affairs, was a supporter of the General Agreement on Tariffs and Trade (GATT), one of the many postwar organizations created to promote a world free-trade system. Both departments were suspicious of the regional solutions to monetary and trade problems that the EPU advocated. Quite simply, the EPU ran counter to the driving philosophy in these circles.

The National Advisory Council on Monetary Policy (NAC), a U.S. organization composed of representatives from the various government departments and agencies, was the citadel of the multilateral doctrine. John Snyder, my old boss from the war and reconversion years, was now secretary of the Treasury and chairman of the NAC. Frank Southard, the U.S. director of the International Monetary Fund, was also a member of the NAC (to some extent dominating its proceedings), as was Willard Thorp, assistant secretary of state. The conflict, as seen in the NAC, was between regional and international sets of rules on monetary and commercial policy.

Southard and Thorp were often bitter critics of ECA policy. Southard was always a free-market man, and while he may not necessarily have been a true believer in fixed exchange rates, he definitely felt that there should be internationally free currency markets and no exchange controls. In his mind, the deliberate creation of a regional bloc in Europe was close to a sin. His dislike of regional blocs and the EPU was so great that he did everything possible to prevent it from coming into existence. More moderate people of that persuasion, like Thorp, felt there was a case to be made for regionalism at a time when there appeared to be an almost permanent dollar shortage in the world. Because the dollar seemed destined to be too strong to allow for a satisfactory world equilibrium, Thorp felt that the EPU was a pragmatic device for its time but that care should be taken that it didn't last too long.

There was a parallel but not quite identical difference of views within the State Department. Secretary of State Dean Acheson and most of the political officers favored a regional approach to unification of Europe. A good many others—among them, interestingly enough, Paul Nitze—felt otherwise. Nitze disagreed not so much because he was a monetary purist or a defender of GATT but because he was convinced that the difficult problems in Europe were primarily internal national problems. He felt that to talk about integration while these problems existed diverted attention from the task of influencing the Europeans to make the domestic policy decisions that were necessary.

I, on the other hand, was very much the regionalist and the integrationalist, as were virtually all elements of the ECA. The Washington office (especially the part of it that I presided over) and the Paris office were in strong agreement. Details of the EPU were worked out in a collaborative effort between Washington and Paris and represented full concurrence between Harriman and Hoffman. This was one area in which there was almost complete accord between the major parts of the ECA itself.

Differences of opinion set the stage for an unpleasant National Advisory Council meeting in the late months of 1949, following my return from Paris, when I submitted the ECA's proposal on the EPU. The necessary actions had been taken to commit a large block of foreign aid for the purpose of establishing the EPU, and there really wasn't anything anybody could do to stop the process. The ECA had taken an important initiative in total disregard of standing U.S. policy, which strongly supported multilateralism, and in spite of opposition from the Treasury, which understandably was infuriated.

Even as late as 1951, when the Marshall Plan was nearing its end, these tensions still existed. In meetings of the National Advisory Council there continued to be heated discussions of the respective roles of the ECA and international organizations like the World Bank that the Treasury was seeking to use as the tool of an internationalist policy. John Snyder was significantly concerned about organizational and policy competition from the ECA and felt compelled to insist on the ECA's obligation to keep the World Bank and the Export-Import Bank fully informed of its activities and to give them first chance to consider loan projects planned under its auspices.[34] Needless to say, by the end of that year there were many in Washington who were not disappointed when the ECA ceased to exist as an independent organization.

The nature of the Marshall Plan had changed drastically when the Communist forces of North Korea invaded South Korea on June 25, 1950. NATO rearmament and other military issues came to dominate the affairs of the Western community to such a degree that a single-minded focus on European recovery could no longer hold the highest priority. This turn of events was a grave disappointment to many of us at the ECA, but even before the onset of the Korean War, it was well understood that the Marshall Plan was never meant to be a wholly altruistic affair. The hope was that strengthening their economies would enhance the value of the Western European countries as members of the NATO alliance, eventually enabling them to assume a defense responsibility in support of cold-war efforts. The initial expectation called for the Europeans to have the benefit of the full four-year program before they had to concern themselves with the reality of a protracted conflict, but the Korean War short-circuited this process. Two years after the beginning of the recovery program, the greatly improved but still fragile economies of Europe found themselves facing considerable military demands.

By the fall of 1950 I had become concerned that our effort to rearm Europe was seriously endangering the program. The burdens of war and the stimulation of aggregate demand that it caused served to heat up the economies of Europe and to increase the inflationary pressures that we had worked so hard to control during the early years of our efforts. While this was frustrating personally, from the standpoint of an economist it made the challenge of European recovery that much greater. Certainly there were many more economic objectives that might have been achieved had the war not broken out, but it was still possible to move ahead with the liberalization of trade, the stabilization of currencies, and a variety of programs to help the process toward European integration.

Hoffman became disillusioned as the ECA's mission was transformed from a predominantly economic program to one very much influenced by the demands of war. He was an idealist and in the postwar years came close to being a pacifist, a position I very much respected intellectually. He was quite suspicious of the arms buildup after the start of the Korean War and did not want the ECA to be diverted from its strictly economic mission. Especially during the first year of NATO's formation, he was insistent that the Marshall Plan concern itself only with economic recovery. The fact that it was not a rearmament program became the subject of a number of his speeches.

People tend to forget that a major crisis arose during the summer following the outbreak of the Korean War, when there was a revival of price controls and rationing at the producers' goods level. This was correctly perceived as a serious problem, and we in the ECA had a real struggle to receive permission to go on writing procurement authorizations for goods the European nations needed because of potential shortages in the United States. The resulting disruption of recovery left Hoffman very unhappy. He took less pleasure in his job, became less effective as an administrator, and, not surprisingly, soon resigned.

Bill Foster succeeded him, and although no hearings were conducted, I was confirmed by the Senate as deputy administrator. I was attending a formal reception at a house in Georgetown high over the Potomac when I learned that my appointment had been approved. Senator Thomas Connolly, who was leaving the party, saw me and said in effect, "Boy, we confirmed you today." I suppose the reason I never forgot those words was that Rev. Endicott Peabody at Groton addressed everyone at school as "boy." I found it quite affectionate of Connolly to treat me the way Endicott Peabody would have treated a twelfth grader.

Meanwhile, Charles Spofford was assigned the task of opening a NATO office for Western Europe that would deal primarily with political affairs. The British were initially opposed but ultimately relented when the decision was made to open the office in London. Averell Harriman suggested that I assist Spofford because of my prior involvement with the Marshall Plan and its mechanics. Though still attached to the ECA, I went to London and spent some time helping Spofford, whom I found a very good person and an able policy maker and negotiator.

For me, the experience brought out into the open the inherent competition between the Marshall Plan and the OEEC, on the one hand, and NATO and the NATO European office, on the other. As soon as the NATO buildup began, it became apparent that one of the ways in which the United States could deal with the foreign-exchange shortage of the Western European countries was what we called offshore procurement: materials for the U.S. military buildup would be attained, when possible, through purchases in Europe, providing the Europeans with much-needed dollars. Offshore procurement had economic benefits for the Europeans, but it was clear that within our government the tide of history was moving from an emphasis on the economic sphere toward the military sphere. From the ECA's perspective, there were better ways to resurrect an economy than supporting the arms industry.

One very foggy December evening when I was in Paris for meetings at the

OEEC, Frank Lindsay, who had worked for me briefly at the ECA, told me regretfully that he was leaving to work for Frank Wisner, who had been given responsibility for forming and heading the Office of Policy Coordination (OPC), a covert-action organization that was administratively part of the State Department but soon merged into the newly constituted Central Intelligence Agency. Without going into great detail, he left me with the impression that its purpose was to engage in the battle against Communism through covert means outside the United States, primarily in Europe. Lindsay's wartime OSS experience in Yugoslavia had convinced Wisner that he was absolutely essential to this new endeavor. I learned about the OPC for the first time that day.

Some time thereafter, Wisner visited me unexpectedly in Washington. Although I don't remember having had any previous contact with him on official business, I had met him socially and knew and trusted him because of mutual friends like Joe Alsop. He was very much a part of our inner circle of people (to use British language)—top-level civil servants who were involved in many of the government enterprises we took on. Wisner explained that he needed money and asked me to help finance the OPC's covert operations by releasing a modest amount from the 5 percent counterpart funds, the local-currency funds generated by Marshall Plan countries as a condition of their participation in the European Recovery Plan. For each dollar in U.S. aid received, the recipient had to contribute an equal amount in local currency, 95 percent of which would be used for Marshall Plan programs and 5 percent (counterpart funds) by the U.S. government and, in particular, the ECA to finance administrative and other miscellaneous costs. Whether anyone anticipated that these miscellaneous costs would include covert activities is difficult to say. This was most definitely a gray area.

I was somewhat baffled by the request since I was very uninformed about covert activities. Wisner took the time to assuage at least some of my concerns by assuring me that Harriman had approved the action. When I began to press him about how the money would be used, he explained that I could not be told. I had direct access to Harriman and could have confirmed Wisner's story with him if I had any doubts, but I assumed that Harriman had sufficient authority and that he probably knew, and approved of, the purpose. Even with my curious nature, I myself was unaware, except in the vaguest terms, what political-action projects were going forward and how the funds would be spent. I don't think any of us were worried that the kinds of things Wisner was doing would jeopardize the recovery program, and I suspect that had we known more we would have regarded OPC's activities as increasing the chances of success.

I ultimately released the funds to Wisner, and it would not surprise me to learn that the 5 percent counterpart funds were used for many OPC operations. It has since become known that the OPC (and later the CIA) financed certain European labor unions, newspapers, and political parties to help them in their fight against Communism. The CIA has been viewed by some as an organization with a knee-jerk reaction against anything politically to the left, while the truth is quite the opposite. The OPC and the CIA helped many left-of-center organizations in the belief that strengthening these organizations would make them better able to battle the Communists for the allegiance of European workers and intellectuals. Vibrant democratic parties, even socialist ones, were preferable to a Communist victory. We in the Marshall Plan were dealing directly or indirectly with quite a number of the people who were beneficiaries of the CIA's early covert political-action programs.

As the Korean War transformed the Marshall Plan, I found myself increasingly exposed to challenging issues of national security and rearmament. One of the ECA's senior officers in Washington, I was a natural choice to serve as a representative on various committees, including the ad hoc group that was created to review the assumptions and conclusions of an NSC paper written by Paul Nitze just before the outbreak of the Korean War. NSC 68 was intended to assess America's ability to confront the Soviets in either a cold or a hot war and to provide a blueprint for corrective measures against U.S. weaknesses. Its conclusions were ominous: "A continuation of present trends would result in a serious decline in the strength of the free world relative to the Soviet Union and its satellites. . . . It is imperative that this trend be reversed by a much more rapid and concerted buildup of the actual strength of both the United States and the other nations of the free world." The paper recommended that several steps be taken, including a significant increase in military spending, expanded use of covert operations and intelligence activities, and an enlargement of our economic assistance programs.[35] My committee work in assessing these conclusions was part of an evolution in my career that would involve me in issues of grand strategy beyond the world of the Marshall Plan.

From its inception the ECA was an aggressive, innovative organization that should perhaps have served as a prototype of how to achieve foreign policy objectives in the postwar era. One can only speculate as to how America's foreign policy achievements and failures might have differed had it been the State Department, not the ECA, that ceased operation at the end of 1951, but there is no doubt that the State Department was threatened by the success and prerogatives of the ECA, and internal documents reveal the extent to which Foggy Bottom personnel were intimidated by the ECA and eager to reassert the department's preeminence in foreign affairs. A memorandum written by Edward Barrett, assistant secretary of state for public affairs, referred to the ECA staff as "boys" who were trying to "keep their large mechanism busy" by moving into the information field. "ECA information officers, Barrett wrote, "have done some disparaging of our operations among members of Congress and others, on the grounds that we are too hemmed in by diplomatic considerations." The ECA staff had no problem conveying this message to their counterparts in the State Department: during a joint meeting set up in January 1951 to deal with conflicts between the two organizations, the ECA's representatives were forthright in suggesting that the State Department would perform better if it reorganized itself. At a follow-up meeting five days later, the ECA representatives stated unambiguously that the State Department's problems were an issue not just of organizational structure but of "caliber and type of personnel."[36]

As the level of conflict rose it came to the attention of Frederick Lawton, director of the Bureau of the Budget, who in a time of fiscal restraint felt that organizational redundancy should be avoided. In a meeting with President Truman, he suggested that the "virtual independence" of the ECA be curtailed and its operations more closely monitored by the State Department. Bill Foster, the ECA administrator, was understandably disturbed, but with the deadline for the ECA's expiration approaching, power was simply slipping away.[37]

Not long afterward, Foster resigned from the ECA and I became acting administrator. A little over three years had passed since Paul Hoffman called me to Washington to begin work on the most important endeavor of my life. Now I was in Hoffman's seat and it was my job to wrap things up. Unfortunately, the ECA's intended life of four years was shortened by events beyond my control. In October 1951 Congress adopted the Mutual Security Act, whose purpose was to create an agency that would coordinate all U.S. government efforts affecting military, economic, and technical aid. To achieve these ends, the act abolished the ECA as an independent government agency several months before it was originally scheduled to terminate. Although it was to become an organizational unit of the Mutual Security Agency, I believed that the ECA would continue in name only.

This turn of events was disappointing. I found myself heading the ECA just as it was about to lose the freedom that made it a unique agency. Nevertheless, the change was a logical conclusion to the increasing militarization of U.S. foreign policy that had occurred with the onset of the Korean War. It was the ECA's success in reviving Europe that had made a reduction of its activities possible in the first place. The time had come for me to leave the ECA and government service. Shortly after resigning I wrote to Harriman, the new head of the Mutual Security Agency, to explain my action:

> The real reason for my decision is the feeling I have often expressed to you that one can be a better citizen and a better public servant if one takes some time away from the government at least occasionally. The importance, intensity, and interest of the work here are so great that it is a very rich intellectual and emotional diet. If one lives on it for too long, one becomes stale and it loses its flavor. . . . I am sure that a short spell outside the government will not only make me fresher, but will restore my own sense of urgency and excitement of the work here. As soon as that happens, I will be only too eager to return.[38]

Since that time, one lesson of the Marshall Plan that has been driven home is the total dissimilarity between the process by which an advanced economy can be revived and that by which an undeveloped economy can be set in motion. Of greater contemporary relevance than the economic process itself is the manner by which the success of the Marshall Plan illuminates the relationships between providers and recipients of aid, the manner in which a collaborative international program of economic development can be organized, and the way in which governments can work together in a field where delicate questions of sovereignty are always present. But even here, the relevance of the Marshall Plan is limited.

The Marshall Plan inspired optimism both about the prospects for underdeveloped nations and about the availability of effective techniques for the more advanced countries to promote the progress of those nations. What is required for success in such ventures is patience rather than urgency. The problem of Europe in 1948 was unlike almost any since. Perhaps the one disservice rendered to the world by the Marshall Plan was the arousing of false hopes that quick and dramatic accomplishments would be possible elsewhere. Inevitably, it has been difficult to shake off the influence of the European experience, which suggested that with enthusiasm and adequate financial resources significant results could be expected rather rapidly. Another view carried over from the Marshall Plan was that economic and political problems could somehow be separated and that it was going to be possible to rely solely on economic criteria to devise programs of technical and economic assistance to the underdeveloped nations; somehow, it was thought, the ugly problems of their internal factionalism and external allegiances would be circumvented. There was no more unfortunate heritage of the Marshall Plan than this view—that economic development can be conducted as a nonpolitical activity involving the furnishing of quantifiable inputs calculated to yield predictable and measurable results within a reasonably short span of time. Nevertheless, it is understandable that as late as 1951 or 1952 it was possible to be optimistic about both the potential pace of development in the underdeveloped world and our understanding of the techniques available for supporting and stimulating it.

There is little possibility that we or the Europeans can play a more active role in assisting the underdeveloped nations. What disturbs me is the not infrequent suggestion that the Marshall Plan approach is appropriate for countries still in the early stages of development. The need of those countries is not for working capital, which by its nature can quickly be supplied if the money is available from some source. Their need is to learn the skills of a modern economy, and those are things that cannot be supplied quickly. It is going to take a long time for these countries to develop the educational and social infrastructure that can successfully communicate these values to the general populace. Looking forward, therefore, the United States should take a more relaxed and detached view of the underdeveloped nations. Their progress is going to be slow and uneven. No really convincing case can be made that slightly faster progress will make a decisive contribution to orderliness and stability. The time is long past for posturing by the United States in an effort to attract the praise of smaller countries. It is time to recognize where power resides and to acknowledge as friends and allies the industrial nations with which we have a fundamental commonality of interest. If a non-Communist Russia is able to join these ranks, so much the better.

Nevertheless, I believe four rules of foreign-aid management can be suggested by the Marshall Plan experience. The first is that the relationship with the receiving government should be placed, insofar as possible, on a basis similar to a buyer-seller contract. The second rule is that subsidies should usually be payments made to finance the purchase or performance of particular goods or the performance of particular activities that are demonstrably identified with the broad purpose being served. The third rule is that a subsidy should customarily be made in the form of a contribution, presumably matched by contributions from other sources, to a common enterprise, in the management of which the United States should share. And the final, most important, and most promising rule is that subsidies should be channeled through such international institutions as the World Bank or the Inter-American Development Bank. By channeling aid through appropriate international institutions, the United States often can reduce the amount needed to achieve a particular end and, above all, can immensely strengthen the institutions without added costs or sacrifices of important alternatives.[39]

The process of extending aid in this fashion made it possible to influence ideas and actions by bolstering notable international institutions like the Organization for European Economic Cooperation. It is doubtful whether the OEEC would have come into being without the Marshall Plan. It would surely have had little force without the backing of the United States, but with that support it became a part of the machinery through which many key government decisions were made in Western Europe. Its importance and effectiveness had to do not with constitutional powers but rather with its providing a clearinghouse for plans and programs throughout Western Europe. It was a forum where any view held by a number of European governments on a matter of common concern could be brought to bear persuasively on other governments.

The ultimate aim of the Marshall Plan was vastly more ambitious than that of merely trying to keep Europe going while the flow of aid continued. The recovery funds accomplished far more than merely making up the deficiency in Europe's resources. They achieved what would otherwise have been a political impossibility: they provided the more progressive and effective groups within each country with bargaining power they could use to carry through the often unpalatable measures of self-help that were so very necessary.

CHAPTER FOUR

Transition

The Ford Foundation to the CIA

The period following my departure from the ECA and its successor, the Mutual Security Agency, was one of transition. In January 1952 I joined the Ford Foundation at the urging of Paul Hoffman, who, having left the ECA in late 1950, had been selected by the trustees of the foundation to be its president and direct its revitalization. As he settled into his new position, he realized the benefit of recruiting his Marshall Plan colleagues, whose experience qualified them to help direct the foundation's disbursement of large sums of money for research and public-service projects. Assisted by Sam Van Hyning, I worked out of a small office in Washington, although most of the foundation's activities were conducted in Pasadena. The arrangement allowed me to work for the foundation while engaging in outside consulting assignments.

I came to the Ford Foundation naively believing that it would be possible with a very wealthy foundation to have a sizable direct impact on events in the public arena. Shortly after joining, I wrote to Milton Katz (another Marshall Planner who had been recruited by Hoffman) that "there is nothing to prevent an individual from exerting as much influence through his work in a private foundation as he could through work in the government."[1] Unfortunately, as the months wore on, my thinking about the foundation underwent a revision. A large part of my job was to screen proposals for research projects and make recommendations. The more applications I screened, the more dissatisfied I became and the more I realized I did not wish to continue in the long term. As a result, my independent consulting work took on greater importance and provided a stimulus that my duties at the foundation did not.

One of my early consulting assignments was to help produce NSC 141, a National Security Council document designed to serve as the Truman administration's last will and testament on issues of national security. The president named Secretary of State Dean Acheson, Secretary of Defense Robert Lovett, and Mutual Security Administrator Averell Harriman to head the effort. They, in turn, named a working committee of senior civil servants—Paul Nitze as Acheson's representative, Frank Nash as Lovett's, and me as Harriman's. The triumvirate of Acheson, Lovett, and Harriman represented the significantly larger group of elder statesmen and other men of outstanding prestige and experience who had guided the administration's international policy in military, economic, and political affairs.

The Truman administration felt there would be major changes in approach and attitude when the Republican administration assumed power. It wanted to leave behind a statement of the policy it would have adopted or continued had it remained in office. One can trivialize its desire, but the statement of policy was meant to convey to the succeeding administration the insights of senior officers who had spent a good many years in international security affairs. It was, in other words, their advice. The notion was to produce the paper in about two months' time, which we did. There was remarkably little difference of opinion among Nitze, Nash, and me, and the report turned out to be a very good document that took a hard line. It assumed that the Communist bloc was enormously powerful, that it would become more so in absolute terms, and that a major continuing effort on the part of the West would be required to keep it in check. The policies recommended by NSC 141 would be fairly expensive and would represent a continuation of the status quo.

In the fall of 1952, I became part of the CIA's Princeton Group of consultants (so named because it met on the university's campus). Working in Washington had enabled me to maintain my close professional relationships and friendships with people like Frank Wisner, Sherman Kent, Desmond Fitzgerald, Tracy Barnes, and Max Millikan, all of whom were in the CIA and close to Allen Dulles. I had met Allen and Foster Dulles through their sister Eleanor, whom I had known while working on the Marshall Plan. She was now active in German affairs at the State Department. I remember being included in a meeting she arranged at her home in 1951 to give Foster Dulles, who was anticipating the 1952 election, an opportunity to meet some of the middle-rank civil servants in the government.

The purpose of the Princeton Group was to allow CIA analysts to interact and exchange ideas with professionals from outside the intelligence sector. The meetings usually took place over a weekend in a highly secure environment overseen by an agency security delegation; they were stimulating in the sense that all participants were able to discuss their views freely. Although the group met infrequently, perhaps once every few months, it provided me with an introduction to the world of intelligence.

As my interest in the Ford Foundation continued to wane, the formulation of my own substantive ideas about foreign policy took on importance and prominence. One area I focused on was the military posture of the United States. I came to believe by the early fifties that it could not be said too often or too emphatically that reliance on overall military strength, and on the threat to use that strength as a deterrent to local aggression, was a euphemism for reliance on the threat to initiate a world war. In early 1953, I produced a paper called "Notes on U.S. Strategy," which I had written not long after the completion of NSC 141. Reflecting on that job and what I learned from it, I felt moved to set down a few rather pessimistic reactions to certain aspects of U.S. military, political, and economic strategy. Over the course of the spring, I circulated the paper to a number of my friends, including Walt Rostow, Max Millikan, Chester Bowles, George Kennan, and Harlan Cleveland. It outlined what I believed to be the weakness of America's defense posture; namely, the U.S. strategy was ill-adapted to deal with the most threatening contingency in the struggle between the Soviet bloc and the Western coalition, which was not a deliberately planned overt invasion of Western Europe or Japan but a Communist-led internal revolution in the weaker states of Asia, Africa, and Latin America. Our defense strategy did not appear to provide, at least on an adequate scale, a means of deterring or countering local aggression. To correct for this, I felt that a modified strategy needed to be developed, "and the only such alternative deterrent could be local forces, perhaps supported by a mobile U.S. reserve, of a sort that can deal with all kinds of limited and local aggression that the Communists have developed."[2]

Another area that interested me was the relationship between economic development and political stability. I was concerned that in both underdeveloped and industrial nations income levels would fail to expand sufficiently in the long run to satisfy the minimum conditions for political and social stability. An opportunity to address this concern arose in late 1952 when Max Millikan resigned as an assistant director at the CIA (where he was responsible for the analysis of worldwide economic trends) to become director of MIT's Center for

International Studies (CENIS). He and I had similar interests, and I was able to get the trustees of the Ford Foundation to fund research at CENIS.[3] Others who would become involved with CENIS included Kingman Brewster, McGeorge Bundy, and Walt Rostow.

My consulting work for the agency and my increasing involvement at CENIS provided me with a number of opportunities to delve into issues of foreign policy. One assignment that proved especially interesting was to explore ways in which the CIA could promote resistance to the Soviets in Eastern Europe; a number of the more intelligent and liberal Republicans thought that it should be possible, without engaging in military operations, to roll back the Iron Curtain. I collaborated on this project with Frank Lindsay, and we were given free license to inquire about ongoing projects, techniques, and procedures of the most extreme sort. In other words, the search was for any kind of cold-warfare weapon or tool that had been overlooked and might be brought out and put in the arsenal. The huge document that resulted suffered the fate of most reports. Nevertheless, its real value was not what it affirmatively recommended but the various avenues that it tended to close off as a result of the investigation. It also strengthened my belief that pure psychological warfare was certainly not going to roll back the curtain.

By autumn 1953 Allen Dulles began putting a lot of pressure on me to come work for him at the CIA. One evening at a fairly large dinner party hosted by Stewart Alsop I took Dulles's arm as he was leaving and mentioned that the special economics project I had been working on at the Ford Foundation was about to end and I was going to have to find a new position. He told me to come see him before I committed myself otherwise. I did, and he offered me a job that was intellectually interesting and very tempting indeed. After wrestling with my conscience for several weeks, however, I reluctantly turned him down.

One reason for my decision was that I could not contemplate living and bringing up our children (who, with the additions of Winthrop and William in 1947 and 1950, now numbered four), on a civil service salary indefinitely. The other was that I remained convinced that freshness in government assignments could be effected only after a period outside the federal establishment. I was forty-four years old, an age that was very nearly the last chance one had in most academic and business organizations to come in as a newcomer lacking previous connections. I concluded, therefore, that to accept Dulles's proposal, though in many ways the easiest and most pleasant path, would be an act of procrastination and that I should instead persist in trying to get myself established outside the government, at least for the next few years. My notion was to return to academia (I inclined strongly toward MIT) by fall 1954 and to engage in consulting activities that would significantly supplement my income. I left other options open as well.

Having reached no firm decision about the future, I committed myself to a CIA project that was scheduled to last at least five months and possibly through August 1954. This was a satisfactory arrangement since it meant my family would not have to move away from Washington until after the end of the school year and I could continue to consider various job opportunities in the private sector. Contrary to my original intentions, however, I remained in Washington and on February 1, 1954, began employment at the CIA in earnest, as special assistant to the director, a title without a specific job description or set of responsibilities. Essentially, I served as Dulles's apprentice, performing a few odd jobs, accompanying him to meetings, and writing some reports.

One of the early meetings I attended with him was a National Security Council meeting that took place not long after the fall of Dien Bien Phu; Secretary of State John Foster Dulles and Secretary of Defense Charles Wilson were among those present. The immediate future of Indochina was broadly known since the French had been defeated and there would be a partition of Vietnam; it was also clear that the United States would become involved to some degree. Foster Dulles would probably have preferred a swift American military response to the crisis, but he made a persuasive exposition of why such an intervention would have been difficult, if not impossible, to execute. He believed such action had been precluded by a lack of adequate justification in international law and by the constitutional constraints imposed on the president in his role as commander in chief. The only way a French defeat could have been avoided was through a massive intervention that would have required a congressional declaration of war. Even if this had been possible, the timetable for its implementation was incompatible with events as the crisis unfolded. Foster Dulles's discussion revealed a great deal about the constitutional approach to foreign policy that Eisenhower and he pursued. His approach is especially illuminating when one considers how more recent presidents have ignored these constitutional issues.

The solution he opted for was to create a legal loophole that would enhance the president's freedom of action within a constitutional framework should a crisis recur in that part of the world. He argued that an appropriate regional treaty would make it possible to overcome obstacles in the future. First, from a domestic perspective, the treaty would have to be debated in Congress and ratified by the Senate, thus providing a legislative history that would clearly augment presidential power of action similar to Truman's response in Korea. Internationally, if a government in Southeast Asia requested U.S. assistance, the treaty would in effect provide both a recognized, published, and public obligation and a legal basis for rendering such support. The main thrust of his argument was that in the aftermath of Dien Bien Phu the United States should work to create a regional body of Asian nations modeled on NATO. The Southeast Asia Treaty Organization (SEATO) was born from this idea. In retrospect, what is interesting about this meeting is how early on American policy makers were preparing for an eventual overt involvement in Vietnam.

I came to know the Dulles brothers quite well, through meetings like these. Although they were very close and largely agreed on policy matters, they differed greatly in personality. The contrasts were never more apparent than during the period of McCarthyism. Foster, in my view, was not very protective of State Department personnel against attacks by McCarthy. Partly he may have lacked courage and partly his response may have been calculated politics. But the real cause seemed to me his somewhat cynical attitude toward his fellow human being, which stood in great contrast to his brother's. I have always felt that to some degree Foster shared McCarthy's deep suspicions about people who had taken unpopular positions that could be construed as insufficiently anti-Communist. I knew a number of men McCarthy attacked who might not have been as staunchly anti-Communist as he or Foster Dulles were, but I was convinced that these men were loyal Americans and anything but Communist sympathizers. Allen Dulles would have perceived as much, and Foster would not have.

Conversely, Allen was quite protective of the CIA during this period. In addition to having personal courage, he was also a warmer and more outgoing person, and he was more receptive to a wider spectrum of beliefs and backgrounds than his brother was. As a result, he was more inclined to judge individuals by their competence and personal qualities and less by their actual or alleged political views. There is no doubt in my mind that Allen's strong stand against McCarthyism and his very able leadership were the key reasons the agency was able to attract so many capable people during the midfifties. Much of the challenge and sense of forward motion had gone out of the other parts of the government, but he was able to keep those elements alive at the agency. The CIA was a place where individuals seeking intellectual discourse and personal challenge could still find a home. He engendered a great deal of loyalty and respect, and I can't think of anybody in the agency who didn't both like and admire him, which is quite a tribute over a period of years.

As part of my early exposure, he invited me to attend the staff meetings that were held in his office about three mornings a week. At the end of these sessions, after I and most other participants had been excused, Frank Wisner, deputy director for plans in charge of covert operations, would be asked to stay and talk further with him. It wasn't difficult to assume that some important operation was brewing, and before long I picked up on a rumor that the agency was planning to overthrow the Arbenz regime in Guatemala.

The Guatemala operation, which became known as PBSuccess, had its roots in the revolution of 1944, in which the thirteen-year dictatorship of Jorge Ubico was overthrown in a coup led by a number of young military officers. Juan José Arevalo was elected president that year in what was perhaps the freest election in Guatemala's history. He undertook an immediate series of reforms that obligated landowners to rent uncultivated land to Guatemala's peasants at reasonable rates and that thereby challenged the privileged position of the landed aristocracy. By 1950 Arevalo was pushing legislation that included a social security system and provided workers with the right to organize unions and conduct strikes. His reforms greatly antagonized Guatemala's wealthy oligarchy and he came to lean heavily on leftist political groups, including the officially outlawed Communist Party, to maintain support for his agenda.[4]

The year leading up to the 1950 presidential election served as a watershed in Guatemalan politics since initially it appeared that the election would be a hard-fought contest between Francisco Javier Arana, the chief of the armed forces, and Jacobo Arbenz, the minister of defense. Both Arana and Arbenz had played important roles in the 1944 revolution and they had even served in a transitional junta together, but they were separated by a wide ideological chasm. Arana, although part of the Arevalo government, was a conservative who came to find increasing fault with the president's politics. Arbenz, while himself not espousing Communism, was a liberal who had close personal relationships with Guatemala's most prominent Communists. His wife, Maria, on the other hand, was very vocal in her support of a number of Communist causes.[5]

Social tensions intensified as the political contest between Arana and Arbenz disintegrated from a public debate into an open feud. As the decorum of democracy disappeared, a group of conservatives suggested to Arana that he lead a revolt before the election took place. Rumors of a pending coup spread throughout the capital, and the national legislature voted to arrest Arana for treason. Responding that he was being victimized by Communist interests, Arana charged that Arbenz was a Communist tool. He made the stunning announcement that a militant radical group had hidden a cache of arms that Arbenz intended to use when he gained power; Arana's plan to corroborate this fact, however, took a fatal turn. As he approached the alleged site, his car was ambushed by twenty gunmen and riddled with bullets. His murder was never solved definitively; suspects included an army lieutenant, who later served in the Arbenz administration, and Maria Arbenz's chauffeur.[6]

With Arana out of the picture, Arbenz's election became almost inevitable. There was great concern about the direction in which he would lead Guatemala. National intelligence estimates in early 1952 showed that the intelligence community was greatly disturbed by Communist infiltration of the Arbenz government. One estimate stated: "The communists already exercise in Guatemala a political influence far out of proportion to their small numerical strength. This influence will probably continue to grow during 1952. The political situation in Guatemala adversely affects U.S. interests and constitutes a potential threat to U.S. security."[7]

By mid-1953 the State Department also became increasingly concerned. Communist infiltration of the Guatemalan government was certainly a problem, but as long as President Arbenz remained independent, there was always the possibility he might be persuaded to fight the Communists. Unfortunately, the State Department's officer in charge of Central American and Panama affairs wrote, the possibility proved illusory: "The trend toward Communist strength [in Guatemala] is uninterrupted. A gigantic May Day celebration was used as a Commie display of strength, and the Communist labor leader Gutierrez made a rabid speech threatening the opposition with destruction. President Arbenz attended this rally, also made a speech (denying that Guatemala is Communistic), and warmly embraced Gutierrez. . . . The Guatemalan Congress stood in silence in memory of Joseph Stalin, the only government body in the Western Hemisphere to do so." Needless to say, Arbenz's protests that he was neither a Communist nor a supporter of Communism rang hollow. Just a few months later, in August 1953, the State Department's Bureau of Inter-American Affairs prepared a paper for the National Security Council on the situation in Guatemala: "In Guatemala communism has achieved its strongest position in Latin America, and is now well advanced on a program which threatens important American commercial enterprises in that country and may affect the stability of neighboring governments. Continuation of the present trend in Guatemala would ultimately endanger the unity of the Western Hemisphere against Soviet aggression, and the security of our strategic position in the Caribbean, including the Panama Canal."[8]

While there may be those today who would question the threat Arbenz presented to security in the Western Hemisphere, documentary evidence reveals that analysts perceived it as real. They were not alone. For example, after having dinner one night with President Arbenz, the U.S. ambassador to Guatemala wrote: "I am convinced Communists will continue to gain strength here as long as he remains in office. My staff agrees fully on this. Therefore, in view of inadequacy of normal diplomatic procedures in dealing with situation, there appears no alternative to our taking steps which would tend to make more difficult continuation of his regime in Guatemala."[9]

I can add that, at the time, the United States regarded Central America and the Caribbean as very much its zone of influence and was hypersensitive to threats in that area. Its view reflected, among other things, the correct judgment that the societies of the Latin American countries were vulnerable, characterized by deep social cleavages that, exacerbated by tensions created by widespread inequities in income, unfair land distribution, and racial discrimination, made the region a fertile area for Communist infiltration. No one in Washington would have questioned that a Communist regime in Guatemala would constitute a major threat to regional stability. It is fair to say that the view was pretty unanimous that Arbenz did represent a threat if he was pro-Communist. I think, however, that a number of people would have questioned whether Arbenz was leading Guatemala toward a Communist regime. In that sense he may have been less of a threat than he appeared at the time.

In January 1954 Guillermo Toriello, the Guatemalan ambassador to the United States, paid a visit to President Eisenhower in the Oval Office. He took the opportunity to address what he knew were Eisenhower's concerns about Communist infiltration of the Arbenz regime and suggested that American assistance might be the best way to help Guatemala fight the problem. Eisenhower replied that the United States wasn't in a position to help a government that had such obviously strong ties to the Communists. He explained in what was perhaps a Freudian slip that the people of the United States hated Communism and that if we helped the Communists there would be a coup against him. A coup was definitely on Eisenhower's mind; the question was merely one of timing. When intelligence sources revealed in May that Communist-bloc countries were beginning to ship arms to Guatemala, the situation turned grave. The SS *Alfhem*, a Swedish-owned ship, arrived in Guatemala carrying approximately 2,000 tons of Czechoslovak arms for the Arbenz government.[10]

In spring 1954 I learned officially about the covert action against the Arbenz government that had been in the planning stage for some time. Approved by Eisenhower, the plan centered on an exiled former Guatemalan army officer named Carlos Enrique Castillo Armas, whom the agency was assisting in building a small rebel army and air capability in Honduras. I was now not only invited to attend Allen Dulles's meetings on the operation but included in Wisner's staff meetings as well. While Dulles's conferences dealt with the broader strategic issues of the operation, Wisner focused on the nuts and bolts of personnel, materiel, and military issues, and I soon found myself taking on odd jobs to assist him.

As the operational date approached, difficulties began to emerge within the agency. Colonel J. C. King, who was head of the agency's Latin American division and nominally in charge of the operation, was a former FBI officer from the days when intelligence activities in Latin America were still a bureau responsibility. When they were transferred to the CIA, King went with them. I don't believe the FBI ever got over its Western Hemisphere operation's being turned over to the agency. King epitomized the old FBI approach, which concentrated almost exclusively on espionage, and was not especially friendly to the philosophy of covert action or to the particular operation. It was inevitable, therefore, that he would get along poorly with its project director, a former army officer named Albert Haney. Haney reported to King, but he represented a different approach. He was young, bold, and enthusiastic about the possibilities of covert action. It suited his temperament, and his boldness and imagination were matched by management and bureaucratic skills that made him effective. For example, he set himself up in charge of what was by CIA standards a rather large headquarters. Located outside of Miami on the Opa Locka air base, it was the site from which the operational direction and control of PBSuccess was exercised and from which Haney also managed personnel throughout Latin America. When the thirty people at the Miami headquarters were combined with the forty or more Americans in the field, the result was a sizable operation by agency standards.

The flow of cable traffic between Haney in Florida and King in Washington was huge and for the most part dominated by a continuing argument. Haney wanted to be more aggressive; King wanted to slow down and pursue a more cautious approach. Their conflict was as irreconcilable as their personalities were, and it was Wisner's responsibility as deputy director for plans to resolve it. His first action was to involve himself more intimately in the details of the operation, but soon a new conflict developed, this time between King and him, over the need to proceed much faster. At some point, perhaps in April or May, the operation was taken out of the Western Hemisphere division and made an autonomous operation, effectively removing J. C. King from the chain of command. A gap remained between Wisner and Haney, though. Wisner's responsibilities were global and he did not have the time to remain closely involved with a high-priority operation like PBSuccess. Nevertheless, after King's removal, he assumed an even greater role in the operation. Before long he found himself in the same position as J. C. King had been in. King had been removed because he was too cautious, but ironically, Wisner came to feel that Haney was perhaps too bold and to lose confidence in Haney's judgment and restraint. I've always thought that Wisner and King were fairly close in their basic thinking; theirs was really a difference in style. As the operation progressed, Wisner became increasingly conservative about the risks he was willing to take. The friction that I recall most prominently in that operation, therefore, was not between Wisner and King but between Wisner and Haney.

With King on the sidelines and Wisner and Haney at odds, Dulles decided to make Tracy Barnes the case officer, or liaison between Washington and Opa Locka, a role he handled very carefully and diplomatically. The line of command changed again—it was now Haney as project officer to Barnes to Wisner to Dulles. At this point Dulles asked me to play a limited role in the operation as a detached observer who could sort out the source of the conflicts and help resolve them. Barnes and I spent half a day with Haney in Miami. By the time we left Haney's office, I had become a supporter of his and thought he was doing a good job. Even Wisner had to admit that Haney ran a tight ship and that his headquarters was very well run. Haney had a clear notion of what the strategy and tactics of the operation should be, and in the end they were the ones that prevailed.

Barnes was very much pro-Haney and gung ho about the operation. I admired his ideas and learned from them some lessons that were perhaps unwise—namely, to be aggressive. In my enthusiasm for what I had seen in Opa Locka, I came to side (along with Barnes and Haney) against Wisner; my support for Haney, however, never caused a rupture in Wisner and my relations. I believed Haney was the right man for the job because the person in charge of an operation of this kind had to be an activist and strong leader. Barnes and I both liked Haney and approved of the way he was running things. No doubt Haney's operation left a positive impression on me, because I set up a project office similar to his during the preparations for the Bay of Pigs invasion.

On June 18, Castillo Armas crossed the Guatemalan border from Honduras and initiated hostilities against the Arbenz regime. Two days later, with the entire operation in danger of failure, Allen Dulles forwarded a CIA memo to the president that outlined the uncertainty of success:

> As of 20 June the outcome of the efforts to overthrow the regime of President Arbenz of Guatemala remains very much in doubt. The controlling factor in the situation is still considered to be the position of the Guatemalan armed forces, and thus far this group has not given any clear indication of whether it will move, and if so, in which way. If the Guatemalan army should move within the next few days against the Arbenz regime, it is considered to have the capacity to overthrow it. On the other hand if it remains loyal and if most of the military elements commit themselves to vigorous action against the forces of Castillo Armas the latter will be defeated and a probability of uprisings from among other elements of the population is considered highly unlikely.

The memorandum is significant not only for what it revealed about the operation but for what it says about the way Dulles communicated with the president. He felt Eisenhower would be best served if provided with the unvarnished truth about the operation's potential for failure. As in the Bay of Pigs undertaking several years later, there was no immediate promise of popular uprisings unless the first, more limited goals of the operation could be met. In Guatemala, a key objective was either inducing the military to remain neutral in the struggle or influencing it to turn against Arbenz and in effect join the rebel forces. Considering that the Guatemalan armed forces were the strongest in Central America and that Castillo Armas and his men numbered no more than a few hundred, the task was not easy. The memorandum also explained the difficulties that needed to be overcome, the means that would be employed, and the limited opportunity for success: "The action of Colonel Castillo Armas is not in any sense a conventional military operation. . . . The entire effort is thus far more dependent upon psychological impact rather than actual military strength, although it is upon the ability of the Castillo Armas effort to create and maintain for a short time the impression of very substantial military strength that the success of this particular effort primarily depends."[11]

Psychological warfare began on May 1, when a radio station that appeared to be run by Guatemalan dissidents but that was actually managed by the CIA took to the airwaves. Although the station's transmitters were alternately located in nearby Nicaragua and Honduras, the self-styled Voice of Liberation seemed to its listeners to be based in Guatemala. The purpose of the broadcasts was to magnify the unimpressive force of Castillo Armas and make an "impression of very substantial military strength." For example, on the day of the invasion, Castillo Armas and his men penetrated about six miles inside Guatemala and then halted. The Voice of Liberation, however, announced that Castillo Armas was leading a military force of several thousand soldiers and that they were heading straight for Guatemala City, the capital.[12]

One of the great accomplishments of the Voice of Liberation was the neutralization of Arbenz's admittedly limited air arm. The station's propaganda succeeded in inspiring the defection of a couple of hundred Guatemalans, one of whom was a pilot in the air force. David Atlee Phillips, who ran the agency's propaganda efforts, was able, with the help of some Scotch, to get him sufficiently relaxed to make an appeal to his fellow pilots to desert and to fly their aircraft to Castillo Armas and the rebel forces. Upon hearing the pilot's broadcast, Arbenz grounded the remaining aircraft.[13] He didn't trust the pilots who were left.

His decision played directly into the agency's hands, and a small agency-run "rebel" air force was able to fly unopposed over Guatemalan skies, playing an important role in the war of nerves that was being waged. In addition to dropping propaganda leaflets on the capital, the air force engaged in widespread miscellaneous bombing, often using empty Coca-Cola bottles, which made a very satisfactory whistling sound on their descent and were harmless unless one hit someone on the head. Of all the factors that contributed to Arbenz's overthrow, I have always believed that the most decisive was the bombing, which did extraordinarily little damage to the city but dealt a powerful psychological blow. The climax of the air war was a successful bombing attack by Castillo Armas's CIA-led planes on a military depot filled with munitions. The explosion caused little loss of life; instead it was a psychologically impressive event, a demonstration of the potential power of even this primitive air force.

Just a few days after the invasion commenced, however, the rebel air force that was so crucial to victory was virtually disintegrating as a viable military force. One reason was the constraints imposed on the agency by the doctrine of plausible deniability (a doctrine that would also later handicap the Bay of Pigs operation), which specified that the only aircraft that could be used were vintage planes the rebels could credibly have purchased themselves on the black market. At the start of operations a few decrepit planes were all that was available. When two of them were grounded by damage from small-arms fire and a third crashed because of malfunction, the operation was perched on the edge of failure.[14]

Tension at the agency was very high, and Dulles continued to hold frequent meetings in his office to discuss the question of resupplying the rebel forces with planes. Wisner and Dulles approached the problem differently. Wisner, it seemed to me, was willing to face the possibility of failure; he certainly was willing to look it in the eye more squarely than I would have been, but his attitude appeared to be almost fatalistic. He was amenable to putting the actors in motion and then letting the cards fall as they might. Dulles, though capable in handling tension, was not willing to accept that possibility. He felt that the agency's reputation and his own were at stake and he intended to fight for both with all his ability and determination.

I went to the State Department to meet with Undersecretary Walter Bedell Smith, the official liaison with whom we dealt on an almost hour-by-hour basis and someone who had great authority to make decisions and take action. Bedell was supportive of the operation, and although he was a gruff military officer he was a friend and ally; one could say that I had a respect for him bordering on the timid. I was seeking permission to obtain four more obsolescent aircraft for the rebel forces. Henry Holland, the assistant secretary, was adamantly opposed and, although Bedell Smith attempted to overrule him, insisted on taking his case to the president.

On June 22, Allen and Foster Dulles, Henry Holland, and President Eisenhower met at the White House to reach a resolution. Anastasio Somoza, the dictator of Nicaragua, was willing to supply the planes, but only if Eisenhower replaced them. Holland was ready to defend his vehement position and entered the president's office carrying several books on international law under his arm.[15] According to Eisenhower, the crucial moment in the meeting occurred when he asked Allen Dulles what Castillo Armas's chances would be without the aircraft. "About zero," Dulles replied. And if the United States supplied them? "About 20 percent." Eisenhower decided to supply the planes needed to keep the rebel air force operating. When the meeting was over and Dulles was ready to leave, the president said to him: "Allen, that figure of 20 percent was persuasive. It showed me that you had thought this matter through realistically. If you had told me that the chances would be 90 percent, I would have had a much more difficult decision."[16]

Once the rebel air force had been successfully resupplied with planes, the operation regained its momentum. Success, however, was in no way assured. I remember a meeting one afternoon in Dulles's office when we were all at our wit's end as to how to proceed. We knew that if the Guatemalan army moved ahead it could push the small Castillo Armas force out of the country and that, generally speaking, there was no force that could overthrow Arbenz's regime. Eventually Haney dreamed up a new maneuver to increase the pressure on Arbenz. He wanted to airlift a small rebel force that had stalled inside Guatemala's border, load the men on a ship, and land them at one of Guatemala's ports. I was given the task of arranging for the charter of an old and unattributable merchant ship to transport the landing party of Castillo Armas volunteers to the attack point. I was about to go to New York to see Granville Conway, whom I had with worked during my years at the War Shipping Administration and who was now president of the Cosmopolitan Shipping Company, when the trip was called off. The Arbenz regime had suddenly cracked.

Arbenz brought defeat on himself. With his air force grounded, his capital under attack, and the Voice of Liberation reporting massive defections from his army, he decided to distribute weapons to the "peoples' organizations and the political parties"—in other words, to what were effectively Communist and labor-led militia groups. The conservative men who constituted the leadership of Guatemala's army viewed this action as the final unacceptable leftward lurch, and they told Arbenz they would no longer support him. He resigned and fled to Mexico.[17]

The CIA was not completely surprised by Arbenz's confrontation with the military and his subsequent resignation. Although the operation had been touch and go in its early stages, events had turned more favorable after the resupply of the airplanes. In addition to Voice of Liberation broadcasts describing major engagements between the Guatemalan army and the rebels, there was enough real (though limited) fighting to give credibility to this disinformation. For instance, there was an actual skirmish near a junction on the International

Central American Railway that resulted in a government train's pulling into Guatemala City with several dead bodies and quite a number of wounded government troops. I have always felt that this vivid evidence of an overt battle, of something more than a mere paper exercise, had a major impact in making Arbenz believe that there was a real war going on and caused him to be very doubtful as to who was on whose side. Adding to these factors was the disruption of Arbenz's entire communications. He didn't know what was happening at the front, and the confusing rumors and radio broadcasts made it difficult to make important decisions. It is my belief that when he was faced with the greatest uncertainty—when he believed that two columns of well-equipped troops were converging on the capital—he caved in.

The agency had good intelligence about how Arbenz was handling the unfolding crisis because the U.S. embassy in Guatemala City, remained open throughout and John Peurifoy, the ambassador, maintained communications with his contacts in the Arbenz regime as well as with the army. This enabled us to take the pulse of the other side as the operation progressed, and, of course, we were also in clandestine communication with many individuals and groups in Guatemala that were opposed to Arbenz.

PBSuccess was by no means destined to succeed; there were many operational components that could and did go wrong. It might be argued that only Eisenhower's willingness to resupply the planes, against the advice of Henry Holland, allowed the operation to achieve its objective. I think, however, that the matter was more complex. One element of the subsequent victory was the successful disinformation campaign; another, equally important factor, one that all of us at headquarters tended to overlook (and that students of the operation still do), was the massiveness of U.S. power viewed from Arbenz's position. We never had any doubts that Arbenz would suspect that the United States was behind the activity. Nevertheless, grappling with continual operational snafus in Washington, we were only too aware of how perilously close to failure we were at any given time. We knew how few and how poorly trained Castillo Armas's recruits were and how difficult it was to get a few obsolete airplanes replaced. It was easy for us to forget that Arbenz felt he was up against the might of the United States and that this was something that might weigh heavily on his mind. He may simply have been persuaded that the United States was earnest in its efforts to oust him and that, if current means proved insufficient, stronger means might be used. This, too, could have contributed to the collapse of his resolve. Although I placed little faith in psychological warfare, the effectiveness of the real paramilitary steps that were taken was enormously enhanced by skillful psychological exploitation.

Many studies of this period have attempted to link the decision to overthrow Arbenz to Allen and Foster Dulles's ties to the United Fruit Company, which had significant properties in Guatemala. Because of its large land holdings and the role it played as a symbol of Yankee imperialism, it had become an early target of the Arbenz government. A major portion of the company's land was ultimately expropriated by the Arbenz regime as part of its reform program. Personally, I would be surprised if United Fruit had any strong influence on the course of events. The Dulles brothers' ties dated back to their days as private-sector attorneys, but at this point in their careers both of them were infinitely less concerned with the fate of United Fruit than with fighting Communism. I never heard Allen Dulles discuss United Fruit's interests. Some of its personnel, equipment, and communications resources were used by the agency on certain occasions and there may have been some contact with the company with respect to the carrying out of the operation, but I had no direct experience with these matters.[18]

Regrettably, the success in Guatemala, combined with the previous success in Iran in 1953, led Washington policy makers to overestimate the agency's abilities in the area of covert action. For many policy makers outside the CIA, covert action became a quick fix, an easy way to deal with hostile foreign leaders and renegade nation-states. Certainly the agency's success in Guatemala against Arbenz influenced its judgment in mounting the Bay of Pigs operation against Castro. There was a great deal of public outcry during the first day or two of the Guatemala operation, but once there was a victory it died away completely. I have made the point more than once, however, that the most one can hope to accomplish with covert action is an immediate operational goal. In Guatemala it was to overthrow Arbenz and put Castillo Armas in his place, but ultimate success depends on how your people (in this case, Castillo Armas and his successors) run the country and how they can make it a productive society.

Some historical accounts of the Guatemala operation have attributed a larger role to me than I actually played. For the most part, I served as either a liaison or a troubleshooter, but this somewhat limited exposure provided me with an opportunity to get an overview of the CIA as an organization, an invaluable experience. As to the question of overthrowing a foreign sovereign government, I would approve the same action today without hesitation. With hindsight, however, I would be more cautious in estimating what would happen as a result of this kind of intervention and whether it was really in the best interest of the United States. I think it is perfectly arguable that U.S. interests over the years might have been better served if Arbenz had remained in power. There is a generalization that is relevant in cases such as these. When I have been asked whether certain operations of the CIA were successful, I have been careful to answer that success must be measured in two quite different ways. First, were the operational objectives of the action achieved? There is not the slightest doubt that in Guatemala they were totally achieved. Second, did the achievement of those objectives (specific operational tasks assigned to the CIA) further or enhance the interest of the United States as it was designed to?

Shortly after the operation I addressed these points in a memorandum that said that we'd have to do everything all over again in the near future if something wasn't done to improve the state of affairs in Guatemala—that is, if other parts of the government did not pick up those tasks that were just as necessary for achieving the desired results. The ball was not picked up in Guatemala. Nobody in the State Department or the Agency for International Development recognized the urgent need to improve that society and no major program was undertaken to accomplish that purpose. In terms of an executive long-term policy, this is a glaring weakness. It was true especially in Guatemala because there we had destabilized a democratically elected government and therefore had a greater moral obligation than we did in most small Latin American countries to try to do something about the underlying situation.[19]

By the end of the Guatemala operation I had overcome my ambivalence about joining the CIA. On August 6, 1954, I wrote to Allen Dulles from Bar Harbor, Maine, just before embarking for a sailing holiday on my yawl, the *Sea Witch*. After a final agonizing appraisal, I had turned down a serious job offer and now, I told him, I was going to be with him "for some time at least."[20] Four months later, I was put in charge of a project that was a revolution in the intelligence-gathering process—the development of the U-2 spy plane.

CHAPTER FIVE

Overhead Reconnaissance

As the Korean War wound down in the early fifties and as economic recovery seemed assured in Europe and Japan, the threat of massive Soviet strategic bombing attacks on the United States received increasing attention from civilian and military planners. The main preoccupation was with the Soviet long-range bomber force and the threat it posed to North America, as well as to Europe. With the memory of Pearl Harbor still fresh, President Eisenhower established the Technical Capabilities Panel, headed by James Killian of MIT and usually referred to as the Killian Surprise Attack Committee. One of the three subcommittees through which it carried on its investigations was the Intelligence Panel chaired by Edwin Land of the Polaroid Corporation. This small group played a major role in initiating the development and deployment of a series of reconnaissance systems that drastically expanded the scope of the whole United States intelligence collection process.

The first system developed was the U-2 reconnaissance aircraft, with its associated cameras and other intelligence payloads. The go-ahead for the U-2 project was given to Clarence "Kelly" Johnson of Lockheed Aircraft by telephone on December 1, 1954, the first official flight of the aircraft was on August 8, 1955, and the first overflight of the USSR took place on July 4, 1956. Twenty months from approval to operation was a remarkable feat.

By August 1956, barely two months after that first overflight of the Soviet Union, Colonel Jack Gibbs and I started defining a successor to the U-2. The key role was again played by an advisory committee, which included most of the former members of the Intelligence Panel, together with the assistant secretaries for research and development of both the air force and the navy. Two years after reiterated design studies by two aircraft builders, the second manned reconnaissance system was given the go-ahead in July 1958. It was the CIA's A-12, known in the air force inventory as the SR-71.

In March 1955 the air force, influenced by Rand Corporation studies, the view of the Killian committee, and by its own scientific advisory board, issued a general operational requirement for a photoreconnaissance satellite, thereby initiating a different technical approach to overhead reconnaissance. A contract for the development of a weapon system was awarded to Lockheed in October 1956 after a three-way competition. Possibly because of publicity concerning this project, in February 1958 Eisenhower canceled the most sensational element, the development of a reconnaissance system using a recoverable capsule. At the same time, however, he decided to continue the task under deep security as a separate high-priority project (with the name Corona) and to make it a joint air force–CIA project on the model of the U-2 program.

The first flight of a Corona vehicle occurred a year later, in February 1959, but it was not until August 1960, after thirteen harrowing tries, that the first wholly successful flight took place. Although there were scattered failures thereafter, there has never since been a major lapse in the flow of intelligence from satellite photoreconnaissance. It is no exaggeration to say that what was accomplished in this period of less than ten years was a revolution in intelligence collection. The desperate rivalry of the cold war, of course, provided the major stimulus for our activities.

Nearly a year before Eisenhower authorized the U-2 project, the air force solicited proposals from four designers for a high-altitude reconnaissance aircraft. A well-defined set of procurement requirements for the design specified a multipurpose plane, not merely a standard bomber with cameras installed in the bay. One submission, by Bell Laboratories, contemplated taking the basic British Canberra in its bomber configuration, giving it different wings, more wing span, and a higher aspect ratio, and lightening it to achieve better performance. The proposal submitted by Kelly Johnson for Lockheed was in conceptual form only, since the engineering was not yet sufficiently complete to produce detailed specifications. Lockheed's proposal called for a single-engine monoplane with a very large wingspan (which results in a wing with a high aspect ratio) and was designed for one purpose—to fly very high. The air force was skeptical; according to Johnson, "they questioned that any engine even would operate at the altitude we were proposing." In any event, the air force rejected the Lockheed proposal and accepted instead Bell Lab's redesigned British Canberra, which could fly up to 55,000 feet.[1] The submission the air force passed on, which was to become the intellectual forebear of the U-2, would ultimately fly at altitudes over 70,000 feet.

Concurrent with the Canberra project, the air force developed a program that called for releasing unmanned balloons near the Soviet border. The apparatus, with cameras attached, was supposed to float across the Russian land mass taking photographs of sensitive military installations. The balloons and cameras were built and many were actually launched, but the Russians picked them up and dispatched a diplomatic protest that effectively ended the operation.

Frustrated with the air force's halting progress, Eisenhower set up the Killian committee in the summer of 1954 to evaluate the threat of surprise attack, presumably by the Soviet Union. The committee's Intelligence Panel received extensive briefings on state-of-the-art optical and camera design, as well as on potential aircraft and power plants; it strongly recommended to Eisenhower that the United States initiate with maximum security and urgency a project to develop an advanced-technology system of overhead reconnaissance. Its recommendation that the United States should build a reconnaissance aircraft capable of flying at very high altitudes and that the plane should engage in overflights of the USSR was regarded as so sensitive that it was omitted entirely from the committee's final report. This conclusion was known only to Killian and a member or two of the full committee and had been discussed with Allen Dulles at the CIA. The proposal, endorsed by the intelligence community and the secretary of defense, was approved by President Eisenhower in late 1954.

The Intelligence Panel had regarded the possibility of overflying the Soviet Union, its satellite countries, and any other denied areas as a means of obtaining timely warning, enhancing the security of the United States, and forestalling the surprise element of any attack contemplated by an adversary. In the course of its work, the panel learned about the air force's reconnaissance program. Reviewing the design options originally presented to the air force and examining the Canberra design that was finally chosen, the members of the panel became convinced that the air force was proceeding in the wrong direction. They wanted to learn more about the rejected U-2 design and so invited Kelly Johnson to meet with them in Washington. Immensely impressed with his ideas and the fact that the U-2's altitude capability made the plane virtually invulnerable to interception, they recommended proceeding with Kelly's aircraft rather than with the air force's Canberra. The Intelligence Panel then met with Allen Dulles and Trevor Gardner, the assistant secretary of the air force for research and development. Those sessions apparently confirmed the panel's belief that an aircraft based on the Lockheed proposal would be a potent weapon for overflights. Dulles conducted a special closed meeting of the United States Intelligence Board, at which only the principals were present, and secured from them (very easily, I must say) their eager support for the project.

In late November 1954, Allen Dulles; his brother Foster; Nathan Twining, the air force chief of staff; Donald Putt, the assistant chief of staff for research and development; and Secretary of Defense Charles Wilson met with Eisenhower to discuss funding for the U-2. Allen Dulles made a strong case, and considering that the United States Intelligence Board had already given its backing, Eisenhower's decision was almost inevitable. Andrew Goodpaster, Eisenhower's staff secretary, noted in a memorandum of that meeting: "Authorization was sought from the President to go ahead on a program to produce thirty special high performance aircraft at a cost of about $35 million. The President approved this action. Mr. Allen Dulles indicated that his organization could not finance this whole sum without drawing attention to it, and it was agreed that Defense would seek to carry a substantial part of the financing." The president did, however, add an important caveat to his approval. "After listening to our proposal and asking many hard questions," James Killian comments in his memoirs, "Eisenhower approved the development of the U-2 system, but he stipulated that it should be handled in an unconventional way so that it would not become entangled in the bureaucracy of the Defense Department or troubled by rivalries among the services."[2]

Not long after that meeting, Allen Dulles summoned me to his office and handed me a packet of secret documents. He brought me up to date on the U-2 project (which until then I had been unaware of), informing me that it had received presidential approval that morning and that I was being put in charge of agency participation. I was to work with Herbert Miller, a specialist on the Soviet atomic program, who would represent Dulles, the director of central intelligence. Miller was bright and very competent, but he liked R & D jargon, which annoyed some of his colleagues on the analysis side of the agency, who found it pretentious. He played a constructive and helpful role as my general assistant during the first nine or ten months of the program, but as officers were assigned to specific duties, he gradually became less active and eventually his role diminished. He was instrumental, however, in getting the work started on the base we established near Groom Lake, Nevada.

My official duties on the U-2 project commenced the following week with an initial organizational meeting in Trevor Gardner's office at the Pentagon. Among the dozen men present were several air force officers, including Donald Putt; Clarence Irvine, the assistant chief of staff for materiel; Osmond Ritland, the air force's chief liaison officer; Herbert Miller; and the CIA's general counsel, Lawrence Houston. There was a fairly orderly discussion of who would be responsible for what. It was clear that there had to be a new procurement of the airframe and payloads since there was nothing like them in existence. It was agreed that the air force would divert the necessary number of Pratt & Whitney J-57 engines from ongoing procurement contracts to the U-2 program in a reasonably private, if not covert, fashion and that the CIA would be responsible for security. Then the question arose as to who was going to pay for the new airframe, which would probably cost in the tens of millions of dollars. I was sitting near the middle of the table, and as I turned to my right, everyone was looking in my direction. As I turned to the left, everyone on my left was looking in my direction as well. I got the point pretty quickly and said I would recommend to Dulles that funding for the project be provided from the CIA's contingency reserve, a reserve appropriated and voted on by Congress. The rules for its use were that withdrawals had to be authorized by the director of the budget and approved by the president on the recommendation of the director of central intelligence. This required a policy paper (or enabling document), which I am sure I drafted and prepared for Dulles's signature.[3]

Larry Houston recalls how adamant I was that we keep knowledge of the project limited to just a few individuals—even in the CIA. I called him later and said I wanted him and no one else in his office, to do the legal work. In carrying out my instructions, he had to handle a wide variety of tasks, from fund transfers to contract negotiations. He remembers meeting with Kelly Johnson in early 1955: "We sat down and started to draft out a preliminary procurement proposal and I remember I was scribbling away. . . . Two points of argument came up. One, I said, 'Kelly, you know when you get doing a program of this size, you get all sorts of people with ideas of how to change, improve, or otherwise make a different procurement. That almost always adds on to the cost. If we do that, we're probably sunk. If you say that no costs will be added without us conferring to make sure we had funds for it, I think we can do it.' The other main point, of course, was the security." When Kelly explained the unique nature and operations of Lockheed's Skunk Works, a highly secure facility for aerospace design, Houston was reasonably satisfied.[4]

In the ensuing months we started the procurement of airframes, cameras, other secondary payloads, and a simple, compact celestial navigation system. With the support of the air force, the CIA took the initiative in obtaining presidential approval for a small, specialized operational and training base in Nevada, to be used for test and development flights, and in constructing that facility. By midsummer it was clear that the roles of the air force and the agency should be defined in writing, and I negotiated an agreement with Hank Everest, the air force deputy chief of staff for operations, that was eventually signed by Allen Dulles as director of central intelligence and Nathan Twining as chief of staff of the air force.

The agreement enabled us to work together with remarkable harmony and effectiveness throughout the life of the project. The Air Force supplied engines from Pratt & Whitney—first the J-57 and then a more advanced slant number of that engine, followed by the J-75 for a slightly modified higher-performance airframe. It also facilitated the recruitment of pilots who would serve as civilian employees of the CIA. This arrangement satisfied the condition laid down by the president that no U.S. military aircraft could penetrate Soviet airspace. In addition, the air force furnished personnel who were assigned to the CIA (in accordance with a long-standing agreement between the agency and the department of defense) to man the operations and logistics functions in several U-2 detachments and the project headquarters. Finally, the strategic air command assigned a training group to the Nevada base. Its members, after qualifying themselves as U-2 pilots, supervised the training of the operation's "civilian" pilots. When the first field detachment of just over a hundred men and three aircraft approached a state of readiness, it was the strategic air command training group that devised and supervised a simulated combat exercise involving a number of long-range reconnaissance missions over the United States. At the end of the exercise they concluded the unit was combat-ready. The active participation and support of the air force continued throughout the life of the U-2 project, and without its many contributions the project could not have been carried through.

The preliminary planning within the agency was highly compartmented, with very few agency personnel other than those assigned to project headquarters cleared for access. I reported directly to Dulles and served as the channel to him and his deputy Pearre Cabell, who was responsible for day-to-day affairs in the agency. Cabell was more involved with administrative matters that were above my level and of concern to the director, but we had a close relationship, and as an air force general he was very much interested in the program. I have always been grateful to him for allowing me to run it and not second-guessing me or attempting detailed supervision. I am sure one of the reasons he found it possible to leave most of the initiative in my hands was that I was usually eager to seek his advice and counsel. He kept a low profile in the conduct of the project yet deserved his fair share of credit for what was accomplished.

During my early years in the agency I talked to Frank Wisner about various people in the agency and their functions. I recall his saying that he sometimes felt that Cabell had not worked out for himself what his role ought to be in the agency and more generally in the intelligence community, which is not surprising. Dulles had a habit of getting involved in whatever came up from day to day that seemed to merit his concern and of doing so in ways that weren't always in accord with a tidy line of command; any deputy working for him would have had a difficult time figuring out an appropriate role.

Dulles relied heavily on Cabell, however, to deal with the business of commercial air proprietaries, notably Air America and Civil Air Transport. Dulles expected that, along with Larry Houston, who was in a sense the case officer for those programs, Cabell would keep an eye on administrative matters and perhaps to some extent personnel. I think it is fair to say that most of the men who were deeply concerned with the operations side of the agency did not regard the smooth handling of administrative matters as especially important. But Red White, the deputy director for support, was good at it, and Dulles left a lot of it to him.

The U-2 project began its life in an aging office building on E Street, close to the Lincoln Memorial. The premises were so rickety that the installation of even basic office machinery threatened to bring down the second floor, and the need for expansion soon became obvious. Replacement quarters were found downtown in a suite of offices on H Street, across from the Metropolitan Club; the new arrangement was particularly satisfactory because the building was mostly occupied by ordinary businesses. The headquarters was relatively small but self-contained, with sections for finance, procurement, and security, a communications center, and operations rooms. The total staff in Washington was under a hundred. Access to our offices was by elevator, and a receptionist checked badges, logged in names, and took care of general protocol and security. I spent only part of my time on H Street; my principal office was on E Street, in what became the administration building, which was where Dulles also worked.

Dulles assigned me responsibility for managing the U-2 program even though I had no previous experience in avionics. I immediately found myself immersed in all the engineering details of airplanes and engines. Fortunately I worked with Kelly Johnson, who was an artist in his field, a superb technician, and a brilliant engineer. He is commonly acknowledged to have been one of the top American airframe designers, if not *the* top. A very personable man, he became a good companion and ultimately a genuine friend. He was a marvelous person to work with and we complemented each other well. Johnson's main attribute as a designer was his decisiveness, which allowed him to take shortcuts and render quick judgments without jeopardizing safety. He would study a problem or obstacle that had not existed in earlier programs, take a certain amount of time to make up his mind, and then, knowing clearly what had to be done, go ahead and do it. For incompetence and government bureaucracy he had very little patience.

I imposed no schedules on the U-2 project, but Johnson himself targeted the first flight of the aircraft for the first week of August, nine months after the go-ahead. Because of the working relationship we had developed, he felt comfortable pushing for what I felt was an almost unrealistic date. Lockheed had by then become personified by Johnson and could be trusted not to abuse the government's interest. The CIA, as the procuring organization, was willing to delegate major authority to him and to Lockheed. Thus he and I were able to cut through layers of red tape and reporting procedures that would have slowed the project down. We kept our regular monthly progress reports to about five pages, for example; had the same program been developed for the air force, it would have required the preparation of a document one inch thick. If the project officer of an air force plane decided a change was required, he had to check with Wright Field, a couple of different laboratories, the budget office, the regulations office, and so forth—that was one reason it was difficult to receive prompt, clear answers that would not be subject to repeated reviews. The agency's way of working, as it evolved, was a dramatic contrast and an effective one.

About two years after the U-2 was up and flying, the officer in charge of procurement for the air force met with Larry Houston to inquire into the CIA's unique ability to support the rapid development and deployment of an aircraft system. The explanation that it was accomplished simply and centrally caused the officer to express surprise that the agency used the same procurement office for wings as it did for the engine. He said the air force could never do that.[5]

Some years later, in the successor A-11 and A-12 programs, I employed the same informal decision-making process to solve a problem Pratt & Whitney had with a fixed-price contract for the J-57 engine. Len Mallet, the president of Pratt & Whitney, came with some others to plead their case. Although he admitted he had no legal basis for his request, because the contract was a valid one, he said he was in deep financial trouble and wanted to obtain a price increase for the engines. At the end of the meeting I told him I wasn't going to bail him out completely, because I didn't think that was proper, but I offered to see what I could work out. I told him I would speak to my associates and get back to him within a day or two. He then asked a question: "When we get your decision, is it final or is it then subject to review by others?" I told him it would be final. A few days later he was informed that we would raise the price by half of the difference between what it had cost Pratt and Whitney and what they had agreed to charge. That was a way of doing business that permitted clean and prompt decisions; it appealed to Kelly Johnson and it appealed to me. It worked.

All this day-to-day business was facilitated by the covert manner in which the agency was able to operate. I worked behind a barrier of secrecy that protected my decision making from interference. As General Leo Geary, my air force deputy, succinctly puts it, "We had security that just would not quit." With some wonder he also notes that "the U-2, for example, was built and flying before the commander of the air force research and development command ever even heard of it. If you wanted to see one ticked-off air force major general, you should have seen this guy."[6] Indeed, the air force would have had a technical board and various high-ranking officers reviewing the process and discussing it every step of the way. I, on the other hand, did not have to have my decisions approved at any higher level within the agency.

I think the major contribution the project office in Washington made to the program's success was to obtain for Johnson, when he needed them, firm, clear decisions that were not going to be second-guessed by anyone else. He could get answers from me on the telephone without delay. As a result, I relied heavily on his judgment in technical matters. My rule to him was simple: "When you face a decision, I want to know about it, I want to pass judgment on it," I said. "But I've got to rely on you to tell me the potential consequences and costs of these decisions." No doubt more of the decision making in the U-2 project was made by the contractor than would have been in an air force or other military procurement program. I felt, however, that the urgency of our mission required our kind of working relationship. Johnson said to me several times that whenever he provided a quote for the air force he would be happy to quote 10 percent less for the agency. This was his way of providing a discount for our elimination of red tape. Many years later he remarked to me that he had made an acceptable, very low-grade engineer out of me. I have always taken that as a compliment.

Arthur Lundahl, who played a crucial role in providing photointerpretation for the U-2 project, recalls how some years after I had left the government Johnson lamented the passing of the good old days:

> The SR-71 had been built, the satellites were flying, and as we ate lunch together, Kelly was saying to me, "What's happened to the days of Richard Bissell? . . . I could come in to this town with a brief folio which describes a brand-new idea which is a considerable advancement over anything that's going. I could sit with Bissell. He would quickly get it. We'd move from his desk . . . to one or two other desks, and almost before I left Washington, I had a commitment. He understood what I was after. He understood how we were going to do it. They approved and I went home satisfied. . . . Now when I come to this town without Bissell, I can't find the office. When I do find it, it's filled with people most of whom don't know anything at all about the past of this kind of project. All have got arguments and complaints against it. And I could spend days going around through various bureaus and undersecretaries, talking to them, and go home and not realize whether I had made a yard or not in this ball game. I'm not coming back to Washington anymore."[7]

Johnson concentrated on the technical issues of the U-2 while I spent most of my time establishing an organization, managing the bureaucratic process, and dealing with the policy matters involved in producing this radically new aircraft. Within two weeks of our establishing the project office, the organization was in place, with a dozen officers identified and given designated responsibilities. James Cunningham, for example, handled administration; Douglas Ogan, finance; George Kucera, contracting; a succession of men, the security section; and so on. "We were collectively trying to make sure that everything we did was aimed at keeping the flag flying on the Hill," says Art Lundahl. His feeling (and mine) was that we "didn't give a damn about the air force flag or the CIA flag or the navy flag." We wanted "the American flag up there." In fact, though, not everyone shared that feeling, and I frequently ran into roadblocks with various agencies of the government. It was necessary to reason, to barter, to show people what the gains would be. With the military especially, I had to demonstrate the acumen to bring something off that they couldn't accomplish themselves. As Lundahl correctly remembers, I wasn't put off by the bureaucratic restraints that would have stopped many other people.[8]

The feat of getting the U-2 operational was formidable and I conducted a search throughout the country to obtain the best advisers and experts in fields like optical science and upper-air medicine. Perhaps one factor that contributed to my success in the project was that I greatly enjoyed learning and talking about science and technology. I had particular respect for Kelly Johnson, W. O. Baker, and Edwin Land, who were precise in their words and willing to quantify their confidence that something would work or would fail. The intellectual qualities of people like these created a stimulating work environment. In the middle of the program, for example, my staff and I went to visit Din Land at his house in Boston. Art Lundahl recalls "sparks flying and scintillating, cutting-edge ideas" coming from all sides. Was there anywhere else, he wonders, where "this mixture of science and friendship and understanding" could have been experienced "in such a nice fashion"?[9]

Having procured the plane, cameras, and film, we now required a secure air base for flight testing and pilot training. With Lockheed test pilot Tony LeVier at the controls of a small passenger plane, Herb Miller, Kelly Johnson, and I began the search for a suitable location. Geological survey maps spread across his lap, Johnson directed our flight from California to Nevada. He suggested exploring several dry salt-lake beds in the Sierra region whose hard-packed dirt could serve as good landing strips. The area near Groom Lake, Nevada, which seen from the air was approximately three to four miles in diameter and smooth as a billiard table, appeared to Johnson a promising location to accommodate the long landing requirements of the U-2. Descending for a closer look, we saw evidence of a temporary landing strip, the kind of runway that had been built in various locations throughout the United States during World War II for the benefit of pilots in training who might have to make an emergency landing. Faced with the option of landing on this strip or on the lake bed, LeVier chose the lake bed. Once on the ground, we walked over to the airstrip to see if it was viable. The closer we got, the deeper we sank into soft, sagebrush-covered soil. Had we attempted to land on it, we most assuredly would have crashed. In any event, Groom Lake would prove perfect for our needs.

When I returned to Washington, I recommended to Eisenhower that he add a piece of adjacent land, including Groom Lake, to the Nevada test site of the Atomic Energy Commission. The commission's work was already highly classified, and enlarging the site area would be the easiest way to prohibit overflights of the new U-2 base without arousing attention from outsiders. Eisenhower approved the proposal, and work began immediately to improve the facility. Three hangars were constructed, a paved runway leading down to the lake was built, accommodations for two hundred were erected, and a well was dug to ensure a potable water supply. An air force DC-4 was soon assigned to make daily rounds from Lockheed's airport in Burbank, California, for personnel and supplies.

Art Lundahl's eloquent expositions had convinced Din Land's panel that the photointelligence obtained from overflights of the Soviet Union would greatly help protect the United States from surprise attack. Recruited by the agency's intelligence directorate, Lundahl was the driving force behind the creation of photointelligence. He had been with the U.S. Naval Photographic Intelligence Center before joining the CIA in 1953 and had served as a photointelligence officer during World War II.[10] As he tells it, his introduction to the U-2 program was abrupt:

> One morning I got a message from Allen Dulles's secretary. It was rather cryptic but alarming. It said, "Mr. Lundahl, you're relieved of all your duties. Come to the director's office right away." If that didn't grab you! So I galloped up the hill from the street level to the high location of the central building and there, for the first time, in 1954, I met Richard Bissell and Allen Dulles together. Collectively they pulled back the drape, so to speak, and showed me the oncoming U-2 aircraft. . . . I was under a totally different line of command in CIA, but here, without portfolio and with nothing more than a handshake, I'm now working for Richard Bissell. I had to make a "storefront" so that all the people in CIA who wanted measurements on a picture could go there and get services. It was a funny part of my life. I was getting my fitness reports and my ratings from a bunch of people who never saw me, and I was working on a confidence, trust, handshake level with Bissell, who saw me every day, and trying desperately to get all these elements to come out right.

Lundahl's experience suggests the kinds of management problems created by the compartmentalization of knowledge to protect sensitive information.

The "need to know" doctrine meant that his colleagues and superiors (except Deputy Director of Intelligence Robert Amory) were unaware of his activities. Lack of widespread information lessened the chance of a potential security leak. Within the constraints of this highly partitioned organization, Lundahl built the infrastructure needed to support his work. His first problem was space: "[We] were dealing with a huge industrial process—thousands of gallons of processing material, chemicals, thousands of feet of film, huge volumes of consumables which were going to be going into this aircraft to provide pictures of unprecedented proportion and quantity. . . . This was not something that could be accomplished out of a locker in a bus depot."[11]

I provided him with a budget commensurate with his important assignment and gave him permission to establish a headquarters. He required not only fifty thousand feet of office space but a discreet base of operations in keeping with security regulations. We found the ideal location on the upper floors of a Ford repair shop on Fifth and K Streets, in the Steuart Building. The dilapidated exterior—and the grim neighborhood—effectively masked the most high-tech photointelligence center in the world.[12] The next step was to give the operation a project designation, since it was not at office-level status. Lundahl wanted to call it Automat because he intended to run it on the model of the places he'd seen in New York that were open practically round the clock. The service he was going to offer was the intelligence equivalent of an Automat, with people coming in twenty-four hours a day for every sort of subject imaginable. Then a man from security stepped in and said a code word couldn't start with a vowel. Lundahl said he didn't give a damn and told him to put something else in front of it. His security officer, Henry Thomas, hung an *HT* in front of *Automat,* and the project became known as HTAutomat.[13]

In addition to Lundahl's operation, I established an ad hoc requirements committee, headed by James Reber. Chances for a successful overflight of the Soviet Union seemed very good, and it was obvious there was going to be a large flow of intelligence—high-quality, we hoped—from a wholly new source. Since there would also be a lot of competition for it from various parts of the government, we needed to prioritize their needs—that is, to establish intelligence requirements. I myself was not vastly interested in this aspect of the program, but Reber proved to be exactly the right man for the job and he kept it until after I left the agency. He was orderly, discreet, easygoing, and diplomatic—in short, a person who could not only help preserve the security of the program but also maintain friendly relations with the various claimant agencies.

My notion in establishing the committee was to get the whole business of intelligence requirements into the hands of a group of people who were competent and interested. The committee's main task was to draw up a list of collection requirements, primarily for the U-2 but also for other means of collection that had prioritized targets, according to their ability to meet three major national objectives with regard to the Soviet Union—the gauging of long-distance bombers, of guided missiles, and of nuclear energy.

Recently Reber has raised some good points about how the cold-war mentality caused us to overlook industrial and agricultural targets that might have helped us better evaluate the Soviet Union's true economic capacity and anticipate its decline. Locked into a mindset that focused on military targets, we didn't raise the right questions, according to Reber. From his perspective, the entire intelligence community should have developed the requirements needed to evaluate the economic stability of the Soviet system. Had we focused on such targets as "all of those physical photographable elements of a transportation system," we would have learned that the Soviets were putting little money into the nonmilitary productive resources that truly make a nation strong.[14]

To preserve the secrecy and expeditiousness that Eisenhower and Allen Dulles insisted on, I argued for removing the U-2 project from the agency's organizational chart and setting it up as a stand-alone organization. As a result, the entire project became the most compartmented and self-contained activity within the agency. The Development Project Staff, as the U-2 operation was known, was the only part of the CIA that had its own communications office and operational cable traffic. This office was supplemented by an outlet at each of the deployed overseas detachments, one at the Groom Lake test site, one at Lockheed, and one or two in California for the other contractors. All cable traffic came into Washington. No one saw copies of cables except on my release. In the normal course of business, copies received by the agency, no matter how sensitive, automatically went to the director's office. Dulles did not insist on seeing U-2 cables, however, and because of the volume, I marked for his attention only those that seemed to me to have policy implications. It was in this way that Dulles participated in all the important decision making of the U-2.

The organizational structure of the U-2 operation began to take its final form in 1955, with about one-third air force personnel on active duty (but assigned to the agency, so that I was actually their commander), one-third agency personnel on active duty, and one-third contract employees, mainly from Lockheed. I received a very liberal education in their different terms of employment and their privileges and duties. Forming harmonious teams out of these groups took a surprising amount of time and attention.

The focus of the first several months of 1955 was heavily on the development of the aircraft. Basically, this involved a long series of experimental and development flights that initially emphasized the airframe and engine and later the various subsystems, including the cameras. We encountered a number of small problems during this stage, the biggest and most disturbing of which was the unreliable behavior of the J-57 engine above 60,000 feet, where it was plagued with flameouts. In the development stage, these were not necessarily dangerous, because the engine could be windmilled by the pilot and restarted above 40,000 feet. Until the problem could be resolved satisfactorily and permanently, however, it would have been risky to fly the aircraft over enemy territory. We attempted a number of small fixes but were not successful. It wasn't until the first detachment had been declared operational that we got a new slant number of the J-57 engine. It proved virtually immune to flameouts up to its maximum altitude. Once we became operational, all personnel associated with the U-2 had great confidence in its reliability. My exposure to the plane had mostly been with drawings and proposals, but it was a very exciting object to see in person. To stand at the end of a long wing and be able to lift it off the ground a little bit was an extraordinary feeling.

On August 8, 1955, just as Kelly Johnson had scheduled, Tony LeVier piloted the first official flight of the U-2. It was uneventful and the landing was absolutely perfect, except that the plane ended up about ten feet off the ground. Mercifully, LeVier didn't do himself or the aircraft any harm, but his postlanding comments were most interesting. Because the U-2 was essentially a powered glider, when it got into ground effect it could glide for miles; the pilot's most difficult task with the aircraft, he said, was going to be to get it down and keep it down at the end of a flight.

There was no comparable plane in existence. Other aircraft may have achieved altitudes as great as those of the U-2, but to my knowledge none was able to go into a cruise climb close to 70,000 feet and remain in that regime until nearly 75,000 feet. Virtually the entire mission could be carried out at that altitude. Combined with the aircraft's prodigious range, this meant that photographs could be taken deep in the Soviet Union and China. That, of course, was vital to us.

My favorite story about the U-2's gliding capability took place during the preoperational phase. A routine training flight would begin in Nevada and range over the United States, covering a 2,000-mile radius and a 4,000-mile range. During the developmental phase, there was always the chance that a flameout or some other problem might develop, so contingency plans using the strategic air command organization were put in place for emergencies in which pilots might have to abort a flight. Their orders were to land at the nearest strategic air command base, where all commanders had a coded alert and sealed orders they were to open only if a mysterious aircraft appeared or if they were notified one was going to appear.

One afternoon I was in my office in Washington when a call came from Groom Lake announcing that a pilot on a long training mission had just reported an engine flameout over Tennessee and that he was heading for the air force base in Albuquerque. He believed he could make the base in about half an hour on a long, flat glide. I got on the telephone to the commander of the Albuquerque base and told him that in about thirty to forty minutes he should expect a special aircraft, a U-2, to land; he was to move it to a remote part of the base as quickly as possible, have a tarpaulin put over it to disguise its shape, and post a guard. I can only imagine his surprise at receiving a call from the CIA, but forty-five minutes later the phone rang and he reported that the flight did indeed land, my instructions had been carried out, and the pilot was available to speak with me, which he did. We talked a little about the incident and how fortunate we were to be out of it. A few days later I visited the U-2 base in Groom Lake and was shown the offending aircraft. Nothing had been done to it as yet and I reached up into the tailpipe of the engine and picked out pieces of metal, the biggest and largest of them about the size of an index finger. This was the debris that was left when a blade disintegrated in the engine; it had caused the flameout and prevented a restart. The engine was eventually shipped back to Pratt & Whitney for teardown, examination, and repair.

To meet the ambitious goals of the program, we needed cameras as technically innovative as the Lockheed airframe. By December 1954, a few weeks after the go-ahead for the project, Hycon, a firm with which Trevor Gardner had had a previous connection in California, was designated as our principal camera contractor. Perkin-Elmer was selected to develop and build a small tracking camera that could photograph all the ground flown over, mainly to corroborate navigational information. Maintenance of the Hycon-designed cameras was ultimately assigned to Perkin-Elmer because of quality-control problems at Hycon. In spring 1955 we approached Thompson-Ramo-Woolridge about procuring electronic intelligence (Elint) equipment. We purchased two systems from them that temporarily replaced the cameras during Elint flights.

Very few aircraft, I learned from Kelly Johnson and from my own experience with the project, come through the development phase without a fatal accident. I would say that something on the order of five pilots died in the course of the U-2 program and that at least one or two more were killed in Europe after deployment for reasons unrelated to enemy action.[15] Whenever there were fatalities Johnson, of course, made a complex diagnosis of what went wrong, why, and how and what could be done to prevent a reoccurrence. Early on, fatalities were caused by the inability of the pilot to restart an engine after a flameout at high altitude. Usually the engine would restart as one came down through operating altitude, and even if it didn't, the plane had such a huge radius of action as a glider that the pilot could usually find a place to land. In one accident, in Germany, that was initially inexplicable, it was finally discovered that the pilot had taken off and gone into a very steep climb and that the aircraft appeared to explode as he approached operating altitude. Johnson's subsequent diagnosis proved that if a pilot climbed too fast the nearly sea-level ambient air pressure in the gas tanks was more than the structure could sustain at altitude. If, instead, the ascent was made gradually, the inside and outside pressures would not differ as much. The installation of a simple relief valve took care of that unfortunate problem.

The project continued to develop according to plan and my personal relationship with the air force was excellent, but the aircraft soon attracted the jealous eye of General Curtis LeMay, commander of the strategic air command, who wanted to take control of the program. A serious controversy erupted between LeMay and the agency in the summer of 1955 and resurfaced again in 1957, when the U-2 program was in limbo because of Eisenhower's reluctance to allow primary missions over the Soviet Union. This controversy affected planning and budgeting so seriously that I was finally compelled to request that the director and deputy director of central intelligence push for a decision on whether the U-2 was to remain in civilian hands or be given to the air force. Up to this time there had been no formal written agreement between the air force and the agency defining our respective roles. Briefing papers I wrote for Allen Dulles argued that continued CIA control of the project was the best way to maintain security and enhance plausible denial of U.S. responsibility. The disagreement with the air force over who would run the program became evident to personnel down the ranks, and even Art Lundahl in photointerpretation sensed the problem: "Air force [officers] would come to this small division I was creating and want to know how many people I aimed to have there, how many copies of the reports were going to be made, what was the security system going to be called, how were the reports going to be distributed, who had the priority on the input to the reports, were there footnoted minority opinions. . . . They were hoping for a bigger role; they were hoping for control of the project."[16]

Fortunately, LeMay had difficulty rallying his air force colleagues to his cause. A fair number of people in the military resented the primacy of the strategic air command in their affairs. There was, nevertheless, little doubt in most people's minds that the command was the primary arm of the air force and that what it wanted it would get. I remember a visit Dulles and I paid to the tactical air command in Colorado Springs. LeMay flew out to see him, and we had a grim session in Dulles's room. LeMay said in effect, "You fellows can't be serious in wanting to conduct these operations." We replied that we were. Dulles told me later that the tactical air commander had spoken to him privately as they were walking between buildings and offered the following advice: "Don't let LeMay get his cotton-picking hands on this project."

I didn't intend to. I wanted this project very much—it was a glamorous and high-priority endeavor endorsed not only by the president but by a lot of very important scientific people on the outside. It would confer a great deal of prestige on the organization that could carry it off successfully. I also knew that Dulles wanted to keep it within agency control. For these reasons, I conducted a fairly vigorous bureaucratic guerrilla campaign that resulted in my negotiating a satisfactory agreement with Air Force Chief of Staff Nathan Twining and his deputy, Hank Everest, early in autumn 1955. It resolved the short-term problem of the agency–air force conflict and also set up a joint project organization that proved to be an effective long-term solution. Strategic air command pilots would be used for training, and while the director of central intelligence would appoint the head of the project, the air force chief of staff would appoint a deputy. The first person who agreed to assume the deputy position was General Osmond Ritland, who earlier had assisted me as a support officer. Our relationship, although now more formal, continued to work extremely well and we became close friends. Most important, we developed an effective collaboration between the agency and the air force that I've always considered to be one of the real achievements of the U-2 program. I remember almost no differences or schisms between the agency and air force that arose after this point.

There is an epilogue to this story. Although I had fought hard for agency control of the project in 1955 and had improved relations with the air force to the point where LeMay was more comfortable with our management, Dulles almost gave the program away in 1958. Always a fiscal conservative, Eisenhower had become concerned with the size of the agency's budget and was looking for ways to save money. After discussing the budget with him, Dulles, much to my chagrin, raised the idea of transferring the U-2, or at least its support elements, to the air force. Even more disconcerting, Eisenhower seemed to think there might be some merit to this proposition. He figured that moving operations to the air force might reduce the number of contractors in maintenance work, which air force personnel could conceivably handle.[17]

A few days after this meeting, I swung into action. As Andrew Goodpaster reported, I came by the White House to offer a different perspective. I explained that the U-2 should be "kept in a small autonomous organization, so as to provide security, direct control, and extremely close supervision"—in short, kept the way it was. I also argued that the savings would probably not be even a fourth as much as the president and Dulles anticipated. And in the process of cutting costs, I explained, the operation's high standards of maintenance could suffer. Eisenhower seemed to backpedal a bit when Goodpaster next spoke to him. Although he had considered transferring the U-2 to the air force, it wasn't because he wanted them to perform flights over Russia—that would always be strictly a civilian affair—but merely because in late 1958 he didn't envision many flights, if any, over the plane's effective remaining life. The president was all for saving money, but he decided not to press the transfer.[18] The U-2 remained entirely an agency-run operation.

By mid-1956 we had performed several test flights over Soviet-bloc countries and were sufficiently satisfied with the plane's performance to take the next, more serious step, penetration of the Soviet Union itself. Allen Dulles and I went to the White House in June to obtain permission from Eisenhower. Andrew Goodpaster and John Foster Dulles were also present. Upon completion of our presentation and discussion, Eisenhower dismissed us, saying that he would inform us of his decision through Goodpaster. Everyone left the room except Foster Dulles. I have always assumed that Eisenhower wanted to give him a chance to express his views in private.

The president appeared supportive during the meeting and as we awaited his answer there were details to be worked out. On June 21, I met with Jim Killian and Andy Goodpaster. Although Goodpaster's declassified memorandum of this meeting is a textbook example of circumlocution (the target of the flights is never mentioned), I am reasonably confident, based on the historical chronology, that the memo refers to the first overflights of the Soviet Union. We covered the potential intelligence yield of the operation, operating conditions, altitude, and malfunctions. Goodpaster relayed Eisenhower's concerns that the flight path "cover all that is vital quickly" and that "during the phase of deep operations" he receive operational updates.[19]

Less than two weeks later, on July 2, I met with Goodpaster again and expressed my desire to begin operations. He had briefed the president, who decided the best way to proceed once the go-ahead was given was to have a ten-day period of operations, followed by a report. The next day he told me that the president had given the go-ahead and that the ten days would run through July 14. Along with the briefing reports, Eisenhower wanted me to provide a review of operational security during the period.[20]

Always a hard bargainer, I asked Goodpaster if I could take the ten days to mean ten days of good weather. "Absolutely not!" he replied. "It's ten calendar days, period. You'll have to take your chances with the weather." I grumbled a bit but accepted the limitation. I believe Eisenhower arranged things this way to keep our activities on a short leash. His idea was that we should try to get two or three flights off in the next ten days and then pause to assess the results. This proved to be sensible, as the overflights were indeed an exceedingly sensitive act so far as the Soviets were concerned.

Although we had experienced poor weather conditions just days earlier, we were soon able to send off our first flight. Checking the weather was part of a sequence of decisions that would determine whether or not the U-2 would fly. About noon, if the weather seemed likely to be favorable, I would be so informed and the detachment would be alerted to the probability of a flight. Around six or seven in the evening I would stop at project headquarters on my way home, and if indeed the weather was good, a second signal would be sent that said "high likelihood of a mission." Then, close to midnight, the decision had to be made and transmitted. I would go to project headquarters, look at the weather maps, and talk to Operations, after which it was literally a one-word message, "Go" or "No-go." In Wiesbaden, where the flight would originate, it would be about 5:00 a.m. Knowing there would be no word until morning, I would go home and sleep (perhaps unwisely) the sleep of the just.

On July 4, 1956, the U-2 left Wiesbaden for its first mission over the Soviet Union. It flew over Poznan, Poland, where riots had occurred just a few days earlier, then to Belorussia and to Moscow, which it passed over twice before heading north to Leningrad. Major targets of this flight were the naval shipyard that was the center of the Soviet submarine program and an important Bison jet airfield, both near Leningrad. After photographing these key military installations, the U-2 returned to Wiesbaden via the Baltic coast. When I saw Allen Dulles early the next morning and told him a mission was about to land at any time, he seemed somewhat startled and horrified to learn that the flight plan had covered Moscow and Leningrad. He asked whether it had been prudent to take such a risk the first time out, and I explained that this flight would probably be the safest one we would experience since it had less chance of being intercepted than any subsequent one. I was able to call him later that morning to say that a cable had come in confirming that the mission had ended successfully.

We had lucked out on the weather, and the photographs were remarkable. We obtained perfectly beautiful high-altitude photographs of Leningrad and Moscow in which one could literally count the number of automobiles in the streets. (Later, with a higher-resolution, lesser-coverage camera, I saw photographs of our own Capitol in which the photoanalysts not only counted the number of cars but identified their makes—all this from about thirteen miles up.)

Our success represented the climax of two years' work and I was excited and gratified beyond words. From what I learned from Andy Goodpaster, Eisenhower was similarly impressed. He had strongly backed this risky project and it had paid off. The U-2 was doing what it was designed to do. It was getting superb information on the Soviet Union, and it was doing so at what was recognized even then as a very modest cost. The aircraft were around $1 million each; the total personnel assigned to the project at its peak (both abroad and domestically) was about five or six hundred, excluding contractors.

The early flights pleased Eisenhower for yet another important reason. The intelligence that was brought back showed that the threat from Soviet long-range Bison bombers was considerably less than had been estimated. As a result, Eisenhower was able to turn down the air force's proposals for increased

B-52 production, secure in the knowledge that national security was not being compromised. Because of these factors, the agency scored very heavily with him. He also liked the feeling that he had direct and immediate control over the operation, which he did.

July 5, the day after the initial Soviet overflight, was one of the few times in the history of the project when I authorized double missions to take advantage of good weather. There were two nearly simultaneous takeoffs, one plane headed for central Russia, the other for the Ukraine. The U-2 made approximately six flights over the Soviet Union that week, and beginning with the very first, we were aware that the plane was being fairly accurately tracked on Soviet radar. According to Leo Geary, who had by this time replaced Os Ritland as my air force deputy, "East German radar picked it up and passed it on to the Soviet radar (which is a difference in name only), fully expecting that it would never come back." Later that day East German radar picked up the plane again on its return flight. The East Germans must have been startled and surprised that it hadn't been shot down.[21]

As might be expected, the Soviets used diplomatic channels to protest vigorously our highly provocative actions. The notion that we would overfly them at will must have been deeply unsettling, yet the note of protest was puzzling: the Soviets did not blame the U.S. government directly; rather they cited "certain circles in the United States" who planned to aggravate relations between the two countries. In the Soviet view of events, these "reactionary circles" in our government would do anything to interfere with the "improvement of relations." Pointing a finger at the air force in particular, the Soviets said, they expected that "steps will be taken . . . to punish those guilty for the said violations." Surprisingly, they misidentified the plane as a twin-engine bomber.[22]

It is my belief that the Soviets always made their protests privately because they did not want to admit to their citizens that the United States could overfly them with impunity and that the government was powerless to do anything about it. This tactic suited us very well, as we did not want public exposure to produce an ultimatum for the Soviets that the world press would convert into a cause for war. What actually happened was that the two governments, even in their deep hostility, found it convenient to collaborate and keep the flights secret.

The Soviet protest had the desired effect on Eisenhower, at least in the short term: Eisenhower wanted the project slowed down and it was quite a few months before he was ready to approve another. The stand-down lasted until autumn (and the Suez crisis), when we went to him seeking renewal of the flights. From that point forward, Eisenhower continued to authorize all flights on an individual basis.

In mid-November 1956, Dulles and I went to the White House to meet with Eisenhower, Goodpaster, Herbert Hoover, Jr., and Admiral Arthur Radford. The president was concerned about sending more flights over the Soviet Union. As a result of the Soviets' recent invasion of Hungary, he believed that the United States had gained a place in the world's eyes it hadn't held since World War II. He was uncertain whether the potential intelligence from future overflights was adequate compensation for the loss of this new position. To underscore the point, he said the U.S. "must preserve" a place in the world "that is correct and moral"; he ordered us to "stay as close" to the border "as possible and still cover [the] fields."[23] A few days later, on November 20, the U-2 renewed its overflights of Soviet territory.

In many ways the pattern established during the first flight continued throughout the program. Allen Dulles, Foster Dulles, and I would meet with the president and give him a map showing the proposed flight plan; he would ask some questions. On at least a couple of occasions he exercised his authority as commander in chief by suggesting the flight plan be altered. He was a cautious man who liked to have contingencies under his control. I never knew him to make a direct decision in meetings about the U-2 at which I was present. He would instead deliberate in private, probably in consultation with Foster Dulles, and his decision would be transmitted that day or a day later, usually by Goodpaster.

I always found Eisenhower businesslike and even-tempered. He was well-informed, wanting to know everything about the question before him, and an intent and intelligent listener. I never saw him exhibit anger in any discussion of policy. Originally I had some doubts as to whether he was fully knowledgeable about what his administration was doing and whether he was in control of it; I realized my initial judgment was wrong, however, once I began to have direct contact with him.

When Eisenhower approved or disapproved a mission, his decision was largely influenced by the circumstances surrounding the mission rather than by any details of the proposed flight itself. There would be a period shortly after each mission had been flown when he would be reluctant to authorize another until the issue of provocation had cooled off. He would consider whether the mission had gone undetected or been accurately tracked and whether there had been a diplomatic protest. I think that his actions reflected a desire to reduce risk and that he did not wish to continue flights that would increase our exposure unless the objective was highly valuable military intelligence. This was the motivation behind all his decisions regarding the U-2. He wanted to know exactly what the objective was and whether it was worth it. He would then authorize only that specific objective and that specific flight.

Andy Goodpaster sees Eisenhower's military background—his experience as a field commander and the importance of intelligence when he was supreme Allied commander—as influencing his interest in and active management of the U-2 project. His understanding of the various intelligence disciplines made him acutely sensitive to the critical role U-2 intelligence could play in maintaining national security. At the same time, the Battle of the Bulge—where, unknown to his own intelligence operators, the Germans amassed a major force—impressed on him the limitations of intelligence and the danger of being caught off guard. Almost every morning, Goodpaster used the CIA's overnight intelligence report to brief him. The president would form and reform his views on the basis of new intelligence. If something was of particular interest to him, he would call for more intelligence on the subject. He would then take this information and fit it into a worldview that had been shaped by years of "reviewing and studying and pondering."[24]

Preparations for overseas deployment of the U-2 began soon after the plane was flight-tested successfully. The next critical step was to obtain permission to operate the U-2 out of strategically placed bases in secure, friendly countries. I embarked on a series of trips to gather agreements on security and cooperation with various host countries. My goal was to maximize the intelligence benefits of the U-2 during its expected useful life, which no one in the agency realistically thought would be extended.

My first such trip was to the United Kingdom, where I met with Prime Minister Anthony Eden and received his permission to base a squadron of three U-2s in a segregated hangar and workspace at Lakenheath, a World War II base where the U.S. strategic air command had retained operations. This site was very satisfactory and fit well with our original intent to begin overflights from Britain. Although we were able to initiate a few practice flights into Eastern Europe, an unfortunate incident altered the situation and adversely affected our ability to operate out of the United Kingdom. A Soviet cruiser docked in Portsmouth harbor while making a courtesy call, and apparently a British frogman was dispatched to take a look at the signaling gear. A short time later his body was found floating in the bay. There was a great deal of press attention, and Eden's reaction was to rescind authorization for the U-2 to fly over enemy or forbidden territory from the United Kingdom. My recollection is that we kept an aircraft and a few people at Lakenheath for perhaps another month or so, but the base was closed out rather rapidly.

The search for an alternative location took my immediate supervisor, Deputy Director Pearre Cabell, and me to West Germany. As we briefed Chancellor Konrad Adenauer on the operation Adenauer said very little, but he quickly gave his approval for us to operate out of Germany. What we had in mind, and eventually used, was Giebelstadt, a former Luftwaffe base near the East-West border, about fifty miles east of Wiesbaden. Meanwhile, however, operations had already begun from Wiesbaden, where there was a large American air force presence. I believe our first five overflights of the USSR, plus one or two over Eastern Europe, originated from Wiesbaden. In due time we sought and received approval to use the Incirlik base in Turkey, where the U-2 operated for several years and produced several important overflights.

It was after the move to Turkey that I saw a limiting factor in our operations—namely, the ability to obtain the president's permission to conduct the flights. I therefore conceived the scheme of involving the Royal Air Force in the operation on a completely equal basis in the hope that we could contrive an arrangement whereby either the British or the U.S. government could approve an overflight independent of the other. It would be a system that didn't require two signatures to initiate an overflight—the last thing I wanted was to make it more difficult for the political authorities to approve flights. Indeed I wanted to make it easier, of course. We succeeded in accomplishing that goal in 1957 with the approval of President Eisenhower and Prime Minister Eden. During the negotiations I also met with Sir Dick White, the head of MI6 (Allen Dulles's counterpart), and M. L. McDonald, the assistant to the chief of air staff command for British intelligence. The CIA worked closely with MI6 and regarded its people as close allies.

British involvement was implemented, and three or four RAF pilots were brought to Groom Lake, where they received the same training as U.S. pilots did and associated freely with members of our detachments. I remember an overflight out of Incirlik that most likely covered the Soviet Union and that was technically conducted by the RAF. It was important in the sense that it enabled us to try out our procedures from the beginning of a mission to its conclusion—

making the proposal, obtaining approval, conducting the mission, and finally handling the processing of the exposed film. As a convenience to the RAF, the film was taken to Rochester, New York, for processing at Eastman Kodak and then returned to the British. The intent was for these missions to be conducted as if they were operations initiated by the RAF with approvals within the British government and results going to U.K. intelligence. I do not believe the CIA withheld, retained, or censored film at any time during this arrangement.

My diplomatic trips to see the British and Germans resulted in important agreements and bilateral cooperation on intelligence matters. I also made a less successful trip to France. Ever concerned with increasing the productivity of the U-2, I decided late in the program to add another partner. My previous trips had been made in consultation with the Department of State and with agency colleagues, but I embarked on this venture without such prior discussion. I met with President Charles de Gaulle and explained my proposal. Much to my surprise, he wanted no part of the operation. Although the outcome was disappointing, it may have been fortunate: when I returned to Washington and explained the nature of my trip and the surprising French reaction, virtually none of my agency colleagues thought the idea had been a good one. Evidently the French were held in lower esteem as intelligence partners than I realized; had de Gaulle accepted my proposal, not only would I have had to face a fight back at the agency, but I could have created a potential diplomatic problem if an agreement had been reached and later had to be broken.

Soviet protests had ended our flurry of overflights on July 10, 1956, but by the time the U-2 had been deployed at the Incirlik air base in Adana, Turkey, we were ready to try another penetration of the Soviet Union. This attempt, which occurred on November 10, 1956, was not successful. Although the U-2 overflew Soviet airspace, mechanical problems forced the pilot to cut the mission short and return to Adana. The pilot was Francis Gary Powers.

Nearly all the best operations were conducted from Incirlik, including the one that gave us the first look at a major Soviet missile development site at Kapustin Yar, north of the Caspian and east of the Volga. Incirlik was an attractive base for operations because for some time Soviet radar defenses were considerably weaker along the USSR's southern border with Armenia and we were tracked less frequently.

In summer 1957 Eisenhower agreed to permit some flights over peripheral areas in the Soviet Union such as the Kamchatka Peninsula and Lake Baikal in central Siberia. The hope was that these overflights could be staged from

Pakistan so that Soviet airspace could be entered from the "back door"—that is, from Chinese or Iranian territory rather than from Western Europe. Anthony Marshall, one of my personal assistants, met with the president of Pakistan, Iskander Mirza, and received his permission. Shortly thereafter, operations staged from Pakistan commenced.

A procedure called Quickmove, developed by Stanley Beerli, the detachment commander at Incirlik, permitted operational flights to be staged from a temporary advanced base supplied from Adana; on more than one occasion, Quickmove originated from Pakistan. Its goal, of course, was to hide any clues to the location of a U-2 takeoff or landing. The procedure involved deployment of a U-2 either from a remote airfield, in which case the plane would return to the detachment base, or from the detachment base, with a landing at a remote airfield. A flight staged from the main base at Adana, for example, meant that two C-130s would fly to the remote base to meet an arriving U-2; the twenty-person Quickmove ground crew, brought in on one C-130, would refuel the U-2 from the fifty-five-gallon drums stored on the second C-130 and reload the C-130s while a spare pilot flew the U-2 back to Adana.[25] When the C-130s followed shortly thereafter, there was no trace of any activity's having taken place. When Quickmove was used to stage a mission from a remote base, a C-130 Hercules would take off from the detachment base ahead of the U-2, carrying equipment, fuel, food, a spare pilot, and communication equipment, and would fly to the landing site at dusk. At the same time the U-2 would take off, follow the C-130, and rendezvous with it. The crew chief and ground staff would check out the U-2 during the night while the pilot remained in the C-130 for his preflight preparation. The aircraft would take off on its assigned mission at dawn.

Beerli says a C-130 was used because "we wanted to have the smallest profile we could when we arrived at the base, and C-130s . . . flew into bases very frequently. It was a normal cargo airplane. The whole operation was . . . compact and . . . beautifully run." Everything was kept to "the minimum." There was no margin for error. If a plane had mechanical difficulty, there would be no rapid way to make a repair. "In clandestine operations," Beerli observes, "you just plan and have 100 percent operational confidence." Quickmove achieved all its goals, and various "listening posts" confirmed that there was "no really high level of interest" in the C-130s as they went about their business.[26]

The first Quickmove launching out of Peshawar, Pakistan, was a mission to

Lake Baikal. The C-130 flew to a tiny village in Iran that had a landing strip within a couple of miles of the Afghan border. The U-2 landed after it, and with a minimum of maintenance and refueling and the substitution of a fresh pilot for the U-2, both planes returned to Incirlik. One important mission staged out of Peshawar produced excellent photography of sizable atomic installations in central Siberia, and another, over Chinese territory and the Semipalatinsk nuclear test site in Soviet Kazakhstan, provided the first glimpse of a peculiar radar installation near Lake Baikal, which enormously interested the electronic experts in the Washington intelligence community. The installation came to be called the henhouse.

On most missions pilots had virtually no freedom to deviate from their assigned course unless they had a compelling reason. We were concerned that burning more fuel than necessary might jeopardize the pilot's life and the mission. Nevertheless, one of the rare occasions when a pilot left his pre-established route proved to yield among the richest intelligence finds of the entire program, the discovery of Tyuratam in Russia, the first test site for full-scale intercontinental ballistic missiles. In June 1957, three months before the launch of Sputnik, a U-2 pilot flying over Kazakhstan spotted something in the distance that caught his attention. Departing from his course, he stumbled on the crown jewel of Soviet space technology, whose existence had not even been suspected. Within a week of the U-2's return, a team of intelligence analysts, photointerpreters, and photogrammetrists had built a scale model of the Tyuratam test site. Photointelligence also allowed analysts to determine the size and power of Soviet rockets based on burn marks and the configurations of the pads for exhaust gases. One of the ironies of history is that months before the launching of Sputnik, an event that would shake American self-confidence, the United States was flying with impunity above this most secret of Soviet military locations.

Overhead reconnaissance of other selected areas of the Soviet Union provided extremely valuable intelligence on the strength of the Soviet bomber fleet and the rate of production. By looking at pictures of a site, photogrammetrists were able to determine how many planes of each type there were. These calculations did not make for a watertight case—since Base A might be photographed one week and Base B not until weeks or months later, and there was no way of telling how much movement had occurred between them—but they did assimilate a great deal more solid evidence on Soviet bomber strength. If not many planes of a certain type were found, it was reasonable to conclude that they were just coming into production or that production was very low. Through this work we discovered that there were fewer Soviet bombers than the air force had claimed, and fears of a bomber gap diminished.

Later in the program, there was great concern about a missile gap. Photoanalysis enabled an extraordinary amount of intelligence to be collected on the progress of the Soviets' program and the characteristics of their missiles and launch systems. Having good photography of their sites greatly deepened our knowledge of the purposes and uses of various Soviet installations and the military strengths they represented.

Approximately two years after overseas deployments were started, we established a base at Atsugi, Japan, where the main target was Communist China and the eastern Soviet Union. A few missions were flown over Communist China from Japan, but we also entered into an agreement with the Chinese Nationalists to train their pilots and eventually turn two U-2s over to them. With our help and logistical support, they operated U-2 flights over the mainland for a number of years, obtaining valuable photointelligence of the military, industrial, and atomic complexes in northwest China. On occasion we also operated U-2 flights through an Alaskan base, which involved flying an aircraft from California to Alaska, conducting a mission, recovering the aircraft in Alaska, and ferrying it back to California.

In the latter part of the 1950s, I developed the idea of deploying the U-2 off aircraft carriers. Navy officials seemed interested when I approached them, but the air force refused to participate. Although the air force may have suspected otherwise, I did not want to take the operation away from them. I simply believed that if we were to run out of available bases it would be prudent to be able to operate off U.S. territory a hundred miles out from any coast in the world. After I left the agency the issue was reopened and the air force finally agreed to the experiment. The U-2 was modified for carrier operations and then tested several times. Carrier capability was thoroughly established, and I take some credit for that.

From the beginning of the Suez crisis in 1956, we staged numerous overflights of the Middle East in Adana, even though the primary role of that detachment was to mount overflights of the Soviet Union. In the course of a month or more, we mapped virtually all of Iraq, Syria, Lebanon, and Israel and most of Egypt. One mission I remember with particular clarity occurred not long after Egypt closed off the canal to international shipping. We had already begun mapping the area, and the pilot on this particular mission had a routine but complicated course laid out that involved several legs from Adana to Cairo, where the military airport was his turning point for Israel. When the photographs were developed, the first shots of the airport showed a tranquil scene with Egyptian air force planes lined up neat and tidily. When, having made its turn, the U-2 flew back over the airport some ten minutes later, the place was in flames. In that short period the British and French attacked and largely destroyed the airport—in effect we had a damage assessment within minutes of the attack. "Twenty-minute reconnaissance," Eisenhower evidently commented after Art Lundahl briefed him and he saw the photographs. "Now that's something to shoot for."[27]

Operations over the Middle East were less carefully allocated by the president than those over the Soviet bloc. We were, in effect, encouraged to obtain any coverage that might be useful. We took full advantage of the situation to improve our intelligence of the region.

Although photointelligence was at the heart of the U-2 program, the missions produced a lot more than pictures. One of our most successful and interesting flights was staged from Bodo, Norway. It was an all-Elint mission that was flown at night without any camera on board. The pilot started down the Russian-Finnish border, flew near Leningrad, continued along the Baltic coast, and then followed the Russian-Polish border south to the Black Sea before landing at Incirlik. The purpose of the mission was to provoke Soviet radar, tracking, and communications along the entire border and make sophisticated recordings for later analysis. A complex radar receiver and recorder took in a large array of signals, locking onto each separate one and recording them on time-marked tape. When this accurate flight-path information was brought back, the analyst could tell where the aircraft was at any given time and could evaluate the extent to which the aircraft was bathed by radiation during its run. Putting these two factors together enabled the analyst to locate Soviet radar with a good deal of precision. Because the signal characteristics of different Soviet radars were pretty well known, it was also possible to determine what type of radar was at which location. We estimated that during this flight almost sixty Soviet fighters were launched against the U-2 yet failed to intercept it. Elint flights along the Soviet border were an important part of the program.

By the beginning of 1960 there were signs that the Russians had made considerable improvements in their air defense system. The possibility of losing a U-2 received serious consideration in policy circles. We told Eisenhower that it was most unlikely that a pilot would survive if shot down, by which we meant that a pilot would not survive a direct hit, because the U-2 was a very light aircraft, more like a glider, and would disintegrate on impact. We believed that if a U-2 was shot down over Soviet territory, all the Russians would have was the wreckage of an aircraft. We did not give sufficient weight to the possibility that a near miss might incapacitate the aircraft but leave the pilot uninjured and able to bail out.

There was unanimous agreement that the big rolls of film aboard the plane would not be destroyed, even if the plane was hit. They were virtually indestructible. Their nonflammable base would prevent them from burning, and they could be dropped from a height of ten miles and survive. We always knew that in the event of a crash there were going to be a couple of rolls of film lying around and there was not much we could do about it.

Eisenhower frequently expressed his concern. According to Andy Goodpaster, "he had the clearest understanding of the excitement . . . and the furor that would occur within the United States." At every meeting he would receive a briefing from the Defense Department: "the Defense people would talk about such things as . . . the assessment of Soviet capabilities and air defense, whether ground-to-air or radar, and what their capabilities for intercept would be." He would review those points each time, and with his excellent memory, Goodpaster says, he covered them quite thoroughly. The Defense Department representatives would inevitably conclude that the Soviets "did have the capability to track but they did not have the capability to intercept, nor did they have an air-to-ground weapon that would be capable of shooting [a U-2] down."[28]

Although these briefings may have allayed the president's concerns to some extent, the documentary evidence indicates that they were never far from his mind. At the end of 1958, for example, when he met with his Board of Consultants on Foreign Intelligence Activities, he once again expressed his periodic ambivalence about continuing U-2 overflights. Not only did he voice his concern that the intelligence produced might not be worth the resulting international tensions, but he worried about tracking of the U-2. Members of the board, however, felt the intelligence was "highly worthwhile."[29]

By early 1959 there was renewed talk in Congress about Soviet intercontinental ballistic missiles. At a meeting after the National Security Council met, Defense Secretary Neil McElroy asked the president to reconsider allowing more U-2 flights over the Soviet Union. He cited the opinion of the Joint Chiefs of Staff that the Soviets still could not shoot down the plane. General Twining supported him, saying that the Joint Chiefs would indeed like additional information. Again Eisenhower was troubled by the potential for a crisis. In a revealing moment, he remarked that nothing would make him "request authority to declare war more quickly than violation of our air space by Soviet aircraft." He concluded that, while one or two flights "might possibly be permissible," he was "against an extensive program."[30]

Eisenhower remained ambivalent. On April 7, I went to the White House at his request to discuss certain overflights to which he had given tentative approval the previous day but had subsequently retracted. If a plane was shot down or detection of the intrusion caused an international crisis, we couldn't "in the present circumstances afford the revulsion of world opinion against the United States that might occur," he said. He was already looking toward the possibility of a summit with Khrushchev and he didn't want to spoil the international climate.[31] During the summer, however, the need for intelligence on the Soviet missile program was so great that the president relented and the mission was flown.

Meeting with Eisenhower in February 1960, his Board of Consultants on Foreign Intelligence Activities proposed that overflights "be utilized to the maximum degree possible." He countered by saying that he had "one tremendous asset in a summit meeting," his "reputation for honesty," and that, "if one of these aircraft were lost when we are engaged in apparently sincere deliberations, it could be put on display in Moscow."[32] By the beginning of 1960, we were *all* growing concerned about the U-2's future and there was considerable discussion of how long it might be before the Soviets developed the capability to shoot one down. We knew that the Soviets could track the plane and send a missile up to the proper height to intercept it. We were equally aware that a Soviet modified surface-to-air missile had an estimated altitude capability of at least 70,000 to 75,000 feet, which was very close to the altitude of the U-2. The air force was asked for a new assessment of Soviet air defenses; its analysis concluded that the surface-to-air missile represented the greatest threat to the U-2, but only if the U-2 was detected early enough in its flight to alert the missile sites properly.

A flight over the Soviet Union at the beginning of April 1960 revealed that the U-2 was indeed being targeted at a very early stage. Even though all efforts to intercept the plane failed, the incident should have served as a warning. Had we given it more attention, we might have decided to suspend future overflights. Instead, we relied on a national intelligence estimate that concluded that although a surface-to-air missile could indeed reach the U-2's flying altitude, it was optimized for 60,000 feet. Above 60,000 feet its accuracy would fall off very rapidly because there wouldn't be air dense enough for its control surfaces to bite on. The Russians could get a missile up, but they couldn't control it or bring it in for a kill, or so we believed.

Our earlier concerns about the U-2's vulnerability led us back to Skunk Works at Lockheed to find a way to redesign the U-2 in a manner that did not interfere with its effectiveness but would prevent the Soviets from successfully tracking it. Kelly Johnson worked hard to try to cut down the radar cross-section of the aircraft. Wires and coatings of special kinds were attempted, but they all reduced the aircraft's performance. Ultimately the pilots who risked their lives flying the plane decided they would rather rely on the safety of the altitude, which kept them out of MIG range, than hope to elude Soviet radar through cross-section improvements. Ben Rich, one of Johnson's assistants, points out that "it is always bad to fix something that is already designed. It's easier to start with a clean sheet of paper."[33] But we didn't have the luxury of starting the U-2 from scratch, and our operation continued with the knowledge that one day the Soviets would be able to hit the U-2 either with a surface-to-air missile or with a plane of their own. I began preparations for a successor aircraft. I was also hard at work, though, to develop another revolutionary tool for intelligence collection—the reconnaissance satellite.

Aerial photography from the U-2 flight in early April 1960 had shown that the Soviets were moving quickly to deploy an operational intercontinental ballistic missile in the area of Plesetsk, approximately six hundred miles north of Moscow. A second flight verifying this deployment became critical, but time was of the essence since a mission over Plesetsk could be flown effectively only between the months of April and July because of the sun's angle in the northern latitudes.[34] If a flight could not be conducted during this three-month period, the opportunity would be lost for an entire year.

From Eisenhower's perspective the need for intelligence about the Soviet program had both a military and a financial purpose. If information brought back by the flight revealed that Soviet capabilities remained limited, he could use it to fight against increased defense spending. The information would be useful to have at the upcoming Paris summit, but that was a less important factor, according to Andy Goodpaster, who recalls that the president "was resisting a lot of pressure from Congress and from the other part of what he called the military-industrial complex. A great deal of pressure in the press [was] generated by the production complex and by the military, particularly the high leadership of the air force." In addition to ascertaining the number of operational sites, it was necessary to know how the Soviets deployed their intercontinental ballistic missiles. If they were truck-mounted, which meant that the entire Soviet highway system could be a deployment mechanism, that had the making of a serious problem. A big tractor-trailer could, as Art Lundahl says, "pull up on any highway, erect the back end, and fire an ICBM." If, however, the operation was tied to railroad spurs, which required a lot of iron and scouring up of the countryside, it was easier to locate where the firing was going to come from before it occurred. Although a rail-served system seemed to the experts all but certain, the system's degree of fulfillment still needed to be known.[35]

My recollection is that we requested permission for the flight in mid-April and received it from the president reasonably promptly, with the limitation that approval expired in two weeks, around April 25. Consistent cloud cover over the northeastern part of the Soviet Union prevented the mission's being flown before the deadline. Frustrated, I went to Andy Goodpaster and asked if there could be an extension. I did not have a meeting with Eisenhower; instead Goodpaster interceded and negotiated directly with him. That day, April 25, Goodpaster wrote a memorandum for the record that stated: "After checking with the President, I informed Mr. Bissell that one additional operation may be undertaken. . . . No operation is to be carried out after May 1."[36] This memorandum disproves the later allegation that the flight was flown without presidential approval. It is important to note that Goodpaster's memorandum did not specifically authorize us to undertake a flight on May 1; it authorized us to fly a single mission anytime through May 1. It looks to have been a grave mistake to have given us the general authority to fly so close to the summit, but the decision was an explicit one on Eisenhower's part. All of us, including the president, had become a little too confident about the success of the U-2. I am sure that Eisenhower's decision to grant us the week's extension was greatly influenced by the fact that the Soviets had been unable to shoot our plane down earlier in the month. They had seen a lot of planes by now, he probably thought, and to send one off a week before the summit wasn't going to be any worse than two weeks before, which he'd already agreed to.

The weather finally broke and we decided to take our chances. The flight plan was the most daring yet. Up to this time the U-2 had never flown more than about midway across the Soviet Union. Typically, it would fly that far and then turn around for the journey home. This mission would have been the first to transverse the entire Soviet Union. Aptly enough, it was called Operation

Grand Slam. Francis Gary Powers, the pilot, was to deploy from Pakistan, using Quickmove, pass over Tyuratam, then fly north to Sverdlovsk, northwest to Plesetsk, and back to Bodo, Norway. The mission was to be the longest U-2 flight to date. The decision as to whether the aircraft could accomplish the flight plan as drawn was left entirely up to the operations section at headquarters. Stan Beerli, who was now chief of the operations section, recalls that a great deal of our confidence relied on a successful Quickmove deployment. For the Powers flight, Quickmove was planned for both deployment and recovery. Beerli feels that it wasn't executed properly and that the slipup may have contributed significantly to the mission's failure.

In his memoir, *Operation Overflight,* Powers describes how he spent the days preceding his mission. On April 27, Powers took off from Turkey for Pakistan and a Quickmove deployment. After arriving in Peshawar, he and his support team tried to get a good night's sleep before the mission, which was planned for the following day. Stan Beerli arrived in Norway on April 28 and went directly to Bodo in preparation for Powers's scheduled landing. Bad weather caused the flight to be postponed that day. According to Beerli, the entire mission team should have been brought back to the detachment base in Turkey at that point to preserve security and the element of surprise.[37] Unfortunately, that isn't what happened.

Weather conditions continued to delay the flight over the next few days. Instead of the entire Quickmove team's returning to Turkey, the U-2 was shuttled back and forth while Powers and his team encamped at Peshawar. With little else to do, they played poker and loafed around.[38] By the time the mission was given the go-ahead on May 1, security had been compromised.

After Powers's unsuccessful flight, the foreign minister of Afghanistan met with a representative of the U.S. embassy in Kabul to protest the violation of Afghan airspace. He explained that he had received details of the flight from the Soviets. The embassy representative recorded that the only detail the foreign minister provided was that Powers, during his four days in Peshawar, had been "entertained socially by his Pakistani officer opposite numbers, who knew all about his mission."[39]

On May 1, Beerli was in position and ready in Bodo to meet Powers on his return. About an hour after the expected arrival time, it was clear that Powers would have been out of fuel if he had flown the mission. For security reasons, Beerli and the others couldn't use the telephone, so they waited. After about five hours, Beerli realized something had gone wrong and he flew back to Oslo. He was supposed to call a man in Oslo and tell him they had a great party last night—the code that Powers had arrived. Unfortunately, that was one call Beerli was never able to make.[40] The Powers mission was well within the range capability of the U-2, and all the usual safety factors had been considered. Our luck just plain ran out.

As events transpired and history has documented, the Soviets shot down Francis Gary Powers and the Paris summit ended in disarray. An important opportunity for an early detente had been lost. There is now no doubt we should have been more sensitive about planning a flight so close to the summit date. As Eisenhower explains in his memoirs, he approved every flight with the fullest understanding of the "stern diplomatic consequences" the United States would face if there was ever a successful downing of a U-2 over Soviet territory. Although I was a strong advocate for U-2 overflights, Eisenhower recalls that we were in agreement on this point: "I . . . consistently expressed a conviction that if ever one of the planes fell in Soviet territory a wave of excitement mounting almost to panic would sweep the world, inspired by the standard Soviet claim of injustice, unfairness, aggression, and ruthlessness. The others, except for my own immediate staff and Mr. Bissell, disagreed."[41]

I happened to be out of town when the U-2 was shot down. I returned to Washington to find a message telling me to go to the project office at once, and that was when I learned that the flight was missing and very probably shot down. Bob King, one of my special assistants, was the administrative officer that weekend and was at home on Sunday when the phone rang and Carmine Vito, a retired U-2 pilot who was the operations officer said, "Bill Bailey didn't come home. You better find the man quick." Bob knew I was out of town visiting Walt Rostow, but he didn't have Walt's telephone number. When Bob tried to get Rostow's number, the operator just wouldn't give it to him. Bob started screaming, "It's a goddamn national emergency," so the operator put him through. When Rostow answered the phone, Bob explained that we had "lost a bird." Rostow told him I was already on a plane flying back to Washington. Meanwhile, downtown, there was chaos in the office. Bob remembers the scene distinctly:

> Everybody was running around like the proverbial chicken when Bissell strolled in (he tends to walk kind of like a stork, pretty fast). . . . He almost sauntered, as I recall, and everybody said (if not out loud, at least to themselves), "Whew, now we're off the hook because he'll take

> charge of this mess." . . . He came in as if he were about to assemble a Monday staff meeting—"Hmmm, hmmm, yeah, OK, we'll talk about it." Not excited. I don't know whether from a management standpoint that was an act or whether he really was in control intellectually and emotionally. Everybody calmed down when he walked back in because we knew he would take care of it—the president, the U.N., or anything else.[42]

My recollection is that I felt a sense of disaster about the entire affair and thought the program would probably be terminated. After about a week, Khrushchev announced that Powers was alive, which was another great shock and the last thing any of us expected. Having always assumed that the pilot would perish in a crash, we issued our cover story, formulated in advance, that the U-2 had been on a weather flight along the Soviet border and might have strayed into Soviet territory. We were ready to concede that the U-2 had come down in their territory, but if the Soviets claimed it had crashed not near the border but in the middle of the country, we planned to accuse them of moving it to a site that they had selected for propaganda purposes. All of this might have worked if Powers had not survived. When it was announced that Powers had been taken prisoner, it was apparent that the cover story had broken down. It is interesting that the first photographs the Soviets made available to the press were not of the actual U-2 wreckage but of another type of plane. Why they did that is something I have never understood.

I remember spending several hectic hours with Secretary of State Christian Herter, one or two of his lieutenants, Allen Dulles, and others from the agency, drafting a statement that could be either made by the president or released in his name. In the frenzied discussion it became clear that the president had only two options: he could claim that he knew nothing about what had transpired and lay himself open to the charge that he didn't control his own government or he could announce that he knew about it and authorized it. The second, of course, is the option he ultimately took, as I was pretty sure he would. There is nothing more damning for a president than to have to admit that a covert operation was conducted by his government without his knowledge. Eisenhower was the kind of president who would insist he was in control (as indeed he was) and who would not want to make a statement to imply the contrary. Eisenhower maintained tight control over the project, but especially over the actual flights.

What happened on the flight is now pretty well established. The Soviets fired their surface-to-air missiles at the aircraft. One missed entirely, one shot down one of their MIG interceptors, and a third was a near miss that came close enough to damage the empennage and the control surfaces. Much of the plane was still intact and went into a flat spin. Centrifugal forces in the cockpit made it very difficult for Powers to jettison the canopy and release himself from the seat. Exactly as instructed, he was not going to press the destruct button until he could get clear of the aircraft. He finally managed to eject himself, but in the tussle and wrestle of doing so, he was unable to activate the destruct mechanism. The plane came down in large pieces.

The issue of whether a U-2 pilot should be told, in effect, to commit suicide had been addressed fully during planning discussions. I distinctly remember approving standing instructions to the pilots that they had this capability available but that the decision was left entirely to their judgment. They were under no orders to do away with themselves. I am sure that these generalized instructions were at one time or another communicated to all the pilots. But the fact is that we felt there was very little chance that a pilot would be shot down and live. We were not well-prepared for what happened.

Those of us in the agency who were close to the project felt that in all probability Powers behaved perfectly correctly. The impression did form in the minds of some senior officials, however, that Powers had been ordered to take poison and that his failure to do so was an improper action. There is no such evidence. The pilots were not briefed to kill themselves, as I have always stated. The choice was theirs. Even while Powers was a Soviet prisoner a preliminary inquiry found no evidence of impropriety on his part. It is simply human nature to find someone to blame when things go wrong, and certain U.S. officials were willing to blame Powers. I never did.

When Powers returned in February 1962, the matter underwent review by a more formal board of inquiry, whose members were Barret Prettyman, a retired federal judge; John Bross of the CIA; and Lieutenant General Harold Bull. Leo Geary, my air force deputy, served as a technical adviser to the panel and sat through many days of testimony. Although the panel ultimately cleared Powers, he unfortunately did not receive a ringing endorsement. Geary thinks it is important to state for the record that "Frank Powers made that mission because he was the best navigator we had."[43]

Eight days after the plane was shot down, Eisenhower remarked at a meeting of the National Security Council that the incident had produced a "great storm" but that it had been inevitable that reconnaissance activity would be revealed. On May 20, reviewing the speech Henry Cabot Lodge would give at the United Nations, he reflected that the only real mistake he saw was in the way the government handled itself in the days immediately following the incident. He felt that "statements were made too soon" and that the "administration and training of some of our intelligence units were weak."[44] It is difficult to dispute this assessment, considering how poorly coordinated our handling of the cover story was.

Gordon Gray, the special assistant for national security affairs, met alone with the president on the last day of May, when, according to Gray, Eisenhower commented on how he approached management of the U-2 program, saying that "he had deliberately held the matter on a tight although informal basis. . . . He had felt this important from the point of view of leaks and in that respect success has been achieved. He said he felt that the only thing to do now is to ride out the storm."[45] And ride out the storm was what we did.

All of us were saddened by the downing of Powers and the collapse of the Paris summit, but I think I was more concerned at that moment with the future of the operation and the agency and with the action the president might take. Given the unfortunate circumstances and considering how much Eisenhower was personally hoping to achieve a breakthrough at the summit, both he and Herter were most understanding. There were no recriminations or criticisms. Eisenhower simply announced there would be no more overflights of the USSR. If one or two occurred, they would have covered Kamchatka in the far east but nothing in the central or western Soviet Union.

The U-2 program had enhanced our national security politically, militarily, and economically. From a political perspective, the intelligence collected allowed Eisenhower to remain calm during a period of great international tension. He was able to avoid bellicose rhetoric or acts of aggressiveness secure in his knowledge that the Soviet bomber and missile threat was significantly less than the public sometimes feared. One consequence was that his stature grew as an international statesman. Militarily, the U-2 provided invaluable information on the Soviets' capabilities and the deployment of their forces. In the event of war, we would be equipped to strike at the heart of their military-industrial complex far better than they at ours. The U-2's contributions to our economic security are also important to recognize. In *The Rise and Fall of the Great Powers,* Paul Kennedy argues that great nations often fall because they succumb to imperial overstretch. In essence, they build a defense establishment so great that its cost undermines their economic strength, which is the true source of national power. Empowered by U-2 intelligence, which proved there was neither a bomber gap nor a missile gap, Eisenhower repeatedly frustrated the attempts of America's military-industrial complex to gain financing for larger and more expensive weapon systems. An economically strong America, unhobbled by huge budget deficits, was one of Eisenhower's greatest legacies. In my view, the achievements of the U-2 belong very much to Eisenhower. He had the courage to support the program and take the many risks associated with each flight.

The other great legacy of the U-2 was the way it changed intelligence collection forever. The fact that we could learn as much as we did by looking down from above was one of the key contributions of the program. It whetted the appetite of the U.S. government for such intelligence and increased the willingness of policy makers to develop systems for this sort of collection. I am especially gratified to know that the U-2 continues to contribute to our national security: during Operation Desert Storm in 1992, it provided important military intelligence during overflights of Iraq.[46]

Like the Marshall Plan's Economic Cooperation Administration, the U-2 program was given the authority, the freedom of action, and the best people available to achieve an important national objective. It is not a coincidence that these programs were highly successful and contributed greatly to national security. Later, with the Bay of Pigs, what is noteworthy was the lack of a similar delegation of authority.

A month after Powers was shot down over the Soviet Union, Andy Goodpaster spoke with Eisenhower about whether or not we should go ahead with the U-2's successor plane, the A-12. Not surprisingly, Eisenhower was unenthusiastic. He said that he did not think the project should be pushed as a top priority. He even thought his advisers might conclude that "it would be best to get out of it if we could."[47] Fortunately, he was merely considering the possibilities; he would ultimately stay the course. Although there were many cost overruns and missed deadlines, the A-12 would prove to be nothing less than a revolution in aerospace technology.

By the time the U-2's first overflights of the Soviet Union had ended in late summer 1956, I had become convinced that a successor program had to be initiated immediately to ensure that our reconnaissance capability would not lapse. In August 1956 I began working on one with Colonel Jack Gibbs. In 1957 I suggested to Dulles that to help move the project forward we establish an advisory committee similar to the one that had assisted the agency in the development of the U-2. A committee was formed with Din Land as its chair.

Successful Soviet tracking of the U-2 indicated that a successor plane would need more than height to evade radar. I hired a contractor to study how changes in a plane's speed, altitude, and radar cross-section affected its stealth. The results determined that it would be impossible to eliminate totally either detection or the possibility of a plane's being shot down. On the other hand, if a plane could attain and sustain supersonic speed it would be possible to greatly reduce radar detection and missile threats.[48] Further studies revealed that the U-2's successor should be able to operate at altitudes over 80,000 feet and at speeds over Mach 3. If a plane could be built with these characteristics it could outfly any missile the Soviets might build, even if it couldn't evade their radar.[49] Din Land's advisory committee confirmed the conclusions of the other vulnerability studies: "The successor reconnaissance aircraft would have to achieve a substantial increase in altitude and speed; be of reduced radar detectibility; suffer no loss in range to that of the U-2; and be of minimum size and weight."[50]

Even before the committee offered its assessment, I began a search for contractors. Although Kelly Johnson was a close friend and Lockheed's Skunk Works had an exceptional track record, I felt I had to seek competing proposals. In the end, three designs were submitted and considered. The least likely was one developed by the navy for what was essentially a high-speed balloon. The more serious competition was between Lockheed and Convair. Convair's proposal, which proved to be impractical, required two aircraft—a plane that could fly at Mach 4 and one that could lift it to its operational altitude. In late August 1959, Lockheed won the contract with its twelfth operational design. Johnson wrote in his diary: "The Agency accepts our conditions that our method of doing business will be identical to that of the U-2. Mr. Bissell agreed very firmly to this latter condition and said that unless it was done this way he wanted nothing to do with the project either. He and Allen Dulles stated following conditions: (1) We must exercise the greatest possible ingenuity, an honest effort in the field of radar. (2) The degree of security on this project is, if possible, even tighter than on the U-2, and (3) We should make no large commitments, large meaning in terms of millions of dollars."[51]

The A-12, or what the military would later call the SR-71 (and the Skunk Works crew would nickname Blackbird because of the coat of black paint covering it), could fly at well over three times the speed of sound, or about 2,600 miles an hour. When the plane flew at high speeds the surface temperature of the skin got hotter than 500 degrees Fahrenheit; near the engines the temperature would shoot up to over 1,000 degrees. As a result, the skin had to be made of titanium, a metal that was not readily available in large quantities and that was difficult to mold but that allowed the plane to withstand blast-furnace heat. Although Lockheed was able to obtain some of the titanium from traditional suppliers, an irony of the cold war was that some also came from the Soviet Union, one of the world's largest producers. The CIA used a series of shell corporations and cutouts to get it.[52]

Because the A-12 was such a revolutionary plane, it practically spawned its own industrial base. Special tools had to be developed, along with new paints, chemicals, wires, oils, engines, fuels, even special titanium screws. By the time Lockheed finished building the A-12, they themselves had developed and manufactured over thirteen million different parts. Developing the fuel was one of the more challenging aspects of the plane's development since it had to be able to withstand variations in temperature ranging from -90 degrees Fahrenheit during midair refueling to over 650 degrees Fahrenheit when the plane reached supersonic speeds. Fortunately, James Doolittle, who had connections at Shell Oil, came through for us.[53]

Designing these tools and parts was an impressive accomplishment, but since their need was largely unforeseen at the beginning of the project, Johnson began to fall behind schedule and I began to lose patience. He informed me in spring 1961 that he was at least four months behind on several important components of the plane. At this point I was also deeply involved with the planning for the Bay of Pigs invasion. My response was sharp (and in retrospect it seems needlessly rude): "I have learned of your expected additional delay in first flight from 30 August to 1 December 1961. This news is extremely shocking on top of our previous slippage from May to August and my understanding as of our meeting 19 December that the titanium extrusion problems were essentially overcome. I trust this is the last of such disappointments short of a severe earthquake in Burbank."[54] And indeed it was.

The A-12 had its first official flight in April 1962. I had resigned my position at the CIA just weeks earlier and attended the ceremony as Johnson's guest. I watched the flight with pride. I had developed an effective partnership between Lockheed and the CIA, not to mention the special CIA-Air Force operation that built the U-2 and now its successor. When the A-12 (and its military version, the SR-71) was retired in 1990, it had distinguished itself as the one plane in U.S. military history never to have been shot out of the sky by enemy fire.[55] However important its accomplishments, though, I believed that development of spy satellites would be an achievement as great and certainly as challenging.

We were already pushing intelligence into outer space when Powers was shot down in May 1960. "The very day that Francis Gary Powers was standing in the dock in Moscow taking his sentence was the very first successful day the satellite was flying over Moscow taking pictures from above," says Art Lundahl. "We had now gone from Mata Hari to the U-2 and we were in the space age, and the results were coming right in while we watched."[56]

The idea for a program of satellite reconnaissance was first considered seriously in a 1946 study produced by the Rand Corporation. Subsequent studies and the Killian committee's support resulted in the air force's being charged in March 1955 with development of a suitable satellite. As articles about the program began to appear in the aviation press, serious concerns were raised about its security. Officials began to question the air force's ability to manage the program, and soon other military services began to pursue their own space and satellite programs. Eisenhower decided to reevaluate the entire project and take corrective action.[57]

The possibility of a Soviet advance into space did not surprise me, and by late 1956, less than a year before Sputnik was launched, I knew that our national effort to put any kind of satellite into orbit was lagging badly. A Soviet launching would qualify as a major psychological setback and have serious ramifications for our own space program. With this consideration in mind—and given my keen personal desire to implement a successor program to the U-2—I approached Allen Dulles and urged him to take action. He gave me permission to meet with Deputy Secretary of Defense Donald Quarles to inform him that the CIA was interested in accelerating the development of a satellite. Perhaps threatened by my approach, the Pentagon added a modest sum of money to the navy's budget to speed up its work, on the grounds that its satellite was the most promising of the candidates for an early flight. Unfortunately, the additional funds accomplished little. Neither the navy nor any other U.S. organization flew a satellite before the Soviets, and we suffered the adverse consequences of being second in the space race.

The Soviets' launching of Sputnik 1 in October 1957 created an atmosphere of crisis in the government, as well as in the country at large. Although the United States had reason to be proud of its achievements in technology, its self-confidence was fragile enough to be broken by a Soviet satellite that carried no scientific or military equipment and weighed less than two hundred pounds. The day after the launch, the war between the agencies that I had witnessed so many times before began to heat up in earnest. The army announced that it had a Redstone rocket that could have put a satellite in orbit long before Sputnik.[58] The navy complained about its budget problems, and the air force offered excuses for the delays in its programs. The Soviet headstart in space was so disturbing that Eisenhower considered revealing the capabilities and achievements of the still-secret U-2 program to allay the fears of the nation. Instead, he became determined to intensify America's satellite program. Eisenhower acted quickly. In January 1958 he issued a National Security Action Memorandum establishing the development of a working reconnaissance satellite as a national security objective of the highest order.[59] The next step was to select the appropriate organizational structure to implement the directive. Most likely having been influenced by the success of the U-2, he assigned this responsibility to the CIA.

The first reconnaissance satellite to become operational had the cover name Discoverer and the agency project name Corona. It also had other names, like the Keyhole series. The air force began design and development of this satellite under a program called WS-117L, the existence of which was completely unclassified, although the designs were not. In early 1958, President Eisenhower, prompted by Edwin Land and other members of the Intelligence Panel of the Killian committee, decided that the satellite part of the WS-117L project should be turned over to the CIA–air force operation responsible for managing the U-2. Eisenhower's decision was as unexpected to me as the U-2 decision had been in November 1954. I became head of the joint project, which was also working on the A-12. It operated under very tight security.

My codirector, General Osmond Ritland, had been a test pilot for the air force, and at least one very bad crash had left him badly burned and somewhat disabled. Very active and energetic nevertheless, he was an ideal choice and one that made it fairly certain that Corona could proceed effectively as a joint project. Finances and procurement were again handled through the agency's contingency fund, which enhanced our ability to make expenditures swiftly and secretly (just as it had in the U-2's). The most ironic similarity, however, was that we chose to move forward with a design that the air force had rejected earlier as unworkable—a capsule that would be fired out of orbit and would bring the film back to earth.[60]

Our first goal was to put the genie back in the bottle. Because of all the press speculation, Ritland and I had to invent an elaborate cover explanation.

The best we could do was to control the public perception of the project. We organized a purported cancelation of the "old" project, obtained authorizations from the secretary of defense and other interested policy makers, and notified contractors and subordinates of the air force that the satellite element of the WS-117L project was eliminated. We also had to have a plausible cover story for that part of the project's development that couldn't be hidden from public view—hence the Discoverer program, a peaceful space pursuit of science. We continued to know it as Corona.

At the same time, Ritland and I faced a major technical decision because we had doubts about a spin-stabilized satellite, which called for small rockets that spun it up like a rifle bullet and kept its altitude unchanged as it orbited around the earth. It was proposed that photographs would be taken through a lens in the side of the camera in such a way that an image would be laid down on film transversely, producing a series of photographs covering the full extent of the camera's coverage on the ground. The alternative to this system was to stabilize the capsule with jets and to use a camera that would move within the capsule, taking pictures in a way very similar to the procedure used with the cameras in the U-2 and other reconnaissance aircraft. Eventually we decided that the latter was the way to go, and we replaced Fairchild's spin-stabilized system with a much more convenient camera from Itek.

While the National Security Council continued to grapple with the security implications of developing an appropriate space policy, we moved forward with our plans. By mid-August 1958, the council's thoughts had crystallized into a document called "Preliminary U.S. Policy on Outer Space," which the president approved. It explained that "reconnaissance satellites are of critical importance to U.S. national security" and that satellites would play an essential role not only in missile targeting but in the policing of arms control.[61]

The quick success we achieved taking the U-2 from concept to reality was not repeated with Corona, and we were not able to meet the president's goal of a successful flight by the end of 1959. We experienced disappointment after disappointment. The first satellite launch, scheduled for January 1959, was aborted because of technical errors. The concept required that the exposed film be wound on a reel in a recovery capsule, which could then be separated from the reconnaissance vehicle itself. The recovery capsule would drop and eject parachutes that would slow its descent as it came into the atmosphere. The capsule would drop into the ocean and then be recovered. We had all kinds of trouble with this system.

When the satellite was finally launched several weeks later, the stabilizing system malfunctioned, so that the satellite fell out of orbit and back to earth. The next satellite made it into orbit and successfully ejected its film—never to be found. The next two didn't even make it into orbit. After significant problems with the fifth launch, the sixth one was at first successful, but the film capsule released by the satellite failed to send a beacon signal. As a result, the plane sent up to catch the capsule couldn't find it. The seventh launch, like the first one, crashed to earth after the stabilizers failed to operate properly.[62]

Malfunctions in an experimental satellite system, as I discovered, are exceptionally frustrating to the designers and operators because there is never any human observer to see and evaluate what went wrong. If something failed on a U-2 test flight, unless it was a fatal crash, the pilot could come back and relate what happened. This was not the case with satellites. They spun out of control, burned up in the atmosphere, crashed, hopelessly lost, in the ocean, or exploded. Because the whole system was destroyed on reentry, it was often impossible to retrieve it and do an assessment. One relied on telemetry while the satellite was still in flight—sometimes it was possible to infer from the telemetry what went wrong; quite often it was difficult. You would simply have to try again and hope for the best. As failures continued to mount, I found the experience increasingly heartbreaking and frustrating. We were all aware that every one of these flights was hideously expensive. It took a certain amount of fortitude to keep going and going, hoping that it would finally work.

In late 1959 and early 1960, the pace of launchings increased. There were launches nearly every month, but malfunctions continued to plague the program. Corona 10, launched in February, failed to even make it into orbit. Corona 11 achieved orbit and appeared to function, but tracking stations lost it. The next Corona fell off the launch pad.[63] There would be a long stand-down after each attempt to enable some modification in the equipment to be made. This would be followed by the wretched business of another flight that still didn't work. Once we cured a particular malfunction, a new malfunction would occur and the whole guessing game would begin again: what went wrong and what can be done to fix it.

Finally on August 10, 1960, on the thirteenth try, the first successful Corona flight occurred. The satellite achieved and maintained orbit, the camera turned on when it was supposed to, and it turned off when the signal was sent for it to do so. The film was then ejected. Because of cloud cover, however, the airplane sent up to catch the film capsule was unable to rendezvous and the capsule landed in the water. Eight days later, while Powers was being tried in Moscow, we made another launch, number fourteen. It was about one year and ten months since the first attempted launch, but instead of disappointment this launch brought great elation. Not only did the satellite achieve and sustain orbit, but the film capsule was successfully retrieved in midair. The twenty-pound roll of film brought back by the capsule contained pictures covering over a million square miles of the Soviet Union—more coverage than all the pictures of that country taken during the entire U-2 program. Although Sputnik had beaten us into space by over two years, Corona, in the words of historian William E. Burrows, "would do quite a bit more than go beep in the night."[64]

The next two flights were failures, but after that, Corona turned into kind of a milk run, where success was repeated flight after flight with intervals of about a month or six weeks between them. Eventually the Corona system itself underwent enlargement and improvement, and later Lockheed converted the basic launch vehicle into an upper stage called the Agena, which was used for a number of different programs. Development moved on in many other directions, notably toward so-called real-time photography, in which the image is transmitted electronically. Transmission would not necessarily occur as the satellite recorded because it would be over the USSR and whatever was broadcast couldn't be heard in friendly territory. Rather, the image would be recorded on a transient storage medium in the system and then rebroadcast over friendly territory. This was the beginning of the satellite age.

The CIA's overall role in the space reconnaissance program was relatively minor. The basic vehicle was developed and procured by the air force. The agency had responsibility for the payloads in the early systems, but its authority was systematically challenged by the air force. Launches were conducted from air force bases, using air force personnel. The CIA did arrange for the retrieved capsules to be taken expeditiously to Eastman Kodak for developing, but it had almost no role in the operational phase beyond photointerpretation.

The satellite, of course, was fundamentally different from the plane as an intelligence tool. Once launched and put in orbit, it had a predictable and unalterable path. In essence, therefore, one was committed to the photography that could be obtained on the preprogrammed path of the vehicle. Also, because photography was the main objective, the system could operate only during daylight hours. With an aircraft, on the other hand, one could, at least theoretically, learn at noon that something might be happening in the USSR that would be interesting to film. If the system was nimble enough, an aircraft could be dispatched immediately to cover the area. That ability to photograph or obtain targets on short notice and at selected times was something that could not be achieved with a satellite. In the view of the intelligence community, there were clearly two different kinds of missions and two distinct needs—for the satellite, with its repetitive and very extensive coverage, and for manned reconnaissance aircraft that could be dispatched to any point of interest at any time.

Satellite reconnaissance turned out to be enormously productive, but given my state of mind in the late 1950s and faced with the choice I had then between the satellite and the A-12, I was more interested in the latter, especially since I had complete control of that program. There is no doubt that satellites came to be the more important of the two, if only because from the start the Soviets did not choose to regard satellite overflights as the infringement of their sovereignty that manned reconnaissance flights were. One cannot contend, after all, that one controls a wedge of space going into infinity. The fact that with a satellite one could cover prodigious areas anywhere in the world without meeting political and diplomatic resistance was very exciting for American policy makers. It made satellite reconnaissance even more attractive.

The information produced by these satellites proved invaluable. While the U-2 flew across and photographed only a slice of the Soviet Union, a single satellite mission could collect photography of an area several times as large. The satellite allowed us to map missile silos, railroad lines, highways, and military bases across the Soviet Union. Satellite photography itself represented some retrogression in the quality of the finished product. Cameras were later introduced, however, that were designed to have much narrower coverage and achieve much better resolution. The knowledge we gained from the satellites caused us to reassess dramatically the view we had of Soviet military strength. For example, the 1960 election had been filled with rhetoric about a missile gap between the Soviets and us. The information brought back by our satellites would prove no such gap existed. As a matter of fact, in September 1961 my old friend Joe Alsop broke the story that fewer than fifty Soviet missiles were capable of reaching the United States. We, on the other hand, possessed almost 250 missiles capable of reaching the Soviet Union.[65]

The 1950s and early 1960s were a unique period of special accomplishments in intelligence. To begin with, there was an extraordinarily effective, often informal collaboration among individuals of many skills and backgrounds: scientists, engineers, managers, and operators drawn from the aerospace industry, from civilian agencies of the government, from the military services, and from academia. There was cooperation among these individuals and among the organizations in which they worked. Furthermore, the program's two major players, the agency and the air force, learned to work together in very difficult times. Progress on the U-2, for example, was unimpeded by infighting or jealousy among government offices and private firms or by outbreaks of "not invented here" syndrome.

There was also an unusual degree of trust between procurement offices and private contractors, partly, I believe, because the projects were carried out by a small, moderately self-contained office that exercised full authority to make operational and developmental decisions. Thanks also to the highly classified nature of the projects, there were few disruptive reviews by outside entities. Project directors had a free hand in cutting corners and simplifying procedures. It should also be remembered that there was strong support at the highest levels of the government. Even members of Congress approved when informed about the projects.

What produced the enthusiasm, cooperation, and selflessness that animated these activities was a recognition of, and devotion to, a major and vital national goal by all concerned. In the case of the U-2 and the SR-71, we prototyped, built, and deployed aircraft that could fly higher and faster than any others in the world. Innovative camera lenses and films set new standards of excellence. This technology was later taken into space, where satellites provided a flow of intelligence information essential for our national security. As revolutionary as the new means of collection were the accompanying techniques for photoanalysis.

During my tenure as director of our overhead-reconnaissance programs, I did not spend a lot of energy trying to quantify and evaluate the rewards associated with them, because I had not been in the reconnaissance or the intelligence business. My interests were always those of an operator, and it is no exaggeration to say that I was concerned less with what the planes and satellites might bring back than with the process of getting it. As soon as we had a few successful overflights, however, it did occur to me that, if you could demonstrate to an enemy country that you could overfly it with impunity and it couldn't do a goddamn thing to prevent you, that in itself would be a good deterrent. I believe this strongly, and it's a point that has never been made about the history of the U-2. The U-2 was a deterrent because it showed that the United States possessed a significant technological capability that the Soviets could not match. That was a great accomplishment.

CHAPTER SIX

Crises

As the last year of the Eisenhower Administration drew to a close, the tempo of conflict between the Soviets and the United States began to escalate. The downing of the U-2 and the resultant collapse of the Paris summit contributed to a sense of impending crisis. The Soviet threat to Western Europe had been thwarted by the establishment of the Marshall Plan and NATO, and although Communists exhibited strength in France and Italy, it was apparent that they would not take over by majority vote. As the struggle between the two superpowers reheated, the focus of the contest moved to the Third World.

For policy makers, the paradox of dealing with the Communist threat in the less-developed regions was all too evident. The social and economic problems that made these areas such fertile ground for Soviet adventurism could be addressed only by long-term solutions that would require property redistribution; improvements in agricultural productivity, health care, and education; and greater democratization. In the meantime, decisions had to be made weekly. Had circumstances allowed our government to formulate a long-term response, the job would have fallen to the State and Treasury Departments; to a considerable degree it fell to them nevertheless.

Our active struggle with the Soviets was in the nonmilitary dimension. They were our rivals in ideas, economic activity, diplomacy, and perhaps most of all, the use of force. Like the Communists, we thought it essential to influence the course of events in the Third World. Unless we were prepared to meet these challenges locally, we would be forced to meet them at a level of escalation and risk that we greatly preferred to avoid. This imperative dictated unconventional policies and actions falling outside the tradition and competence of the existing departments in the executive branch—hence the large role assumed by the CIA.

Many criticisms have been leveled at the CIA for its activities during the 1950s and 1960s, especially in the field of covert action. Having rethought this policy many times since then, I am convinced that the agency acted in the government's best interest in attempting to preserve the highly desired principle of democracy. From today's perspective, many episodes might be considered distasteful, but during the Eisenhower and Kennedy years the Soviet danger seemed real and all actions were aimed at thwarting it.

My responsibilities as deputy director for plans encompassed crises all over the globe. Africa was one field in which the forces of East and West were destined to clash; the Congo, which had gained its independence from Belgium on June 30, 1960, was on the verge of civil war. As the summer began, newspaper headlines blared: "African Nations Wooed by Soviets," "Khrushchev Hastens to Hail New States," "Two Tribes Battle in Capital of Congo," "Khrushchev Warns of Rockets." In all of underdeveloped Africa, which really meant southern Africa up to the Sahara, the Congo was the most important prize in the contest between the Soviet Union and the United States. Political disorganization rendered its government ineffective, yet its size, location, production of strategic materials, and enormous economic potential rendered any crisis a matter of grave concern.

Sharing borders with nine other countries, the Congo had a land area equal to the United States east of the Mississippi and produced many minerals vital to aerospace production—we obtained approximately 75 percent of our cobalt and 50 percent of our tantalum from the Congo—as well as bauxite, iron, manganese, zinc, and gold.[1] The importance of the Congo's natural resources, combined with the most primitive (indeed, nearly nonexistent) political arrangements anywhere in the world, rendered central Africa the kind of political vacuum into which power flows. This set of conditions set the stage for an immediate critical threat.

Long built-up resentments were evident on independence day when the new prime minister, Patrice Lumumba, a charismatic leader with primary allegiance to himself and Moscow, addressed the nation. He quickly denounced Belgium's colonial policy as inflicting "atrocious sufferings" and "humiliating bondage" on the Congolese people. Colonialism had ensured that the populace would be as dependent on the Belgians after independence as it had been before. There had never been any provision for training the Congolese for positions of any importance in the government. In fact, approximately 9,000 top- and middle-level officials were still Belgians, and all the officers of the 25,000-member Force Publique, the Congo's national security force, were European and most of them Belgian. Lumumba's attitude towards Belgium was understandable, but that did not lessen the dangerousness of his early postindependence policies. The first two months were filled with turbulence and uncertainty. On July 2, tribal disturbances began to tear at the nation's social fabric. Three days later, Congolese soldiers mutinied against their Belgian officers. The Belgians requested that they be allowed to send in troops but Lumumba refused. By July 9, they had grown tired of watching the situation deteriorate in a nation where many Belgians still lived and where Belgian companies had significant stakes, and they began to intervene unilaterally. To make matters worse, on July 11 the mineral-rich Katanga province of the Congo proclaimed its own independence.[2]

Belgium's intervention led to disaster. To forestall a worsening of the crisis the United Nations requested its withdrawal and sent in peacekeeping forces. Meanwhile, Lumumba arrived in Washington at the end of July to negotiate for economic aid. Although his meetings with Secretary of State Herter were somewhat successful, Lumumba quickly undermined his initial achievements by raising the possibility of inviting Soviet troops into the Congo to force Belgium's withdrawal. His threat was not idle, and soon the Soviets were airlifting supplies and support technicians. CIA intelligence personnel in the field became greatly concerned about Lumumba's intentions. In August, one intelligence officer cabled: "Embassy and station believe Congo experiencing classic Communist effort takeover government. Many forces at work here: Soviets *** Communist Party, etc. . . . Decisive period not far off. Whether or not Lumumba actually Commie or just play Commie game to assist his solidifying power, anti-West forces rapidly increasing power Congo and there may be little time left in which take action to avoid another Cuba."

A week after this cable was received, Allen Dulles had a meeting with President Eisenhower and the Special Group (the body that authorized covert operations) at which Eisenhower expressed "extremely strong feelings on the necessity for very straightforward action" regarding Lumumba. The minutes note that the Special Group "agreed that planning for Congo would not necessarily rule out consideration of any particular kind of activity which might contribute to getting rid of Lumumba." The next day, Dulles cabled the Congo station: "In high quarters here it is the clear-cut conclusion that if [Lumumba] continues to hold high office, the inevitable result will at best be chaos and at worst pave the way to Communist takeover of the Congo with disastrous consequences for the prestige of the UN and for the interests of the free world generally. Consequently we conclude that his removal must be an urgent and prime objective and that under existing conditions this should be a high priority of our covert action."[3]

In 1975 the Senate Select Committee on Intelligence, headed by Frank Church, questioned the intent of this cable as part of its investigation of CIA assassination attempts on foreign leaders. To prepare for my testimony I was shown a copy of the original cable, and seeing it again fifteen years later, I was at first baffled that it had been signed off not by me but by Richard Helms, the chief of operations in the clandestine service and the deputy to the deputy director for plans. Dulles did occasionally draft a cable personally, but when he did he would always want Helms and me to see it, know its content, and have an opportunity to argue for a different course of action. It turned out that I was on vacation during this period and Helms was the officer in charge. In reviewing what had transpired during my absence, Dulles explained, I remember, that he had drafted the cable after returning from a National Security Council meeting attended by the president where the subject was discussed at length.

While the meaning of the cable may seem open to interpretation, in that period of history its meaning would have been clear. Certainly the cable doesn't say, "I want Lumumba assassinated"; it says, "I want to get rid of him." It also makes clear that almost any conceivable means could be used to accomplish that overriding purpose and that its accomplishment was sought "in high quarters," a term that would be correctly read in the field as meaning the president. Does this authorize assassination or doesn't it? That is in the eye of the beholder. Nevertheless, I believe the recipient of such a message colors it with his or her perception of the policy climate as revealed in recent communications and uses personal judgment about the situation. The message was no doubt drafted in an intentionally ambiguous fashion to avoid attributing a decision to the president that could become an embarrassment. As it is in many other areas related to intelligence and covert activities, this function is an important part of plausible deniability. I believe, however, that if you had asked Eisenhower what he was thinking at that moment he probably would have said, "I sure as hell would rather get rid of Lumumba without killing him, but if that's the only way, then it's got to be that way." Eisenhower was a tough man behind that smile.

The CIA prepared to deal with Lumumba, but as events unfolded the agency was relieved of having to implement any kind of executive action. After losing a struggle for the leadership of the government to President Joseph Kasavubu and Joseph Mobutu, chief of staff of the Congolese armed forces, Lumumba fled to the United Nations forces in Leopoldville. Mobutu's troops captured him in early December as he attempted to reach his stronghold in Stanleyville. He was imprisoned and killed in early 1961 by his own people.[4]

At about the time of Lumumba's capture, Eisenhower was briefing John Kennedy, the president-elect, about Laos, warning that it had to be defended against the Communists at all costs. Its central location in the Indochinese peninsula, its dense jungle and rugged mountains, and its 300-mile stretch of the Mekong River made Laos crucial to preventing the Communists from gaining logistical access to Vietnam, Cambodia, and Thailand and thereby escalating their ascendancy in that part of the world.

The history of events leading up to the situation of the late 1950s and early 1960s is complicated and convoluted. Following the return of the French in 1946, a Communist independence movement called the Pathet Lao was organized by Prince Souphanouvong with the support of Ho Chi Minh in northern Vietnam. Its forces were used to foment a civil war in Laos that was resolved in 1954 with a division of territory that effectively ceded the two northern provinces to the Pathet Lao, while the royal regime retained the rest. A few years later, Souphanouvong and his half brother, Prince Souvanna Phouma, the royal premier, agreed to reestablish a unified government with participation of the Pathet Lao and integration of its forces into the Royal Army.

The election of 1958 was an important turning point in Laotian politics and American involvement in the country. Souphanouvong's party and his allies won most of the assembly seats up for election. Because he was believed to be a fellow traveler of the Communists, his continued success was unacceptable to the United States. Washington was alarmed enough to have the CIA set a covert operation in motion. A CIA-sponsored political front called the Committee for the Defense of National Interests (CDNI) was created to support the conservative anti-Communist faction in Laotian politics. With CDNI support, Phoui Sananikoune formed a new government in August 1958. In so doing, he dropped two Pathet Lao ministers who had been in the previous government and appointed four CDNI members. By 1959 he had added Phoumi Nosavan and two other military figures as well, moving his government farther to the right.

Over the next several months, backed by the United States, Phoui took actions that would ultimately lead to civil war and provide the Soviets an occasion for more open and active support of the Pathet Lao. In February 1959 he repudiated those parts of the Geneva Accords that limited the level of foreign military assistance that Laos could receive. While the Soviet Union protested, the United States was eager to have an opportunity to increase its level of anti-Communist support. Phoui became increasingly aggressive in his dealings with the Pathet Lao, but he was unwilling to order a total military effort to crush them. He did not want to plunge his nation into an all-out civil war from which it might not recover. When his CDNI ministers placed increasing pressure on him to take military action, he dismissed them. At this point, Washington shifted its support to Phoumi Nosavan, who led a coup against Phoui's government.[5]

Thus, by the beginning of 1960, the country's fragile peace was broken. Renewed armed conflict and the specter of a Communist victory supported by the Soviets forced U.S. policy makers to look for a strategy, but they vacillated between Souvanna Phouma, Phoui Sananikoune, and Phoumi Nosavan. Souvanna Phouma and Phoui Sananikoune favored a neutral Laos but differed in their concepts of neutrality and their approaches to attaining it. Souvanna Phouma believed a strict neutrality that included Pathet Lao participation in government was the best method; Phoui Sananikoune, who was pro-Western, believed the ideal neutrality would exclude the Pathet Lao. Phoumi Nosavan, on the other hand, wanted to destroy the Pathet Lao and secure an alliance with the United States. I believe the cause of America's shifting allegiance can be found in the friction that developed between policy makers at home and our representatives in the field.

My concern with Laos began when I became deputy director for plans and inherited the ongoing project on a small scale. The three agencies dealing with the situation—the State Department, the Defense Department, and the CIA—did not necessarily have congruent policies. By and large, though, they were able to hammer out instructions from Washington to the field, but the three corresponding groups in the field were equally successful in agreeing on a policy that differed from Washington's. The resultant mix of policy inputs was not helpful to the cause.

It is clear with hindsight that U.S. support should have gone to Phoui Sananikoune, who advocated pro-Western neutrality; our failure to support him reflected Washington's inability to understand the ground situation in

Laos. Instead, we ended up supporting Phoumi Nosavan because of his staunch anti-Communism and pro-Western stance. Had Laos been better understood, we would have realized his goals were unobtainable in the context of that nation's politics. Had we also shown more open-mindedness (which is not always compatible with crisis management), the advice and perceptions of experts on Laotian politics, history, and culture might have received more attention. My personal level of confidence in seeking to promote a pro-Western solution in Laos could possibly have been changed in that I might have been persuaded to believe that the most we could realistically hope for was a neutral government that would not readily condone, still less encourage, political and military activities blatantly favorable to Communist interests.

The first weeks of the Kennedy administration were greatly absorbed with the crisis in Laos. Even before Kennedy took office, more destabilizing coup attempts had occurred, and early February witnessed an increasing deterioration. In particular, a nationalist paratrooper named Kong Le was battling Phoumi Nosavan for control. To compound matters, the Pathet Lao had occupied the Plaine des Jarres, one of the country's prosperous agricultural areas, and was being supplied by a continuous Soviet airlift. Kong Le aligned himself with the Pathet Lao and also received aid from the Soviets at his base in the Plaine des Jarres. Opposing the Pathet Lao and Kong Le were the thinly positioned forces of Phoumi, who was attempting to defend the approaches to Vientiane and the southern panhandle. President Kennedy's response was to create the Laos Task Force, which reported to him daily.[6]

I attended one of the first meetings of the National Security Council after Kennedy took office, at which a decision was made to increase the level of assistance to Phoumi. The Joint Chiefs presented an overview of a U.S.-designed military operation that Phoumi would soon execute with the Royal Army to regain the Plaine des Jarres. As I listened to General Lyman Lemnitzer describe the plan, I could not help but feel that it had very little likelihood of success. In fact, it was impossible. Having recently returned from Vientiane, I was convinced by my brief contact with reality in the field that we were dealing with a situation a million miles from the precision, order, and purposefulness of the Department of Defense. The proposed plan included elegant lines of troop deployment, bold military maneuvers, and a prediction that the Plaine des Jarres would be seized by parachute troops on approximately the tenth day of operations. I found this assessment and briefing almost surreal. My close involvement for well over a year had persuaded me that the Laotian Royal Army could never carry out such a fine-tuned operation, and when the attack actually commenced they didn't. The failed attempt in February 1961 merely worsened an already hopeless situation.

Unfortunately, I did not express my views at this meeting, since I did not pretend to be an expert on Laos and there were people present from the State Department and elsewhere who knew more about it. Later, when I would make similar presentations to the president about our covert military plan to overthrow Castro, the Joint Chiefs chose to remain silent about their reservations. This was quite simply the etiquette of bureaucracy, and it exemplifies the way ingrained Washington habits are sometimes detrimental to policy making.

There was general agreement among Kennedy's advisers that the Communist threat in Laos had to be dealt with before any serious consideration could be given to an acceptable solution for the country. The plan that evolved required first that Phoumi defeat the Pathet Lao. Then, with the Soviets' agreement, Laos would be declared neutral. This two-prong approach would avoid the larger strategic problem of Communist control of the Ho Chi Minh Trail, which provided access to the rest of Southeast Asia, particularly South Vietnam.[7]

Later, when Kennedy decided to let Averell Harriman try to negotiate a cease-fire and a neutral Laos, I remember protesting to Walt Rostow, the deputy national security adviser (with whose essentially hawkish view I tended to agree), that we were effectively throwing away all U.S. assets in Laos. Rostow replied that he sympathized but that the president's position was that we could not win in Laos. It was the wrong place. Rostow said with considerable emphasis (and I assumed with Kennedy's agreement) that what happened in that part of the world would be decided in Vietnam. That was where the action was going to heat up and where U.S. resources could be deployed effectively. Practically all of Vietnam was within reach of carrier aircraft, whereas almost none of Laos was. Vietnam was a thin strip of land along the coast where the United States could use its naval dominance and carrier forces to conduct amphibious operations. This made Vietnam a vastly more promising theater than Laos.

During the early months of the Kennedy administration, I sat in on a number of White House discussions of Laos and Vietnam. It is my feeling the president chose to take a stand in Vietnam and not Laos because he believed a local victory in Laos would be meaningless unless we could win in Vietnam. A victory in Vietnam, pacifying the country under a friendly government, would make Laos almost irrelevant. I believe that his decision was entirely valid, but it presupposed that we *were* going to win in Vietnam, which of course was the view at the time.

My involvement with Vietnam derived not from any urgent crisis—for as long as I was at the CIA, Laos, not Vietnam, was the active area—but from the fact that I was a member of various interagency committees, sat in on White House meetings, and became an early organizer of our counterinsurgency doctrine in the first year of the Kennedy administration. According to Walt Rostow, Kennedy was the only president who took an interest in the planning process, and his interest was very serious. After discussions with Rostow, Kennedy approved a list of nineteen tasks, organized under five headings. In February 1961 I was assigned to head a task force on the number-one topic—the deterrence of guerrilla warfare. In an interview with Richard Neustadt in 1964, Rostow summed up the questions we needed to answer for the president: "How could we organize our military and civil assets—including covert assets—to make guerrilla operations unattractive or to deal with them if they start? What doctrine should we develop? How should we organize the government for the task?"[8]

In early 1962 the task force's work culminated in the issuance of National Security Action Memorandum 124, which set up the Special Group (Counter Insurgency), to be distinguished from the regular Special Group, for ensuring "unity of effort and the use of all available resources with maximum effectiveness in preventing and resisting subversive insurgency and related forms of indirect aggression in friendly countries." The Special Group (CI) would see to it that its mission became recognized as a key goal of our government and that all potentially related programs would be oriented in that direction. The "organization, training, equipment and doctrine of the U.S. Armed Forces and other U.S. agencies abroad and in the political, economic, intelligence, military aid and informational programs conducted abroad by State, Defense, AID, USIA and CIA" were all expected to play a role. The Special Group (CI) would oversee interdepartmental programs related to these efforts and periodically review the ability of U.S. resources to confront insurgencies.[9]

In those early days, members of the Special Group (CI) may have expressed their enthusiasm in ways that rankled the military. For example, in response to their inquiries regarding military training for counterguerrilla warfare, Lyman Lemnitzer, chairman of the Joint Chiefs, briskly observed that "such activities as guerrilla warfare, counter-insurgency, counter-subversion, combat in cities, mob and riot control, civil affairs and military government are not new to the Military Services. From their inception, the Military Services have been faced with these and related problems in varying degrees according to the politico/military climate of the times." More ominously, Lemnitzer concluded that the military services were "taking full advantage of the laboratory-type approach afforded by the current situation in Southeast Asia and other areas of the world."[10] Southeast Asia would become an expensive laboratory indeed.

Just as I had participated in the administration's early discussions regarding Laos, I became an active participant in discussions concerning Vietnam. During the summer of 1961, Bill Bundy, the deputy assistant secretary of defense for international security affairs, organized an interagency group that met for lunch once a week to discuss various foreign policy issues, including Vietnam. Walt Rostow, Bob Amory, and Paul Nitze were among the participants, and we would test out our ideas on one another. At the beginning of October, for example, we considered whether direct talks with the Soviets might be a worthwhile approach. The proposal was "pretty unanimously rejected."

A few days later, I met with Kennedy, Dean Rusk, Robert McNamara, Lemnitzer, and McGeorge Bundy for about an hour and a half to discuss Vietnam. In addition to beefing up the air force component of the Military Assistance and Advisory Group, Kennedy decided to send a presidential mission made up of Maxwell Taylor, acting as his military representative, and Walt Rostow to gain fresh ground information. Taylor was so concerned by the state of affairs he found that he wired the president an eyes-only cable recommending that American troops be quickly deployed to show "the seriousness of the U.S. intent to resist a Communist take-over."[11]

In the first week of November, I participated in a meeting to discuss his recommendations. Taylor opened the meeting by observing that Kennedy was "instinctively against" the introduction of U.S. forces into Vietnam. Nevertheless Taylor advocated that an 8,000-man force be sent to South Vietnam as a show of American resolve. McNamara felt that neither the size of the force nor Taylor's other recommendations could "save" South Vietnam. He felt "small actions without words" would be of little use. What was needed was to determine the nature of U.S. interests in Vietnam and the scope of the broader commitment we were willing to make. If we stated those interests to the world, in addition to using force, that would show our resolve. Undersecretary of State George Ball recommended a larger force. I voiced my support for Taylor's recommendations because they represented "action, not talk."[12]

America's involvement in Vietnam would intensify dramatically after I left the CIA in early 1962. Speaking to John Kenneth Galbraith in late 1961, Kennedy explained why he decided to take a stand in Vietnam: "There are limits to the number of defeats I can defend in one twelve-month period. . . . I've had the Bay of Pigs, pulling out of Laos, and I can't accept a third."[13] It is interesting to speculate whether a victory at the Bay of Pigs would have allowed Kennedy to sidestep Vietnam or if it would have emboldened him to make a more dramatic commitment earlier in the game. Personally, I believe that once committed to Vietnam he would never have retreated. I feel it would have been against his character to pull out. His combative attitude toward Communism and Communists would not have allowed retreat. Unfortunately, the Bay of Pigs would be another matter entirely.

CHAPTER SEVEN

Cuba

Latin America became a frequent battleground of the cold war. My experience with the Guatemalan operation provided me with a lively appreciation of what seemed to be the vulnerability of most Latin American societies to subversion of one kind or another. In countries like El Salvador and Nicaragua, there was no competent middle class performing the function it did in most Western societies. Because of this inherent vulnerability, it was not difficult to perceive the disorder a Soviet-backed country like Cuba could inflict in this hemisphere, and it was natural to want to forestall it.

The general feeling in intelligence circles when Batista fell was that, although Castro's brother Raul was a dedicated Communist, Castro himself was not. It became critically important to confirm or disprove this assessment, and a CIA representative was sent to meet with him on the occasion of his trip to the United States in 1959. He was briefed on Communist penetration among his own supporters in the hope that if he realized its pervasiveness he might take steps to combat it. It was also felt that this information might strengthen his own resolve not to espouse Communism. The effort proved futile. As revealed shortly afterward by his explicit advocacy of Marxism and subsequently by his open alliance with the Soviet Union, Castro was a strong Communist and had been for some time. It is therefore not surprising that there was a great deal of concern in the federal government (eventually proven correct) that he would use Cuba as a base from which to attempt paramilitary and other subversive activities. A Communist government in Cuba, ninety miles from the U.S. mainland, was unacceptable. By January 1960 Eisenhower was plainly intolerant of the Castro regime. Meeting with Christian Herter, Ambassador Philip Bonsal, and Andy Goodpaster, he said that Castro was beginning to "look like a mad man." Furthermore, he was showing an increased willingness to take tough action to incite Castro's overthrow. He suggested that a quarantine of Cuba might be one course of action to consider. He also noted that if the Cuban people "are hungry, they will throw Castro out."[1] On January 13, 1960, a formal decision was made at a meeting of the Special Group that Castro's regime must be overthrown.

The CIA prepared to act. Successful operations in Iran and Guatemala, where unfriendly governments were destabilized and replaced with regimes compatible with U.S. interests, had provided the agency with enough experience and confidence to believe that Cuba would offer another suitable and manageable target. In March, after three months of planning very much influenced by these previous operations, I went to the White House to discuss our proposal with Eisenhower; Vice President Nixon, Secretary of State Herter, Admiral Arleigh Burke, Allen Dulles, and J. C. King were among the others there. Following presentation and discussion of the concept, the president said that he knew of no better plan. As always, he also demonstrated his desire for security and plausible deniability. He stated that "the great problem is leakage and breach of security. Everyone must be prepared to swear that he has not heard of [the plan]." He stressed that "there should be only two or three governmental people connected with this in any way." In the plan we presented, "A Program of Covert Action against the Castro Regime," we estimated that a covert-action and intelligence organization, or a guerrilla movement, could probably be created within sixty days. We left with Eisenhower's approval to carry it forward.[2]

The strategy that was developed included using propaganda as well as political and military means to achieve Castro's downfall. A top priority was to provide the citizens of Cuba with political alternatives, and a program was created to build up a "responsible, appealing, and unified Cuban opposition to the Castro regime." Castro had already begun tightening his grip on Cuban society, and to counteract his control a radio station was established to undermine his popular support. Radio Swan, as the station became known, beamed an anti-Castro message from abroad and played an important part in the plan to overthrow Castro.

The military aspect of the plan that we viewed as the prime vehicle for achieving Castro's overthrow envisioned the creation of a guerrilla force of approximately twenty Cuban exiles trained in sabotage, infiltration, and communications. These initial recruits would in turn become trainers so that eventually there would be a group of 100 to 150 Cuban agents. When this force had achieved a critical mass, a sizable number of them would be infiltrated into Cuba, where they would be placed with various dissident groups, including with students at Havana University who opposed Castro but were not engaged in active resistance and with enclaves in the Escambray Mountains and elsewhere that were.

The plan originally anticipated training the Cuban exiles at the U.S. jungle warfare school in Panama, but because of the State Department's decree against using either U.S. or U.S.-controlled territory, another site had to be found.[3] It was not long before we settled on Guatemala as the location for the training camp. The United States and the CIA had maintained a friendly relationship with that government since 1954 and the arrangement proved to be a good one.

In addition to infiltrating a group of exiles as guerrillas, the plan also envisioned the creation of a small paramilitary force, or brigade, of a few hundred Cubans who would land on the island and detonate a coordinated resistance at the appropriate moment. It was the importance and size of this force that would eventually play a major role in the operation.

Our immediate goal, though, was to model the guerrilla organization along the lines of the underground organizations of World War II. The first step was to create a command and control net on the island whose mission would be to establish safe houses, provide the capability for receiving supplies, and enable the retrieval of infiltrated agents. This would require between 100 and 200 highly disciplined members, all of whom would have to be rigidly trained and able to obey orders. They would also need to be compartmented in such a way that they would not know one another, so that the individuals in the net as well as the integrity of the operation would be protected. Communication would be effected through code names and pseudonyms. There was a firm belief within the agency that it would be possible to build up this kind of underground mechanism in Cuba, and action was taken to implement it.

By late 1960 the agency had received a thorough education in the difficulty of establishing an effective guerrilla organization. There had been a number of successful small infiltrations of supplies and people by boat, but generally these detachments were picked up within forty-eight hours and never heard from again. The reasons for this failure were straightforward and simple. Reliable safe houses to provide food and shelter in the crucial first hours after infiltrators landed on the beaches at night could not be assured, it was soon discovered. Adding to the difficulties, there was no effective organization in which infiltrators could be passed along from village to village until they were able to reach a fighting force. Informers were also rampant. Consequently, the proposed command and control net never functioned as expected and the efforts to build a secure and successful guerrilla network failed abysmally.

In early October 1960, intelligence revealed that Castro had executed twenty men, including three Americans, for counterrevolutionary activities. In eastern Santiago he had begun a successful implementation of what appeared to be a neighborhood spy system to keep the population under observation. Although the people of Santiago might previously have been expected to protest the executions, they were silent. Intelligence reports on such matters, combined with the agency's lack of success in building a guerrilla movement, contributed to our further reliance on the brigade concept and our fear that we had to act quickly before Castro's grip on the island became unshakable.[4]

In spite of this setback, there was no doubt that an active resistance movement existed in Cuba. When the National Security Council met on October 20, 1960, Dulles explained that the CIA believed that "active opposition to Castro continues among scattered groups inside Cuba." He also noted that there were about a thousand poorly armed and provisioned guerrillas in the Escambray Mountains, but they lacked unity and effective popular leadership. Soviet military aid continued, he said, explaining that three shipments had arrived and a fourth was on its way to Castro.[5]

The original plan contemplated building a strong guerrilla organization around such groups, but while the training program for infiltration of the Cuban exiles progressed, Castro (armed with Soviet weapons) embarked on a counterprogram of destroying the local resistance. Even in the Escambray Mountains, the area most promising for active resistance, he had developed a successful strategy for rounding up the local Cuban bands and rendering them ineffective. He deployed enormous numbers of militia around the whole area and in effect starved these people out. Slowly but surely, the resistance in the Escambray was broken.

The failure of the guerrilla infiltration efforts in Cuba was compounded by political disappointments in Miami. It soon became evident to agency planners that the leaders of the Cuban exile community, centered in Miami, were in competition with one another for U.S. funds, supplies, and support. They all claimed to have large responsive followings in Cuba with whose members they could readily communicate. Unfortunately, their assertions proved to be grossly exaggerated. Another factor that perhaps did not receive enough weight was the distinction between a reasonably well-disciplined, security-conscious compartmented underground and an amorphous body of people who would vote against Castro if they had an opportunity. The latter may become important after an uprising is moving along, but in the early stages of a covert operation, it has absolutely no significance.

To make matters worse, by the end of autumn it had become apparent that any hope of molding our exile groups into a unified, cooperative coalition was unattainable. Part of the difficulty was the internecine rivalry among the leaders of the Miami-based Cuban exile community, which prevented them from playing a more active and authoritative role in organizing, training, and directing the operation and meant that it had to be conducted as an American-run enterprise. Moreover, not every leader of the exile community was persona grata to the men in the training camps. Given this state of affairs, we realized that if the plan was to remain viable and have any chance of success, the United States would have to assume all decision making.

Our difficulties also impaired the effectiveness of Radio Swan. Its broadcasting range was wide enough to reach Cuban audiences in Miami, as well as Havana, and for Cubans living under a repressive Castro regime, it was disheartening to hear broadcasts by exile program managers who seemed more concerned with serving the political ambitions of Cubans in Miami than with the situation of those trapped on the island. As a result, the station began to lose credibility with listeners in Cuba.

It was at this point in late 1960 that the "Program of Covert Action against the Castro Regime" approved by Eisenhower underwent a metamorphosis. The administration's determination to deal with Castro remained strong, and when efforts to establish a guerrilla organization proved fruitless, our reliance shifted to the invasion force being trained in Guatemala, the one group that was still considered to have a chance of success. It would have to be expanded and strengthened, however, if it was to meet expectations. It was during the transition period between Kennedy's election in November and his inauguration in January that the concept of Brigade 2506 began to take its final form.

I remember talking several times with Jack Hawkins, a Marine colonel assigned to the agency by the Pentagon for this operation, and saying that, if we were going to place heavy reliance on a landing force as the means for change in Cuba, the less than 500 Cubans we had in training was an altogether inadequate number; another 1,000 to 1,500 would be needed. I always seemed to be advocating a larger brigade while Hawkins appeared not to share my sense of urgency about a further buildup. The potential expansion of the brigade and the increasingly complex issues associated with a conventional invasion meant assigning more CIA personnel. By late fall 1960, I was greatly concerned that the senior officers involved in the operation were overworked and that we were running out of appropriate personnel to fill all the positions.

Other opportunities arose for dealing with Castro. Developing the brigade to overthrow Castro militarily was one option; having him incapacitated or eliminated was another. I believe I first learned about the plan to use the Mafia to assassinate Castro from Sheffield Edwards, the director of the agency's Office of Security. He and his deputy became the case officers for the CIA's relations with the Mafia. Edwards was frank with me about his efforts and I authorized him to continue. The idea did not originate with me (as some authors and historians have claimed it did) and I had no desire to become personally involved in its implementation, mainly because I was not competent to handle relations with the Mafia. It is true, however, that when the plan was presented to me I supported it, and as deputy director for plans I was responsible for the necessary decisions. As Edwards later explained to the FBI, the Mafia seemed a reasonable partner. Since the Mafia had controlled the gambling casinos that thrived in Cuba under Batista, Edwards assumed that Sam Giancana and others would have a powerful motive for overthrowing Castro, as well as the contacts for carrying out such a plan.[6]

I do not recall any specific personal contact with the Mafia, but Doris Mirage, my secretary at the time does: "Bissell got calls . . . from the Mafia and he would not take them, and I don't know how they got the inside telephone number even. We had an outside line, we had a scramble phone, we had . . . the agency line, and they'd come in on the agency line. I remember Joe Bonano offered to assassinate Castro and I remember it was written on a yellow legal pad and Bissell had in the bottom of his box. He wouldn't touch it. . . . Somebody had delivered this yellow paper. . . . He just didn't want to have any part of it."[7]

No doubt as I moved forward with plans for the brigade, I hoped the Mafia would achieve success. My philosophy during my last two or three years in the agency was very definitely that the end justified the means, and I was not going to be held back. Shortly after I left the CIA, however, I came to believe that it had been a great mistake to involve the Mafia in an assassination attempt. This is partly a moral judgment, but I must admit that it is also partly a pragmatic judgment. The more people involved in a project, the greater the chance of disclosure. These were people who were not subject to any kind of security control by the agency, and they posed a great risk.

In Guatemala, meanwhile, a politically volatile situation required immediate attention since the brigade was training under circumstances that could not be maintained indefinitely. The impending arrival of the rainy season, the inadequacy of the training facilities, and the increasingly precarious political position of our sponsor, President Fuentes Ydigoras, all contributed to a sense of urgency. Eventually Thomas Mann, assistant secretary of state for inter-American affairs, was persuaded to request the brigade's departure. Moving the brigade to the United States would have been the most logical and efficient option, but opposition from Mann and others in the Eisenhower administration made that infeasible. They very much wanted to avoid the appearance that the United States was behind the operation. One alternative plan (which seems fantastic now) was to ferry the brigade to an agency training site in Saipan, part of the Mariana Islands, near Guam. This notion was also abandoned and the brigade remained in place for the moment.

In mid-November, while grappling with this dilemma, I was awakened about three-thirty in the morning by the project's watch officer. A cable had just come in from Lieutenant Colonel Frank Egan, our man in Guatemala, communicating a request from Ydigoras to borrow some of the brigade members to put down an uprising against his government. Egan needed an answer within an hour. I reached Tom Mann on the telephone, but he said he could not possibly act on a matter of this kind until he conferred with Herter later in the morning. Ydigoras was levying a request to a local agency representative under a time constraint that made effective referral to the State Department impossible. The department was just not equipped to decide something like that in an hour.

At about five that morning, I sent a cable to Egan on my responsibility saying yes but stating that no soldiers were to be used, only Civil Air Transport pilots, if needed. I took this drastic independent action because I did not feel a decision with such important potential ramifications should be left to Egan. Also, it was possible that the Guatemalan government was in serious trouble, which would endanger the status of the training base. There is no evidence that brigade members were ever deployed in that crisis, but it is an example of how the agency could take action when time and circumstances did not allow more "proper" channels to get involved. Covert operations require that there be a mechanism to allow decisions to be made quickly and decisively. In this case, the State Department was not prepared to take a stand while the agency was.

When the National Security Council met on November 17, Dulles went over the details of the attempted uprising against Ydigoras. He noted that "Castro-itis" was affecting Central America and that, although Ydigoras was able to suppress the present revolt, there was no assurance that he would be able to keep the top on the "Guatemalan political volcano." He then commented on a leftist revolt that had recently been suppressed in Nicaragua and on Communist penetration of the El Salvadoran government.[8]

That autumn everyone had to face the reality of a possible change in political direction. Eisenhower was leaving office after two terms, and depending on which of the candidates, Richard M. Nixon or John F. Kennedy, succeeded him, an entire modification of the Cuban operation and other covert activities might conceivably take place in the near future. About a month before the election, I received a call from an intermediary of Kennedy's who said that the senator would like to talk to me about general issues raised during the campaign. It was probably Joe Alsop who suggested to Kennedy that as a well-informed Washington insider I was someone he should get in touch with. I am sure I told Dulles about the planned meeting, and I probably reported to him about it afterward. I found Kennedy to be bright, and he raised a number of topics on which I had something to say. I made it clear to him, however, that I was still working for Eisenhower and therefore could not do anything of an active nature for him. I also told him truthfully (although perhaps a little inappropriately since I was part of the current administration) that I agreed with most of his philosophy.

The pressures of the fall were beginning to affect my outlook. Days after Kennedy's election, I wrote to my friend Edmond Thomas:

> The election will probably have considerable influence on my life as a bureaucrat, but I have not the faintest idea what it will be. I am glad it came out as it did. I found less to choose between the two candidates than many of my friends, but I think Kennedy is surrounded by a group of men with a much livelier awareness than the Republicans of the extreme crisis that we are living in. . . . What I really mean is that I believe the Democrats will be far less inhibited in trying to do something about it. My guess is that Washington will be a more

lively and interesting place in which to live and work. Even so, I think middle-age cynicism is catching up with me, and I am not sure how much longer I want to stay in this business.[9]

Around Thanksgiving Dulles and I flew to Palm Beach to brief the president-elect on Cuba. We spent the night with a friend of Dulles's and the following morning met with Kennedy at his family's compound. The interview was held by the swimming pool and I remember there was a big table on which maps could be spread out. The presentation took less than an hour and was complete and frank. Kennedy listened attentively but was obviously very careful not to say much. He was sensitive to the charge that he was involving himself in matters that should be left strictly to Eisenhower; a successor needs to appear in the guise of a successful political candidate and not seem to be acting as if he were already in office. When the session ended, I drifted off to another part of the terrace while Kennedy and Dulles transacted other business. Dulles remained in Florida for a day or two after I flew back to Washington.

At the end of November 1960, Eisenhower held a meeting at the White House to discuss the situation in Cuba. He asked two key questions: "Are we being sufficiently imaginative and bold, subject to not letting our hand appear?" and "Are we doing the things we are doing effectively?" Although he did not advocate any particular course of action with regard to the planning of the operation, his key point was that "we should be prepared to take more chances" and be "more aggressive." He expanded on his concerns about organization and wondered whether it would be "useful to have an individual executive to pull the whole Cuban situation together who would knew precisely at all times what State, CIA, and the military were doing and who could answer questions directly."[10]

Intelligence reports of December 1960 brought unwelcome news. One in particular, entitled "Prospects for the Castro Regime," was based on a national intelligence estimate that showed that Castro remained "firmly in control" of Cuba and that "internal opposition" was "still generally ineffective." It also noted that although anti-Castro guerrilla groups were operating in the Escambray Mountains region and in Oriente province, "the regime has reacted vigorously and has thus far been able to contain" them. The report concluded that Castro would continue to consolidate his control over Cuba: "Organized opposition appears to lack the strength and coherence to pose a major threat to the regime, and we foresee no development in the internal political situation which would be likely to bring about a critical shift of popular opinion away from Castro." Although intelligence information seemed to indicate that Castro's popular support might erode somewhat, any such erosion was "likely to be offset by the growing effectiveness of the state's instrumentalities of control." The national intelligence estimate pessimistically determined that the "regime's ability for dealing with internal disturbances and foreign-based incursions are almost certain to improve."[11]

On January 3, 1961, Dulles, Tracy Barnes, and I went to the White House to meet with the president. Eisenhower had called the meeting, which included Christian Herter, Lyman Lemnitzer, and others, to get an update on the situation and on our current planning. There was some discussion of breaking diplomatic relations with Cuba, and Eisenhower expressed his concern as to what would happen to the two to three thousand Americans still living in Cuba if we took such a course of action. He feared that without diplomatic representation we would have difficulty getting information about what was transpiring. The Cubans could, for example, round up Americans in groups of twenty, take them to the hills, and shoot them. There was little more than a week left in his administration, but he took a tough stand, stating that if he learned of such an occurrence we would then "of course go in with our own forces."

The president seemed to be eager to take forceful action against Castro, and breaking off diplomatic relations appeared to be his best card. He noted that he was prepared to "move against Castro" before Kennedy's inauguration on the twentieth if a "really good excuse" was provided by Castro. "Failing that," he said, "perhaps we could think of manufacturing something that would be generally acceptable." For those who were fooled by Eisenhower's avuncular manner, this is but another example of his willingness to use covert action—specifically to fabricate events—to achieve his objectives in foreign policy. He wasn't the only participant at the meeting willing to "create" history. Secretary Herter suggested we stage an attack on Guantanamo.

The conversation then turned to the status of the brigade. Gordon Gray cited a report describing the trainees as the best army in Latin America. Lemnitzer agreed, although he observed that there were some difficulties with the brigade's military equipment. I pointed out that things were indeed going well but that Ydigoras had told us that we should find a new location for training the brigade by the beginning of March. I also noted that our trainers believed that the brigade's morale would suffer if action was not taken by then. Eisenhower felt we had to make a decision. Either we should commit to an invasion in

March or we should abandon the operation. He made it very apparent on which side of the issue he stood, saying that "when we turn over responsibility on the 20th, our successors should continue to improve and intensify the training." Toward the end of the discussion, he raised a question to which all of us should have given greater consideration. He asked, "What are the feasible means of helping to mobilize a stronger invasion force so that a failure in the first effort would not wipe out the whole project?"[12] Unfortunately, as the plans for an invasion continued, we lost sight of this question. Just a few days later, Eisenhower would not be in a position to request an answer.

Two days before Kennedy's inauguration, Ambassador Whiting Willauer sent Livingston Merchant, the undersecretary of state for political affairs, an evaluation of the government's current planning. Willauer had picked up the executive function that Eisenhower had suggested in November would be useful for overseeing the anti-Castro program. He explained that the Department of Defense had been updated on the specifics of the invasion plan. The department's representatives, Brigadier General David W. Gray and Captain Spore, concluded, along with Willauer, that the current plans "might not succeed in the objective of overthrowing the Castro regime." Whether or not such a plan could succeed would have to be a judgment "made almost at the last minute in the light of the then existing evaluation of Castro's capabilities." Willauer assumed that the invasion "would not be triggered unless the U.S. government were prepared to do everything else needed overtly or covertly . . . in order to guarantee success." The new administration, he said, would have to resolve several issues before deciding to go ahead with the plan. Could U.S. air bases be used for air strikes, supply, and resupply? How would recognition of a provisional government occur? Who would be in the provisional government and would its makeup be acceptable to the United States? Would recognition allow overt U.S. support to the strike force? Was a mutual-assistance pact with the provisional government desirable? Willauer was concerned that without proper attention to these questions the plan would not be effective and that "the only practical course of action for the *physical overthrow* of Castro will be either: (1) open U.S. war with Cuba, or (2) a seven month overt training by the U.S. on United States soil of a Cuban-Latin American invasion force which will be planned to strike with at least overt U.S. logistical support."[13]

The last weeks of the Eisenhower administration should have presented an opportunity to reassess the Cuban plan. Considering all the problems that had surfaced and all the things that had not fallen into place as originally expected, one conclusion that could have been drawn was that the whole project should be aborted since it was clear that the effort to build up and maintain an underground had failed. By this time, however, a great effort had already been mounted and there seemed to be no pressing reason to call the plan off. The desire to contain the spread of Communism in our hemisphere had grown in the light of ongoing incursions in Africa and Asia. Propelled by the momentum of our planning, the operation had been transformed from a guerrilla movement to a full-scale invasion.

The inauguration of John F. Kennedy provided the prospect of a new beginning for the nation. His vision and message and the vigor with which he undertook his responsibilities created high expectations. While his hard-line rhetoric was inspiring, it also served to raise the stakes in America's global confrontation with the Soviets. His was an untenable position because any prospect of presidential vacillation in the face of Communist expansionism risked a loss of confidence in America's leadership of the West. Complicating matters further, Kennedy inherited certain policy decisions of the previous administration and was under pressure to carry them out. Cuba was destined to become his baptism by fire.

It was becoming impossible to sustain the discipline and morale of the troops in training. Now a major force, they could not be brought back to the United States, they could not be dispersed into smaller groups, and they could not be disbanded. A commitment to action was the only viable course, and time was running out. The frustration of the Cubans was apparent. Many were saying that they were prepared to recapture their homeland without U.S. assistance and that the government was actively preventing them from doing so. Kennedy was understandably reluctant to have his new administration reproached for thwarting or dismantling a major initiative to unseat Castro, and taking into consideration the agency's firm expectation that the Cuban operation would be successful, he authorized continued training and planning.

Dulles requested that a restricted group from the CIA's Board of National Estimates, headed by Sherman Kent, produce a report on everything known about the Castro regime—the state of public opinion in Cuba, intelligence on the morale of the Cuban forces, and so forth. In essence, the report would contain the best available field information the agency had and would represent the collegial opinion of the Board of National Estimates. Two memoranda addressing the question "Is time on our side?" were made available to President Kennedy. These documents were important for two reasons: the answer was an unqualified no, and contrary to future allegations, they provided evidence that the intelligence side of the agency was not entirely ignored by Dulles and me, even though compartmentation had to be preserved. The board had autonomy under the deputy director for intelligence, and when Dulles wanted a select group from the board to give him an estimate on a top-secret, restricted, highly classified subject, he automatically turned to Kent. As a result, the intelligence personnel had an opportunity to state their views. The deputy director for intelligence, Robert Amory, may not have been an active team member, but I believe he was aware of what was happening generally.

The presidential authority exercised by Eisenhower was now renewed by Kennedy in an early series of meetings at the White House. The ongoing plan was reviewed; at each session the president was explicit about authorizing the subsequent steps to be taken. The first meeting occurred only a week after the inauguration, a sign of the anti-Castro program's high priority. Among the issues decided was that the Department of Defense would review the CIA's military plans and provide the president with a prompt evaluation.[14]

On February 3, the Joint Chiefs (through their chairman, Lyman Lemnitzer) responded to the president's request by sending a memorandum of their findings to Secretary of Defense McNamara. Lemnitzer outlined many of the deficiencies in the CIA's plans for a Cuban invasion that would lead to disaster at the Bay of Pigs. Broad in scope, his memorandum addressed questions of logistics, strategy, and intelligence. A three-page executive summary stressed the degree to which operational success was predicated on local Cuban support, and it advised that "this factor should be a matter of continuous evaluation." It was Lemnitzer's judgment that "lacking a popular uprising . . . the Cuban Army could eventually reduce the beachhead," bringing about failure.

In the full report, Lemnitzer enumerated several problems with the agency's plan, yet his executive summary did not fully reflect them and actually ended on a positive note: "Despite the shortcomings pointed out in the assessment, the Joint Chiefs of Staff consider that timely execution of this plan has a fair chance of ultimate success." The apparent discrepancy between the opinions set forth in the main report and the executive summary went unchallenged. One example involved the issue of logistics. In the main report, Lemnitzer concluded that "shipping is limited and allows no margin for miscalculation or unforeseen contingencies." This statement on its own is damaging enough, but an additional list of logistical concerns disclosed that there was no engineering capability, no bridging capability, no floodlight trailers for beach and dump operations conducted in darkness, inadequate shore party personnel and equipment for handling heavy loads over the beach. This list continued extensively. Addressing the amphibious assault itself, Lemnitzer observed: "The amphibious element of the force has received no amphibious training and is not now scheduled to receive any prior to the operation. This deficiency will not be too serious if estimate of unopposed landing holds true. Nevertheless, lack of sufficient trained shore party personnel will complicate control in moving personnel and material across the beaches." The language grows blunter as the document continues: "The personnel and plans for logistic support are marginal at best. This operation may be supported logistically on an austere basis during an unopposed landing. If opposition increases, the logistical elements will rapidly worsen. Against moderate, determined resistance, this plan will fail to provide adequate logistic support."

Lemnitzer's worst fears about the amphibious landing would prove fatefully correct, as would his concern about the unsubstantiated assumption of a popular uprising. He was not satisfied with the information at his disposal, writing that "assessment of the combat worth of assault forces is based upon second and third-hand reports, and certain logistic aspects of the plan are highly complex and critical to initial success. For these reasons, an independent evaluation of the combat effectiveness of the invasion force and detailed analysis of logistics plans should be made by a team of Army, Naval, and Air Force officers."[15]

In the meanwhile, Kennedy was most eager to have his new administration act on a Cuban policy in a unified fashion. He asked in a February 6 memorandum to McGeorge Bundy, his special assistant for national security affairs, "Has the policy for Cuba been coordinated between Defense, CIA (Bissell), Mann, and Berle? . . . If there is a difference of opinions between the agencies, I think they should be brought to my attention." Bundy responded with a memorandum outlining the differences as they existed within the administration and preparing Kennedy for an upcoming White House meeting. Bundy wrote: "When you have your meeting this afternoon on Cuba, I think you will find there is a divergence of view between State on the one hand and CIA and Defense on the other." He characterized the State Department as cool toward the idea of an invasion "primarily because of its belief that the political consequences would be very grave both in the United Nations and in Latin America."[16]

Bundy sent Kennedy copies of memoranda written by Thomas Mann and me to assist him in sorting out the key issues. While my memorandum contained the CIA's familiar arguments for proceeding with the invasion, Mann's advised against it. His view reflected disagreement not with the president's policy on Cuba but with the means of toppling Castro. He believed that Kennedy "would be far better off to do whatever has to be done in an open way and in accordance with the American tradition after preparing public opinion both at home and abroad."[17] The two documents may have represented differing opinions on the Cuba policy, but they agreed on the basic necessity of planning for Castro's overthrow.

Bundy noted that, despite the State Department's attitude toward the invasion plans, "Defense and CIA now feel quite enthusiastic about the invasion."[18] This may have been true for the CIA, but the documentary evidence reveals that the Defense Department definitely was not enthusiastic at the time. Unfortunately, differing administration views were not reaching Kennedy through normal staffing channels.

A meeting on February 8 provided the president with another opportunity to receive opinions, particularly from the Joint Chiefs of Staff. A White House memorandum records that the meeting began with my report that the Joint Chiefs, "after careful study, believed that this plan had a fair chance of success—'success' meaning ability to survive, hold ground, and attract growing support from Cubans."[19] McNamara and the Joint Chiefs were remarkably silent after my summary of the Pentagon's views. The information McNamara and Lemnitzer possessed could have been used to support a strengthened air arm for the brigade or it could have been used to argue for cancellation, yet none of the operational criticisms raised in Lemnitzer's February 3 memorandum came up. It is my feeling that at that very early moment in the administration McNamara was probably diffident about voicing opinions on strictly military matters in the presence of the chairman of the Joint Chiefs, which is understandable. He was a civilian; he had no recent military experience that I am aware of and none at high levels of command. In the presence of a uniformed representative of the Joint Chiefs, a civilian newly arrived in office did well to keep a low profile.

Had McNamara taken or revealed firm opinions in these meetings, I assume that he would have expressed them to the president directly as well. He didn't give any evidence of having strong views, however, and I have no way of knowing to what extent the president consulted him. Kennedy was more apt to look to the Joint Chiefs or their chairman than to Bob McNamara for his information. McGeorge Bundy corroborates this view. He recalls that with regard to the White House meetings "McNamara did not play a major part in the Bay of Pigs" and that the president "tended to ask the Chiefs."[20] Their failure to convey the damning analysis in Lemnitzer's memorandum to McNamara is part of the pattern of incomplete interaction that continued throughout the period leading up to the actual invasion.

None of Lemnitzer's major criticisms received attention, although one issue from his February 3 memorandum was discussed at this meeting; namely, his conclusion that a more thorough evaluation of the agency's military operation was needed. The president concurred, and the Joint Chiefs appointed a committee composed of a senior officer from each of the three services, chaired by an army brigadier general, to carry out an independent review of the CIA plan. It was essential that the military plans be approved since reliance was being placed predominantly on the brigade, and the agency was not an organization with any particular combat expertise or experience. Military personnel were assigned to the CIA, and they were the men who did most of the military training. Our activities to date were at a relatively low level and organizationally would have been classified under the heading of "support" by the Department of Defense, which assisted us in obtaining B-26s from the National Guard, helped our efforts to build an air arm by allowing volunteer National Guard pilots to train Cuban pilots, and permitted us to use an old military base in Miami for logistic purposes.

This midlevel of interaction (with little participation in planning) was changed decisively by Kennedy when he assigned a prominent role in operational oversight to the Joint Chiefs and the review committee. The committee members first studied the provisional military plans and then traveled to Central America and wherever there were operational facilities to obtain a firsthand assessment. It should be noted that, although the Joint Chiefs were acting as advisers to the president and not in the role of an implementing or directing body, they nevertheless effectively had the power to pass or reject the operation as it took shape.

The committee remained in existence to review variations and new versions of the plan, thus involving the Joint Chiefs on a more intimate level. The three military officers worked very closely with the CIA and spent as much time in agency headquarters as they did in the Pentagon. Their job was to oversee and report to the Joint Chiefs; they had no authority over the CIA and the CIA had no authority over them. In practice, however, they collaborated with Colonel Jack Hawkins, who was on assignment to the CIA from the Marines, and Colonel Stanley Beerli, who was in charge of the brigade's air operation, both of whom reported to me. The committee members "could go anywhere they wanted. . . . They could see the operation just the way it was," says Beerli. "Anywhere" included not only Washington but the base as well. "I took the air person from the Joint [Chiefs] with me—Tarwater—and we went and talked to the pilots. We looked at the equipment. [Tarwater] even flew a mission with them. . . . There was no expression on his part in any way that he felt the mission couldn't be accomplished the way we had planned it."[21]

The arrangement allowed the Joint Chiefs to know what aspects of the invasion plan were being revised or reconsidered. Under Brigadier General David Gray, the Committee was in daily contact with the agency and assisted in the planning of the operation. Furthermore, he updated the Joint Chiefs at every scheduled meeting. Some historians have contended that either the Joint Chiefs and their representatives were never fully informed of the plans or they never had a real opportunity to make their views known. It should be clear, though, that once Kennedy became president the military was involved in overseeing the project at the highest levels. Although the information in Lemnitzer's February report failed to surface during regular meetings, the interagency group assigned to study the CIA's plans had every chance to provide useful information to the president had they chosen to do so.

I found Lemnitzer a very good colleague. Throughout the discussions I felt that he was an honest and objective observer, critic, and reporter. He was trying (as the best of U.S. military officers very often do) not to pronounce on or make a policy decision, which is what the decision to do something about Castro was. I never regarded him as overly or improperly critical. The inconsistency between the body of his memorandum and the executive summary did not fix itself in my mind as an important fact at the time. It is hard to speculate why it did not receive more attention.

The beginning of March, just six weeks from D day, found the CIA's planners engrossed in final preparations. In compliance with the president's request, the committee completed its report. The March 11 memorandum and appendix that Lemnitzer submitted for McNamara's review contained conclusions that were as prescient as they were disconcerting. Although surprise was essential to the mission's success, the odds against achieving surprise were believed to be about eighty-five to fifteen. Loss of surprise "could lead to the destruction of part or all of the invasion force." The appendix details not only why surprise was unlikely to be achieved but the most likely operational consequences. For example, without surprise, "one or more of Castro's combat aircraft will likely be available for use against the invasion force, and an aircraft armed with 50 caliber machine guns could sink all or most of the invasion force."[22]

Also on March 11, a meeting was held with Kennedy at which I delivered an update. Four alternatives were proposed: a nighttime amphibious landing, a daytime landing in full force, a daytime landing plus a diversionary force, and a slow buildup. The plan that called for a paramilitary force's infiltration during a night landing was of lesser priority and did not merit much confidence of success, but it was offered as part of an overall package of options. While it had the benefit of addressing the president's frequently stated concern for maintaining a low-profile, plausibly deniable operation, as contemplated it "would run the risk of becoming completely disorganized and scattered in a night landing. . . . Initial ammunition and food supplies would be limited, and it would be wholly dependent on air logistical support." In contrast, the plan receiving our recommendation was a landing that involved a combined "amphibious/airborne assault" during daytime, with concurrent tactical air support and the "holding of a perimeter around the beachhead area. . . . The scale of the operation and the display of professional competence and of determination on the part of the assault force would, it is hoped, demoralize the militia and induce defections . . . impair the morale of the Castro regime, and induce widespread rebellion. If the initial actions proved to be unsuccessful in thus detonating a major revolt, the assault force would retreat to the contiguous mountain area and continue operations as a powerful guerrilla force."[23]

Both the recommended plan and the nighttime operation were predicated on a landing near Trinidad, a city on the southern coast of Cuba near the Escambray Mountains. The former, while representing the best hope, was deemed "too noisy" by Kennedy, and although he was willing to move ahead generally, he could not support a plan that he felt exposed the role of the United States so openly. Resorting to compromise, he gave the agency four days to rework the plans and come up with a "less spectacular" alternative. It is hard to believe in retrospect that the president and his advisers felt the plans for a large-scale, complicated military operation that had been ongoing for more than a year could be reworked in four days and still offer a high likelihood of success. It is equally amazing that we in the agency agreed so readily. Perhaps our compliance reflects the degree of pressure felt by everyone involved in resolving the Cuban problem.

When the new report was ready, McGeorge Bundy summarized the key revisions for the president, noting that the CIA had "done a remarkable job of reframing the landing so as to make it unspectacular and quiet, and plausibly Cuban in its essentials." The major remaining problem, he said, was the air battle: "I think there is unanimous agreement that at some stage the Castro air force must be removed. . . . This is the only really noisy enterprise that remains."[24] There are two crucial points about his memorandum. The first is that at the highest levels there was awareness that air superiority was necessary for success. The second is Bundy's ominous observation that the air strikes were the only "noisy enterprise" that remained in the plan.

There is no question that I should have paid more attention to the views of advisers on the strength of the air arm. On one or two occasions the limitations of our capability due to policy prohibitions were discussed; the main problem was our inability to use U.S. volunteer air crews to supplement the small number of available Cuban crews. Stan Beerli expressed the opinion that everyone was counting on the air arm to do more than it would be able to do, and I think that if I had taken his comment more seriously I might have been stimulated to inquire what would happen if the airstrip at the Bay of Pigs could not be made operational within the contemplated twelve hours. Had I asked, I probably would have concluded that the proposed anti-Castro air force could not provide the kind of cover over the beachhead that we were counting on. I attribute my carelessness to inexperience in paramilitary affairs and overinvolvement in presenting and pressing the case on behalf of the agency. Not reexamining this aspect of the plan was definitely a failing on my part and cannot be put down to any external cause.

On the afternoon of March 15, the revised CIA plan was presented to the president. I gave a briefing that explained the essentials of the operation, now called Zapata, which was designed to disguise American involvement as much as possible and called for the invasion to take place at dawn. One important change (which would be critical to the eventual outcome) was a switch from Trinidad to the Bay of Pigs, a swampy coastal area a hundred miles to the west, which was selected because its distance from a major population center eased the president's concern about noise and attracting undue attention.

Kennedy found the new arrangement still too noisy. He asked repeatedly whether the air strikes were necessary; in effect, he wouldn't take yes for an answer. The move from Trinidad to the Bay of Pigs helped, but he disapproved of the dawn landing. As David Gray described in his memorandum of the meeting, Kennedy "felt that in order to make this appear as an inside guerrilla-type operation, the ships should be clear of the area by dawn."[25] This meant, of course, reverting to a night landing, which had been dismissed as infeasible a few days earlier.

At a meeting on the following day, March 16, the president received a revised plan. The landing would now take place at night, even though a nighttime amphibious landing had only been accomplished once, in World War II. (This issue, never really focused on in our deliberations, should perhaps have received more weight.) The attack would begin with a wave of air strikes two days before the invasion to destroy Castro's air force. Then, on D day itself, there would be a second wave of air strikes designed to destroy those planes that might have survived the first assault and, more important, to destroy Castro's microwave radio links. This disruption of his internal communications network was viewed as a critical element since it would force his top military commanders into open-voice communication. Once this occurred, messages regarding troop deployments could easily be intercepted and used against him. Castro would have to either continue open-voice transmissions or implement radio silence and jeopardize his response to the invasion. Toward the end of the presentation, the president gave his approval for proceeding with Operation Zapata. Once again, however, the approval was ambivalent. He reserved the right to cancel the operation up to twenty-four hours before the landing.

The question arises as to why the Joint Chiefs and the secretary of defense did not, in their oversight role, debate the change of landing location from Trinidad to the Bay of Pigs. One explanation may be that we at project headquarters had become convinced that the new site offered as good a chance of initial military success as the old one. As a result, neither the president nor McNamara received any sort of pressure from me, Dulles or Hawkins in favor of Trinidad. I remember meeting with Hawkins at the headquarters after a long weekend and his saying, "Well, we have developed an alternative plan to meet the president's desire for a quieter landing and we think that you will like it and approve of it. We do, and I think in some ways it's better than the original." So I did not get from Hawkins or any people on my staff a strong feeling that the change from Trinidad to the Bay of Pigs made the outcome more uncertain. What we did not think or talk about much—but should have—was the fact that it hindered the possibility of guerrilla action in the event of an initial setback.

There is no doubt that failure to question the viability of the move had serious repercussions. This is not to say that the CIA planners were blameless. Being responsible for the operation, we had a duty to ensure that the president and his advisers completely understood the impact of the changes. Dulles and I could have used the opportunity to recommend cancellation. There was no doubt that changes made over the past several days—especially the decision to land at night—had greatly reduced the chances of success. Not only were the operational difficulties of carrying out the invasion increased, but the move from the heavily populated Trinidad to the remote Bay of Pigs made a mass uprising less likely and effectively negated the option of a retreat into the Escambray Mountains. Yet the agency was so committed to the Cuban invasion plan and so sure of it at this juncture that Dulles and I were edged into the role of advocates. It must be admitted that we either encouraged or allowed the president and his advisers to believe that in the event of uncontainable pressure at the beachhead the brigade could retire and thereby protect the guerrilla option. I think this is the most clearly identifiable single error that we can be accused of.

The careful development of a contingency plan to deal with an inability to hold the beachhead was also impeded by the need to justify our position before repeated inquiries and inquests. During one briefing, I know I took the view that there was high confidence about seizing the beachhead and holding it, at least for a limited period. We did not take very seriously the possibility of failing to accomplish the landing, seize the beachhead, and repulse any initial modest attacks by Castro's forces. That being the case, we did not have somebody draw up a plan for retreating to the Escambray. If we had, it would have been obvious that there was no easy way to escape to the Escambray from the Bay of Pigs. The concept that had been appropriate for a Trinidad landing was retained even though it was inapplicable to a Bay of Pigs landing. One must keep in mind that plans changed fast—from Trinidad on March 11 to Bay of Pigs on March 14. I have never denied that we were culpable, and I am more than happy to accept the blame personally.

I think it is also important to state that, as far as planning was concerned, it was believed on the basis of available intelligence that Castro's militia would be a very low-grade military force; that the old regular army would be weakened by recent reorganization, the loss of a lot of the officer corps, and divided loyalties; and that the task of the regular army and militia would be to invade a strongly defended site. I still think those were reasonable assumptions on which to base an operational plan. The question we faced was not whether we could seize the beachhead and hold it for a few days (which I always thought was possible) but whether we could hold it for any length of time if Castro had time to bring up two or three times the force.

The physical impossibility of calling off the invasion, as well as the emotional toll that would entail, was an important factor in our actions. It could very well be that the fear of cancellation became so absorbing that I managed to ignore or suppress relevant facts, although I sincerely believed that, even with the plan's faults, as long as we were able to move ahead with the air strikes and destroy Castro's air force, the brigade would still win the day, at least to the extent of establishing the beachhead. It is also possible that we in the agency were not as frank with the president about further deficiencies as we could have been. As an advocate for maintaining the president's authorization, I was very much afraid of what might happen if I said, "Mr. President, this operation might as well be made open because the role of the United States certainly cannot be hidden."

One of the restrictions imposed on the new plan by Kennedy was that hard evidence of direct involvement by the U.S. government had to be concealed and, if exposed, plausibly explained or denied. This requirement lost its validity many weeks before the invasion since there were all kinds of rumors in the press of an imminent attack. We should have been aware of and concerned with the implications of this public exposure. If citizens here and abroad and most friendly governments were convinced that whatever action took place was instigated and presumably controlled by the U.S. government, then the presence or absence of hard evidence (such as up-to-date weaponry in the hands of the invaders) would have little bearing on the public or international reaction. If the United States was sure to be held responsible, then it made no sense to pay a price in terms of impaired operational capability for a result that could not be obtained. Yet that is exactly what we did. It was a major error.

Had this situation been faced up to, other courses of action could have been considered. One would have been to admit a U.S. role openly and take actions that would have enhanced the likelihood of success. Training could have been done on U.S. territory; better aircraft could have been used; above all, U.S. volunteers could have been recruited for piloting and other duties, at least in small numbers. (Our experience was that a large number of true volunteers would have been available.)

I am also inclined to think that Dean Rusk, as secretary of state, could have argued harder than he did against the operation. If he had, it might very well have been completely canceled. Instead, he kept a low profile in meetings, probably in the belief that he was the president's man and knew Kennedy's mind and that it was not up to him to question or go against it.

Everyone in the Cuban operation moved forward without much debate, confident that the fig leaf of plausible deniability was still in place. The myth of disclaimability influenced every move: small old cargo ships with no past connection to the United States were secured; the brigade was restricted to using World War II–vintage B-26s since they were aircraft the Cubans themselves could have procured on the open or black market; air bases in Central America were employed instead of ones in the more convenient and accessible southern part of Florida. This last restriction created a particular hardship because a B-26 leaving from Central America to operate over the Cuban beachhead had to spend up to three hours in transit; in order to have enough fuel for its return flight, it could stay over the attack site for only an hour to an hour and a half. With the limited number of aircraft and crews available, there was really no hope of maintaining constant air cover over the beach until the local airstrip was captured, gasoline and supplies had been landed, and a runway had been cleared so that the B-26s could begin operating there. Providing fighter escorts for the bombers was considered but then rejected on the grounds that the aircraft the Cuban exiles could obtain on their own did not possess the necessary range to operate out of Central America and might have jeopardized plausible deniability. All the above factors emphasized the need to destroy Castro's air force on the ground; no other alternative existed.

By early April, a little over two weeks from D day, Kennedy was ready to make the final decision about whether to proceed with the operation. A meeting scheduled for April 4 was attended by more than a dozen men, including Dean Rusk and Senator William Fulbright. First there was a general discussion of the current plans; then a number of questions were raised about the prospects of an uprising on the island. I believe it was made clear that no immediate wave of rebellion among the population was expected. I explained that once a beachhead was established successfully and held for a time it was hoped that a steady flow of defectors would come into the camp and add to the strength of the brigade.

The president went around the table and asked each individual for his vote to cancel or proceed. I remember the occasion clearly because Adolf A. Berle, the State Department specialist in Latin American affairs, gave a lengthy response. When he finished, Kennedy said, "Well, Adolf, you haven't voted." Berle replied, "I'd say, Let 'er rip." Several people at the meeting ultimately offered inconclusive opinions, saying they had no objection, but I recall that pro votes were recorded by McNamara, Berle, Mann, and Paul Nitze. "Bill Fulbright was fulminating against the whole idea of a big country like the United States taking action against a small country like Cuba," Nitze remembers. "That seemed to me to be quite wrong, to miss the point, so I got angry at Bill Fulbright. . . . I took the opportunity to attack Bill Fulbright's ideas and didn't bring up what was my worry, and that was, Would the goddamn thing work?"[26]

Kennedy and his advisers made the decision to go ahead with the invasion, using the recently altered plan. They were carried along by the momentum generated by their strong commitment to resolve the Cuban problem and their hope that the venture would be a success. Without anyone's realizing it, however, there was something of an undercurrent in the government that was serving to undermine what chances the operation had.

In addition to the president's continued ambivalence about making decisions, especially the ones that resulted in favorable revisions to the plan, there were other problems. On at least two occasions (reported to me by eyewitnesses), some of the Joint Chiefs said they felt the CIA was exaggerating the need for air cover for the landing. I myself recall an incident that occurred at a White House policy meeting on Cuba. The participants were gathered outside the Cabinet Room (which was still occupied by an ongoing meeting), engaged in conversation. David Gray took me aside and informed me about a discussion that had taken place the preceding day in a meeting of the Joint Chiefs. Curtis LeMay (who was sitting in for the absent commandant of the Marines) and several of the chiefs admitted their doubt about the absolute essentiality of air cover. Gray did not voice this as his own opinion but thought I should be aware of it.

I was shocked. We all knew only too well that without air support the project would fail. Bundy's memorandum had also made it clear that the executive branch understood the critical need for air superiority. I remember that when I reported this incident to Jack Hawkins he was exceedingly angry. If any senior Marine officer had participated in that meeting, Hawkins said, he would have totally supported the need for air cover. Hawkins was experienced in amphibious landings and believed that every military officer who knew anything about amphibious operations understood that unless you could count on solid air cover the chances of success were small. I don't know whether the president was ever directly or indirectly subjected to the Joint Chiefs' view, but if he was, that could explain his willingness a short time later to cancel the air strikes so readily.

One could make a case that their view reflected rivalry between the air force and the CIA. The agency's earlier successes with the overhead-reconnaissance programs had disturbed certain high-ranking members of the air force. Friends of mine in the military spoke frankly to me about this. There was no denying that a sentiment existed among the military that all the air activities undertaken by the CIA in the U-2, SR-71, and spy satellite programs should have come under the jurisdiction of the air force. Robert Amory recalled in a 1966 interview that, after I was put in charge of the U-2 program, "essentially, the air force's eye was wiped in you-know-what. And they resented that from the beginning."[27]

Unfortunately, as I perceived it, that resentment never died. For example, as we shifted from the guerrilla-based plan to the brigade concept, I recognized a need for air force officers to help train the brigade's air arm. Beginning in late November 1960, I made at least two requests for air force assistance that went unanswered. These requests did not seem unreasonable, since we had received some support personnel from the air force, but clearly some sort of change was occurring. During a Special Group meeting in December, Deputy Secretary of Defense James Douglas relayed certain air force concerns and questioned the need for the support we already had. By the middle of January, our air force personnel were pulled out of the project.[28] Considering the importance of the air arm to the plan's success, this was a serious development. Perhaps it should have concerned me more than it did, but my job was to move the plan forward. When we were able to get the Air National Guard to step into the breach, we simply proceeded with our preparations.

It is possible to conjecture some thirty years later that this ongoing resentment adversely affected the Joint Chiefs' support for the CIA's massive paramilitary operation, but there is no overt evidence. I have always thought that the Joint Chiefs were mainly influenced by their sense that the operation as a whole wasn't theirs. They didn't dream it up, they weren't in charge of it, they didn't plan it, and they were called in later to pass judgment on somebody else's idea. Not all the military officers felt this way. Gray and his two air force and naval colleagues who inspected the training camps of the brigade became strong partisans of the operation and were very friendly toward it. I think, in other words, that if resentment existed it influenced only a few officers. Certainly

Arleigh Burke, who was acting chairman of the Joint Chiefs when the operation occurred, was highly supportive of it.

The increasing skepticism among the Joint Chiefs about air control was troublesome enough, but resistance to the operation within the agency was also evident. The Bay of Pigs was an attempted covert operation on a scale never before undertaken by the CIA. The old professional hands who were in a sense my opposition (or who didn't really think highly of my way of doing things) might have said that one can be sloppy about a small covert action and if it's blown or it fails it doesn't do much harm but that doing things on such a massive scale renders one's chances of success very slim.

My deputy Richard Helms was not in favor of the operation, although he never expressed his opinion formally. I am sure his reluctance was a result of the cool relationship that had developed between us after I was appointed deputy director for plans in 1959. A number of people in the agency who had a long tradition in the intelligence field felt that Helms deserved the position and that I, an interloper and "superstar," catapulted over him and deprived him of his due. Bob King, one of my three special assistants at the CIA, recalls that although Helms's office and mine were only about thirty-five feet apart we almost never went into each other's offices. "With regard to the Bay of Pigs," he says, "Helms appeared to me to use an eleven-foot pole and stayed the hell away from it because I know that he thought it was a horrible idea."[29] I talked to John Bross, my deputy Tracy Barnes, and Dulles about the situation, and although they understood my relationship with Helms had its difficulties, they all felt it was best simply to persevere. Helms's competence and loyalty were never questioned, but at one point Dulles told me that it might have been better if Helms had been moved to another position in the agency.

The tension of the rivalry continued throughout the planning period. I regret today that I did not take Helms's views more seriously and that I did not encourage sufficient discussion among my colleagues to allow their concerns to be raised. I can only blame my reluctance on managerial style. So far as I knew, Dick Helms never said or did anything disloyal to me, much less to the agency, but I made the mistake of disregarding him. Although we may have represented different schools of thought and philosophy, we really had no direct conflict. There was a tacit understanding between us that he would be responsible for handling certain kinds of matters and I for others. I did, however, attach importance to his judgment on personnel matters. He knew the backgrounds of individuals in the clandestine service extensively and intimately, and I am certain I never proposed a major appointment without first consulting with him.

Asked to comment on Thomas Powers's claim in *The Man Who Kept the Secrets* that the friction between us served as a metaphor for the struggle between human intelligence and technological intelligence, Helms disagreed. He admitted feeling that I was sometimes indifferent to the problems of the clandestine service but said our differences were a matter more of separate vantage points than of any deep-rooted conflict.[30] That is a fair statement.

Helms was privy to almost all the cable traffic regarding the Bay of Pigs and must have been well-aware of what was going on. I am sure he did not feel it was his duty to approach me with his opinions, especially since my own actions toward him over the years had not encouraged that. Even if he had offered his input at the time, I must admit that he probably would have found me unreceptive. The greater obligation was on my shoulders to solicit his views. I did not do that and must assume full responsibility for our rather distant and careful relationship. One of my major mistakes as deputy director for plans, and particularly in the Bay of Pigs incident, was not finding a way to make an ally of Dick Helms. In the years that followed, we made our peace, and I have high regard for his work in the clandestine service and for him personally. I thought he made an excellent director of central intelligence.

In the months leading up to the Bay of Pigs, the tension in the agency worsened. I sensed that a large number of former OSS officers felt that the operation was too large, that there would inevitably be a breach of security, and that it was not the sort of thing an intelligence agency should even be attempting. Since no one brought these concerns to my attention or that of Dulles or Pearre Cabell while events progressed, they were easy to dismiss. If, however, I had been working closely with a deputy who, like Helms, was a bit more cautious and more professional than I was about the maintenance of security and a better judge of the agency's limitations, I might have been persuaded to consider cutting back the scope of the operation in some way.

Tension in the agency was not limited to the directorate of plans. In *A Thousand Days,* Arthur M. Schlesinger, Jr., writes that Robert Amory "was not informed at any point about any aspect of the operation." This sweeping statement has been subject to misinterpretation. For a variety of reasons, Dulles decided that the directorate of intelligence, headed by Amory, was not to be made officially knowledgeable of or involved in the operation. Nevertheless,

Amory was not, in fact, wholly ignorant of what was going on. He himself has said: "I had all the photo interpretation in the agency under my command, and my [senior] photo interpreter, Art Lundahl, kept me advised on what they were taking pictures of, so I knew informally what was going on." A few days before the invasion, according to Amory, he told Dulles, "I've got duty tomorrow, and whether you know it or not, I know what's going on." He wanted to know what he should do if anything came up. "You have nothing to do with that at all," Dulles snapped. Amory reacted as might be expected: "I came in and opened the cables from Uruguay and Nigeria . . . and went home and played five sets of tennis. I said, 'Screw 'em.' "[31] The day that Amory said "Screw 'em" and went about his business was the day Kennedy canceled the air strikes. One can only speculate what the presence of seasoned hands like Amory and Helms might have brought to the deliberations during that moment of crisis.

Perhaps Helms should have tried to force his views on me, ignoring what would have been my vociferous negative reaction. Perhaps Amory should have argued with Dulles for more active involvement in the operation. I am doubtful, however, whether Amory's wartime military experience would have made much difference; Helms would have had much to contribute as the operation was being planned and developed, but his exclusion is the sort of risk one takes in a probably overzealous effort to maintain compartmentation.

In contrast to my relationship with Helms, that with my deputy Tracy Barnes was always friendly and agreeable. In the split between those people who wanted to emphasize intelligence collection and those who were more interested in the possibilities presented by covert action, both of us fell in the latter camp. Barnes's views certainly supported my inclinations toward covert action, and his agreement gave me more confidence in my views on the matter.

I am not sure that this agreement was entirely beneficial. I think I overestimated the degree to which Barnes really embodied the philosophy of the clandestine service. I know fair and neutral colleagues who felt that he knew little more about tradecraft than I did. Some might argue that for me to rely on his judgment to support my views was to rely on ignorance to support ignorance, but this is a judgment that strikes me as unfair. I always assumed that Barnes brought a certain knowledge and experience to decisions on the projects that we worked on together. I believe that Dick Helms and John Bross had less regard for him than I did, however, and they may have been right, although I always gave him credit for his competence and knowledge.

To a large extent, my confidence arose from the fact that he had served for part of the war with Dulles in Switzerland and had been a candidate for an airdrop of personnel to discuss the surrender of the German armies in Italy. It appeared to me that he had a lot of contacts and experience in covert operations. Furthermore, it was Dulles who used Barnes during the Guatemala operation, and it was Dulles who was pleased to have him actively involved in the Cuban operation. Wanting him to be more of a manager and an executive, Dulles sought ways to give him a broader role in agency affairs. Before the Bay of Pigs operation, Barnes attended meetings of the 5412 Committee (the predecessor of the Special Group) as the agency's representative, and he served as ambassador to other departments as well. If my judgment of him was a little incorrect, it was because it mirrored Dulles's view of him. It is also possible that my personal affection for Barnes may have prejudiced my judgment.

During the training and preparation phase of the operation, Barnes saw the cable traffic and made some decisions, mostly small, in response to operational problems such as recruiting members for the brigade, training them, and maintaining their morale. He also attended planning meetings and offered suggestions. Although he worked as my deputy, we never achieved the neat division of roles that the titles "director" and "deputy" might imply. Whoever was there dealt with the issues as they arose. Thus, attempting to describe and evaluate Barnes's role and responsibilities in the Bay of Pigs is more ambiguous than those seeking tidy answers would suppose.

The consistently upbeat appraisals of my military advisers tended to allay my concerns about the many changes and constraints imposed on the plans by the president. In addition to the reports on the review committee's inspection, I relied heavily on ones coming in through the CIA's cable traffic. Although the December national intelligence estimate had been negative, late winter and early spring witnessed a flow of encouraging cables and intelligence reports. One intelligence report in early March brought news that "many people in Camaguey [province] believe that the Castro regime is tottering and that the situation can at any moment degenerate into bloody anarchy." There was news of uprisings in Oriente province and food shortages among an increasingly disgruntled militia. Later in March, news arrived that in Las Villas province "large numbers of militiamen have refused to fight." This intelligence report concluded that "approximately 75 to 80 percent of the militia units will defect when it becomes evident that the real fight against Castro has begun." Finally, an intelligence report from the first week of April observed: "The Castro regime is steadily losing popularity. . . . The people have begun to lose their fear of the government and subtle sabotage is common. . . . All of Oriente province is seething with hate. . . . It is generally believed that the Cuban Army has been successfully penetrated by opposition groups and that it will not fight in the event of a showdown."[32]

I remember particularly well a series of cables I received from Jack Hawkins on April 13 in which he provided his final evaluation of the Cuban air crews. He said that morale was high and that the group was the equal of any in the United States Air Force. Hawkins's cables reinforced conversations I had had with him in which he stated that the brigade had higher firepower per man than a comparable U.S. formation did.

I never traveled to the brigade training grounds myself, and I depended solely on my subordinates to provide information assessing the combat readiness of the Cuban troops, trainers, and leaders. I had no personal contact with the brigade leadership—Manuel Artime, José de San Román, Erneido Oliva, Enrique Ruiz-Williams. Perhaps if I had formed a firsthand impression of the Cuban contingent, I would have reshaped certain of my views and decisions.

Concurrent with the military planning, efforts continued to build a political coalition of Cuban exile groups that could serve as the basis of a provisional government once the beachhead was established and stabilized. The first attempted alliance proved inadequate, but in March two of the key leaders of the exile community signed an agreement to create the Cuban Revolutionary Council. Made up of members of the original alliance as well as all other groups that had materialized in the interim, it held some hope. The policy of two U.S. administrations was upheld, however, in that former supporters of Batista were not accepted.

Information about the exact nature of the operation was intentionally withheld from members of the council because there was little confidence in U.S. circles that they could maintain a high degree of secrecy. They were aware that a military organization was in training and that this training was being financed, organized, and conducted by the U.S. government, and they undoubtedly knew many of the individual Cubans involved. Three council members even made a visit to the training camp in Guatemala, but they were not told the actual date of the invasion or the details of the military plan. The secrecy constraint was so critical to the operation that, as D day approached, the council consented to be sequestered at a location out of communications contact.

About a week before the invasion, I decided to get another look at the feasibility of the air plan and asked Air Force General Leo Geary for his opinion. He thought it was "a barebones plan, . . . a skeleton." He explained that there are three basic criteria that an officer uses to assess a military plan's worthiness: Is the plan suitable? Is it feasible? And is it acceptable? In April 1961 Geary believed the Bay of Pigs plan was suitable, feasible, and acceptable, "but you had to have the whole thing." I knew it was essential to keep full support for the air plan, so I asked Geary if he would be willing to offer his opinion to Arleigh Burke of the Joint Chiefs. He was a little surprised at the request but agreed. I called Burke to give him some notice, and Geary went over to repeat his appraisal for the admiral. Considering that a few days later Kennedy would order the strength of the first air strike cut and that he would subsequently cancel the second strike, one can certainly argue that the project would have been better served if Geary had briefed the president instead. Since, however, the president had mandated the Joint Chiefs to review the plan and its revisions it seemed reasonable to have Geary brief one of the Joint Chiefs.[33]

On April 12, a few days before the start of the invasion, Kennedy held a press conference in the auditorium of the State Department. Cuba was surely foremost in his mind, but disturbing news on the international front was not far behind. Earlier that day Soviet cosmonaut Yuri Gagarin had become the first man to orbit the earth, and in Laos the Communist Pathet Lao guerrillas had forced the U.S.-sponsored Royal Army into a broad retreat. Someone asked about U.S. intentions toward Cuba. Knowing that Brigade 2506 would hit the beaches in a matter of days, Kennedy publicly ruled out armed U.S. intervention.[34]

The president's sometimes unorthodox organizational procedures and arrangements carried over to a lot of things, including having an attorney general who was his brother and one of his closest advisers. Shortly before the invasion took place, I was asked by the president to brief Robert Kennedy. It was the first time I had spoken with him on a professional basis, and because I knew he had great influence with the president, I was glad he was explicitly being brought into the circle of those who were knowledgeable about the operation. We met alone in his office. The briefing was straightforward and, no doubt, taped. He asked a few questions. I think I said that I thought we had a very good chance of seizing the beachhead and holding it. I am more doubtful about what happened after that and his closing remarks. Picking up on my confidence about holding the beachhead, however, he said, "I hope you're right." Usually such a remark implies that the speaker hopes you're right but is by no means sure you are—I think that at that juncture he probably had a much cooler and more skeptical view of the operation than his brother did.

On Friday, April 14, the day before the first strike was scheduled to take place, Kennedy gave me a fairly ambiguous instruction. He said he wanted to play down the magnitude of the invasion in the public eye and therefore did not want a full-strength strike but a more limited one. As far as I know, he made this decision without consulting either the Joint Chiefs or the secretary of defense. I was simply directed to reduce the scale and make it "minimal." He left it to me to determine exactly what that meant, and I responded by cutting the planned sixteen aircraft to eight.

I believe the president did not realize that the air strike was an integral part of the operational plan he had approved. I don't think we, the planners, made it clear enough to him that, as with most military plans, all aspects of it had to be dealt with. In other words, we should have told him more clearly ahead of time that if he wanted to exclude that part of the plan the whole plan had to be reconsidered.

The half-strength strike was flown the next morning, and while it was fairly successful, it did not completely destroy Castro's air force. The poststrike photography of that day revealed that the runways were damaged but not entirely out of commission, so that Castro's few remaining planes could still take to the air and become an unexpected threat to the invasion forces. The second air strike, scheduled for April 17, D day, became even more critical.

Another unforeseen and calamitous effect of the air strike was the furor it aroused at the United Nations, which was then in session. Adlai Stevenson, our ambassador, had received an incomplete briefing about the upcoming operation. A representative from the CIA had explained on April 8 that a group of Cuban exiles would invade Cuba and attempt to overthrow Castro, but he did not adequately cover the U.S. role in supporting the invasion. As a result, Stevenson was left with the distinct impression that the United States had virtually no hand in the events that were unfolding. Stevenson was able convincingly to defend the United States against charges of aggression during the session on the fifteenth because he genuinely believed he was stating the truth. As the cover story unraveled, however, he became furious. Feeling duped, he took his displeasure directly to the president. Kennedy did not like Stevenson and, I think, regarded him as congenitally soft on tough issues of foreign affairs; nevertheless, Stevenson was still a powerful force in the Democratic party and the president felt an obligation to heed his grievance. Arthur Schlesinger says that it was not that "Kennedy cared so much that Stevenson was in a position to bring about any threats but that he thought Stevenson at the U.N. was a valuable asset. Anyone who would compromise that asset by having him tell lies was making a grave mistake." Imagining himself in a similar position, Kennedy, "sort of identified with Stevenson."[35] I agree that at that moment Stevenson didn't constitute any kind of domestic political threat to the president. The next election was nearly four years away, and nothing Stevenson could have done to Kennedy would have had an effect on him. I believe the president was quite unhappy contemplating the worldwide furor that would be raised if Stevenson were openly critical.

The next decision rendered by Kennedy was late Sunday, April 16, when the ships were well within sight of the Cuban shore and the actual landing was only a matter of hours away. CIA Deputy Director Pearre Cabell was informed through McGeorge Bundy that the air strike scheduled for the next day would be canceled and there could not be another strategic air strike until the landing had been completed, the airstrip was seized, and B-26s were operating from Cuban soil. The main effect of these successive decisions was that *eight* sorties were flown before the invasion took place instead of the hoped-for *forty plus* (which in practice would have been reduced by attrition to perhaps thirty or thirty-five). Cutting the air strikes by 80 percent proved to be the operation's death sentence. This presidential decision, too, was made, I believe, without consultation of the Joint Chiefs or the secretary of defense.

That Sunday evening, Cabell and I met with Secretary of State Rusk, who telephoned the president in our presence and laid the matter before him. Cabell and I heard him tell Kennedy that the CIA felt strongly that the strike was a military necessity. He then gave his own reasons against the strike, explaining that developments at the United Nations made another air strike politically disastrous for the president. Kennedy reaffirmed his decision to cancel.

Rusk offered Cabell and me an opportunity to plead our case with the president over the telephone. Having heard Rusk's side of the conversation, we regarded the situation as hopeless. Cabell said, "I don't think there's any point," and I replied, "I think I agree with that." It was not difficult to see that Kennedy's and Rusk's minds were made up and would not be swayed. Today I view this decision of Cabell's and mine as a major mistake. For the record, we should have spoken to the president and made as strong a case as possible on behalf of the operation and the welfare of the brigade.

Cabell and I returned to headquarters about ten-thirty. I remember the shock and disbelief of our staff when we told them that we had not secured the right to go ahead with the air strikes. They considered them a matter of life and death (as indeed they turned out to be). When Jack Hawkins (who was now back in Washington) and CIA officers Richard Drain and Jake Esterline were informed, their reaction was much like everyone else's. Hitting the table with his hand, Hawkins yelled, "Goddamn it, this is criminal negligence," to which Esterline added, "This is the goddamnest thing I have ever heard of." Cabell, as the senior representative, addressed the group: "I know that some of you have lived very close to this operation for a long time and feel very deeply about it, but when you get a change in the marching orders you have to react now and you have to take your orders and do what you are told."

Cabell was always a good officer. He knew that one made the strongest plea one could, and if it was turned down, one followed one's orders. His was a mental set quite different from that of the more energetic and self-starting members of the clandestine service, however, and as a result his remarks went down poorly. Probably out of cowardice, I allowed Cabell to be the one to deliver the message, and so he bore the brunt of everyone's anger. I think many of the men involved in the operation were not convinced that Cabell was as much on their side as I was. They knew how deeply engaged I was, how much I had to lose, and that when I obeyed the orders, it was with sorrow and reluctance. I had committed a year of my life and an extraordinary number of other people's lives. We had observed all the directives and all the limitations up to a certain point, and I felt a passionate desire to go with everything we had at the time. I don't think it was perceived that Cabell had the same strong commitment to see the operation move forward and succeed.

So emotionally involved was I that I may have let my desire to proceed override my good judgment on several matters. Each new restraint or restriction or cutback was disturbing, but I relied very heavily on Hawkins and his estimates of success. My recollection is that he was in the same state of mind as I was, deeply committed to the plan and eager to have a go at it. I think I retained too much confidence in the whole operation up to the end, more than was rational—but that's the way it was.

At the same time, the political resolve at the White House was far from decisive. One explanation may perhaps be found in Dean Rusk's background. Although active in the deliberations, Rusk had been afraid of the enterprise from the very start. His whole approach to the operation had been conditioned by his experience in active ground-force duty in the China-Burma-India theater during World War II. From that he formed a number of impressions about guerrilla and unconventional warfare that he felt our planning had not considered. He argued to the president and Joint Chiefs that in a guerrilla operation air cover isn't really necessary for a landing (it is accomplished at night in small boats) and that the whole notion of air cover was more flamboyant than the situation called for. He used to ask (quite sensibly, I thought) whether something couldn't be done with "silver bullets." His impression was that even in a well-run covert operation one should try to bribe one's enemies rather than fight them; unfortunately, this would not have worked in Cuba. Rusk consistently argued for reducing the noise level, and his influence prevailed since Kennedy was already acutely sensitive to Stevenson's political weight. The strength of Rusk's convictions was enough to undermine any chances the operation had of succeeding but not enough to actually cancel it. Among the many tragedies associated with the Bay of Pigs, this is certainly one.

Later that same Sunday night, Cabell made another appeal, first to Rusk and then, from Rusk's apartment, to the president. He asked Kennedy to allow navy air cover for the Cuban supply ships as far as the three-mile limit. This proposal was much milder than the request for another strategic strike by Cuban aircraft. Nevertheless, it, too, was turned down. With hindsight, I have taken Kennedy's refusal (as Cabell took it) to mean that had we both spoken to him earlier that evening we would not have changed his mind. I still think, however, that it was a mistake on our part not to have made the attempt.

An authorized second strike was always included in the plan. Dean Rusk says in his memoirs that he thought the second air strike was not part of the plan, but he wasn't sure, because he had never received a written copy.[36] I think it is important to comment on this issue. It is true that he had not seen a tidy, complete operational plan in writing; even I hadn't. Whether they are justified or not, the requirements for maintaining extremely tight security dictate that an absolute minimum be written down in this kind of operation. I believe now that the failure to reduce plans to writing (if only so as to have a record) is open to criticism. There was no big sheaf of documents, tabbed on the edge, containing all the elements of a plan, as there would have been in the military. There wasn't time for it and there weren't enough people to prepare it.

I suspect that if Kennedy were alive today, he would admit to having vacillated. I think that as he got farther into the Bay of Pigs operation and closer to D day or D hour he had growing doubts. I do not believe these doubts really had to do with an assessment of the chances of success. If they had, they would perhaps have been quite rational. Instead, though, I think they had to do with political consequences reinforced by Stevenson's strong views and by Arthur Schlesinger, Richard Goodwin, and, to a degree, Thomas Mann (although by the last call of the National Security Council meeting—the final council of war at the White House—Mann had become either neutral or pro).

The situation reached serious proportions on the morning of April 17, when the invasion began in earnest. The president's decision to cancel the D day air strikes, the limited availability of aircraft and crews, and an air arm forbidden by the president to engage in strategic bombing meant that some of Castro's air force survived and sank two supply ships. This was a turning point for the brigade since the remainder of the supply ships withdrew to a position some fifty miles offshore, where they were presumably out of range of further attack but unavailable to give logistical support. Without resupply and air cover, the venture was doomed.

The Bay of Pigs site had been selected because of a nearby patch of solid ground that was surrounded by extensive marshlands. The only approaches to the beachhead were over three causeways and a road that ran along the south shore of the bay itself. It was thought that, if the brigade could seize the points at which the causeways reached the beachhead area and could rely on strong air support, any columns Castro tried to send across the causeways would be destroyed by air-to-ground fire. Just as the men were ready to hit the beaches, this strategy was nullified by the president's decision to withdraw the air strikes. The brigade was left in severe jeopardy. Not only did the decision weaken our plan militarily, but it gravely impaired the air wing's operational capabilities. As Leo Geary had observed, the air plan was no doubt a "bare bones" strategy, but it involved a carefully designed military operation that required a very specific timetable. Once this timetable was disturbed, the capacity of the brigade's air wing to provide air-to-ground support was all but lost.

While we began D day with a systematic chronology of flights, including a choreographed role for every pilot, maintenance crewman, and so forth, we soon found ourselves improvising. At a time when everything in the operation was supposed to have gone like clockwork, we required new mission planning. For example, once the mission was changed from bombing to air-to-ground support, the bombs that had been loaded on the planes had to be removed and different munitions substituted, a time-consuming logistical operation when one is working out of the primitive base of a covert operation. The original plan allowed rest time for the ground crews; instead, they found themselves working twenty-four hours a day. Air crews that were supposed to be operating out of an airstrip within the beachhead were now shuttling back and forth between Central America and Cuba. The air wing was effectively executing a new plan.[37] In retrospect, it is clear that the number of air crews and bombers that were available for this task would have been stretched thin in the best of circumstances. The president's withdrawal of even minimal air strikes was a high price for the men of Brigade 2506 to pay. And, in addition to everything else, communications with the beachhead were so poor that they greatly impeded our ability to assess events as they transpired and to manage the crisis. Plausible deniability had turned around to haunt us.

Walt Rostow describes the horrible morning of April 18 in his book *The Diffusion of Power*. It was seven o'clock, and Allen Dulles, Pearre Cabell, and I had gone to the White House to meet with Kennedy, Rostow, Bundy, and Ted Clifton, the president's military aide. Sitting in the White House situation room, we reported the desperate news from the beaches. Afterward Rostow asked Bundy if he could assist in any way. Bundy and the president agreed that it would be helpful if Rostow spent many of the next crucial hours at our operational headquarters. What is important about Rostow's recollection of the meeting is the way it fills in the chronology of how events unfolded. There were moments during the Bay of Pigs planning when we overlooked an opportunity to reconsider the situation and take action before it was forced upon us. This meeting provided another such occasion, yet there was no discussion on my part or Dulles's of our fallback scenario. Although the operation was proceeding poorly, no one bothered to ask what we planned to do next. Nobody pushed us for an explanation.[38] It would have been a logical moment to reassess the situation and try to figure out how to get the men off the beaches during the day. Had we faced up to the dreadful situation at this meeting, we might have provided ourselves and, more important, those men with a better ending. By the time of our next meeting in the Oval Office almost eighteen hours later, things were far worse.

Rostow accompanied me back to CIA headquarters, where he had a chance to observe the mood of the staff. "It was terrible," he remembers sadly. "They all turned to Dickie. . . . They were pulling at Dickie's coat, begging him to send in the army. . . . and make good on the covert operation by sheer force. All day long the cables kept coming in. It got worse and worse and worse until finally I said, You'd better tell the president. I called Kenny O'Donnell and said, Bissell has a message for the president." That night Rostow drove me to the White House, where I briefed Kennedy on his remaining options.[39] A gala dinner was in progress, and everyone, including the cabinet members, was in white tie; Arleigh Burke was in dress uniform. All the pertinent people left the affair to conduct an emergency meeting. I would guess we talked for thirty or forty-five minutes, evaluating the desperateness of the situation. It was difficult not to let my passionate belief in the cause influence my assessment of the options at hand, but I was aware of my responsibility to help Kennedy make the best decisions possible, given the appalling circumstances we faced. He asked what word we had. Burke, who was there both as acting chairman of the Joint Chiefs (Lemnitzer was out of town) and as chief of naval operations, was very much on my side and would have liked nothing better than to have been given authorization to use carrier aircraft to ensure that supplies would reach the brigade. Acutely aware of the desperation of those whose lives were on the line, I made another appeal for air support. The invasion was on the brink of failure, but there was still hope. Leo Geary remembers that "we had a carrier with some stripped-down aircraft ready, and it would have taken them maybe forty-five minutes from start to finish to clean out that beach . . . but the president said no."[40]

To my great disappointment, especially in the light of the serious consequences of defeat, Kennedy would not allow the navy to provide full air support, even at this late date. Instead he authorized one hour of air cover the following morning, which would allow the B-26s to resupply the brigade safely. It is worth noting that just forty-eight hours earlier, he had canceled the B-26 air strike because it was too noisy. Now he was allowing the planes to fly air-to-ground support. Why he considered this less noisy is inexplicable.

I hurried back to headquarters and sent off an instruction through channels to expect navy cover during the agreed-on hour. When the B-26s lumbered into the air the next day, however, no navy air cover appeared. It seemed that a misunderstanding about the correct time standard had prevented the air support from being at the target area when expected. As a result, the B-26s were either forced from the field of battle or shot down, the final tragic blow. The situation on the beach worsened as members of the brigade waited for American intervention that never materialized. It had been hoped that if the beachhead collapsed many of the invaders could attempt to make their way into the swamps, whence they could harass Castro from behind his lines. But Castro moved quickly and effectively to deter this action and the entire group was soon captured, proving that the long-touted guerrilla option was as much a myth as plausible deniability.

With the invasion in a shambles, there was little likelihood of inspiring rebellions against Castro, as had been contemplated. No one, right up to the level of Allen Dulles, expected a mass uprising the minute the men hit the beach, but we counted on the possibility of some sporadic incidents that would grow in intensity when the beachhead was consolidated and had been held for three or four days. By that time, if aircraft had been operating out of the beachhead and had successfully prevented Castro's forces from destroying it, there was a very real possibility, we hoped, that significant defections would begin. What actually occurred, however, is that fifty to sixty Cuban peasants from the sparsely populated area came to the help of the beleaguered brigade. It is at least possible that the original plan to land at Trinidad, a city of twenty thousand, would have provided the large uprising needed to support the troops.

There is no question that the brigade members were competent, valiant, and committed in their efforts to salvage a rapidly deteriorating situation in a remote area. Most of them had had no previous professional military training, yet they mounted an amphibious landing and conducted air operations in a manner that was a tribute to their bravery and dedication. They did not receive their due.

Ironically, the public outcry provoked by the operation, as it began to be revealed, had nothing to do with whether one could buy B-26s outside the United States or whether they had to be obtained from the Air National Guard. The reaction wasn't significantly influenced by the fact that U.S. volunteer air crews were employed. The American public was upset and angry because, no matter how you viewed the facts, an action that need not have been undertaken at all or that could have been successful with the limited support furnished by U.S. sources had resulted in a defeat for the United States and an unqualified victory for Castro. Polls conducted the following week indicated that more than 90 percent of Americans supported the idea of a Cuban effort to topple the Castro regime.[41]

Art Lundahl remembers being in my office the morning after the debacle. Kennedy called a couple of times, and at one point I turned to Lundahl and said, "Now, many heads are going to roll as a result of this, but I want you to know that the hard information that you, the photointerpreters, provided to us before we went into the Bay of Pigs was absolutely right. No share of this fault should in any way attach itself to you all. You did your job and did it well."[42] I myself received numerous calls and letters of support from friends, which were gratifying. One of the most meaningful calls came from Adolf Berle, who had wanted to "let 'er rip." He told me, "I voted for this operation; I still believe we should have tried; I'm glad I voted as I did. I think what you did was the best that could be done, and take heart—I think we are better off than if the operation had not been attempted." It is fairly rare that one gets such a supportive message following a dismal failure, and the fact that he took the time to be thoughtful has always given me the warmest feeling toward him. His remarks were very much in keeping with something my daughter remembers my saying at the time: "In the field of intelligence, the opportunities for success are so spectacular and so important that there is only the possibility of total failure or total success. The risks are very high, but people must have the courage to take chances. History deserves that it be tried."

Allen Dulles wrote a paper on the Bay of Pigs, never published, that is very revealing. There is one particular sentence that he reworks over and over in draft form: "Great actions require great determination. In these difficult types of operations, so many of which I have been associated with over the years, one never succeeds unless there is a determination to succeed, a willingness to risk some unpleasant political repercussions, and a willingness to provide the basic military necessities. At the decisive moment of the Bay of Pigs operation, all three of these were lacking." He also refers to the histories written by Arthur Schlesinger and Theodore Sorensen during the sixties: "I deplore the way this is being done. In effect, an attempt is now being made to write history and only a part of the story is available. If what is so written goes entirely unanswered and without critical examination, it will go down as the history of the event. It is not the true story."[43]

Kennedy was shocked by the failure of the Bay of Pigs, but internally, within the government, he did not engage in any kind of vigorous reprimand. In the first heat of anger and disappointment, he probably considered a drastic reorganization of the CIA. Allen Dulles offered his resignation, which was accepted. I was called into the president's office, where Kennedy explained that I could not continue as deputy director for plans. Then he used a phrase that I have always remembered. He said, "If this were a parliamentary government, I would have to resign and you, a civil servant, would stay on. But being the system of government it is, a presidential government, you will have to resign."

Although I had expected no less and accepted his decision as conclusive, he made it clear that he was in no hurry to have me leave. In fact, I don't think he wanted the transition to occur too precipitously and look as if it were a quick reaction on his part or a seeking of scapegoats. As president, he had generously and appropriately accepted full blame for the outcome of the Bay of Pigs. During the summer and autumn of 1961, I had occasion to attend, and be a part of, small meetings with him, and in no way did he behave with me or with Dulles as if there had been a loss of confidence. In other words, he continued to work and consult with us as before.

Early in 1961 I had been offered an opportunity to become deputy undersecretary of state for political affairs. Chester Bowles, a long-standing friend whom I originally knew through my brother, Bill, had recently been named undersecretary of state by Kennedy and was eager for me to accept the position. He and I discussed the possibility at length, and finally I asked him if Dean Rusk agreed with the move. Bowles replied that he did. Then I asked if he thought Rusk really believed in it. He told me to talk to Rusk myself, which I did. Rusk said he would be delighted to have me serve in that capacity and then went on to describe the duties. I remember his saying that if I accepted he didn't think I should be the senior State Department contact with the CIA, since that would be a conflict of interest. Following that conversation I had an appointment with Kennedy. I was already aware that he was comfortable with me and, on the whole, preferred to have me stay in the CIA. It was also no great secret that he viewed me as Dulles's successor. Kennedy didn't go so far as to say he wouldn't approve me for the State Department job, but he clearly thought it was more important for me to remain as deputy director for plans, which I decided to do.

Had I not, of course, my involvement with the Bay of Pigs operation would have ceased before the fateful invasion, my chances of becoming Dulles's successor and director of central intelligence would probably have increased, and I might have continued my career in Washington instead of leaving in 1964 for the private sector. I am content with my decision. I was so deeply immersed in my duties as deputy director for plans and with the details of the upcoming invasion that I felt I could not leave, regardless of how tempting the State Department position was.

On April 22, Kennedy directed Maxwell Taylor to organize and chair a board of inquiry into the reasons for the Bay of Pigs failure. This board, which became known as the Cuba Study Group, or the Taylor Board, also considered ways of improving the government's counterinsurgency capabilities. In the process, it provided an education on covert operations that would have a great impact on Robert Kennedy, who served on the board and would shortly become far more interested in CIA operations. The Cuba Study Group concluded that the "proximate cause" of failure at the Bay of Pigs was a "shortage of ammunition." This was a direct result of our inability to destroy Castro's air force on the ground, a grave shortcoming that allowed his T-33s to sink the brigade's supply ships.[44]

A second critique of the Cuban operation was conducted by Lyman Kirkpatrick, the inspector general of the CIA, an ambitious man who, in spite of paralysis from polio, aspired to the position of director of central intelligence. His illness necessitated a move from the exciting and challenging directorate of plans to the more mundane, bureaucratic position of inspector general, a shift he always resented. His report covered the same ground as the Taylor Board's but was more ruthless in its conclusions and caused an uproar at the agency, especially with Dulles and Cabell.

Kirkpatrick met John McCone, the newly appointed successor to Dulles, at the airport and handed his completed report directly to him instead of going through proper channels. McCone, a fair and sensitive man, was appalled by this breach of courtesy, as well as by the contents of the report. He instructed Kirkpatrick to give a copy to Dulles, who was furious upon reading it. I was also given an opportunity to see the report and was wounded by it. McCone allowed me to rebut it in writing and directed that my response be permanently attached to Kirkpatrick's report as part of the official record.

The report and my rejoinder have been very closely held by (and within) the agency. I have not been able to review them for a number of years and therefore cannot relate much about their contents. As was to be expected and as was appropriate, the inspector general's report dealt mostly with decision-making procedures, personnel selection, and other administrative matters. Kirkpatrick could not and did not offer any new analytic insights to explain the military failure. A number of his critical comments were, or may have been, valid, but that didn't make them any more welcome to me or to Dulles and Cabell.

I remember that one of his conclusions, probably correct, was that the operation, although large and of a sort that the clandestine service had rarely contended with, had been hastily and inappropriately staffed. Specifically, he said that few of the agency's really first-rate people were used and he identified a number of people whom he characterized as second-rate. His criticisms of decision-making procedures were more sweeping, but they were (necessarily) vaguer. He pointed, as did other critics, to the nearly nonexistent documentation of policy meetings, to the failure to put operational plans into writing so that they could be circulated for policy makers' information and comment, and generally to the lack of professional staff work. Much of his characterization was fair, but I have never felt that inadequate paperwork or staffing had much to do with whatever misconceptions arose. The shortcomings of our procedures were mainly attributable to keeping the circle of knowledgeable participants as small as possible. I will say, however, that I found our procedures refreshing in contrast to the stuffy discussions and negotiations that went on among the National Security Council's staff members during the Eisenhower years.

In 1985, twenty-four years after the invasion attempt, I attended a CIA ceremony at which I had an opportunity to renew contact with McCone, by then the former director. Not long after, he wrote me: "Some day soon we will meet again and I would like to get your version of the discussion you and Cabell had with Dean Rusk when you were trying to persuade the President to withdraw the 'stand down' of the air cover you had arranged for the landing of the Brigade. It was this fatal error that caused the failure of the Bay of Pigs operation."[45] Would we have succeeded if the air strikes had not been cut back and the supply ships had not been sunk in the attack? I believe that, even if the supply ships had been able to continue to resupply the brigade, the brigade might not necessarily have established and held the beachhead. Even in the best scenario, the air arm would have been stretched to the limits of its capabilities, and while there would have been no problem in purchasing more B-26 bombers to increase its strength, there were no additional qualified Cuban pilots to recruit. In the latter weeks of the operation it became clear that the only way to bolster the air force was to use U.S. volunteers, but doing so meant violating Kennedy's mandate against involving U.S. military personnel. Given the constraints on the number of air crews that could be recruited and the limited training time, I am not sure that a different and better plan could have been produced with more safety margins built into it. I hold myself responsible for not having had better judgment on some of these features of the plan and for not voicing warnings to Dulles and the president that would have made these risks clearer.

It is important to note that definite plans were made only for the first phase of the operation—the establishment of the beachhead. Planning for the second and third phases was progressively more difficult until the outcome of the first phase was known. Since virtually all public discussion has focused on the first, unsuccessful phase, it is worth commenting on what had been contemplated for the remainder of the operation. Phase two would have involved a defensive ground action to gain a firm hold on the beachhead and, simultaneously, air operations and psychological warfare (such as diversionary attacks, jammed communications, disinformation, and a functioning radio broadcast from the beachhead). In phase three, as perceived by Jack Hawkins, the brigade was to break out from the secure beachhead after a number of weeks and march on Havana, picking up local volunteers and supporters on the way to swell its ranks.

My own speculation differed somewhat from Hawkins's scheme. I believed that securing the beachhead and operating aircraft from its landing strip would have served to confuse and disorganize the Castro regime. A few days of this treatment might have caused it to lose touch with what was going on at the other end of the island and impaired its ability to move troops at will, especially heavy armor. Either Castro's nerve would have broken under these circumstances or important elements of the armed forces (especially the regular army) would have defected from him and gone over to the invasion force. If the beachhead had been held and Castro had proved incapable of driving the invaders out, at the very least a stalemate would have been achieved that would have allowed a provisional government to be flown in and a proposal mounted for new elections to be supervised by the Organization of American States. That in itself would have demonstrated Castro's ineffectiveness and meant a major victory for the United States.

One reason that events did not occur as intended was that Castro had troops at the northernmost beach far sooner than expected, probably a direct result of the president's decision to cancel the air strike scheduled for early Monday morning, which had among its primary targets the microwave radio links that constituted the basic voice communications system for the island and carried much of Castro's military traffic. The destruction of those links would have forced the Cubans into open-voice transmission and provided a considerable advantage to the invading forces. Unfortunately, the microwave links were not something that Cabell and I had in mind when we went to request that the president reinstate the full-strength air strike, and we may have failed to warn him about the additional consequence of his action. As it was, these intact microwave links alerted Castro to the invasion and facilitated his accelerated response. Speaking for myself (and probably for Cabell as well), I felt the issue had been drawn by Rusk on the level of high political policy and that the president was going to decide it on that level and not on tactical considerations.

John McCone wrote me again in 1986, after reading an article I had written on the Bay of Pigs. I found his comments revealing:

> Understandably, entering CIA as its Director shortly after the Bay of Pigs failure, I heard many explanations and analyses of the invasion effort and the reasons that things went wrong. I have lodged in my mind two and only two serious errors by individuals. First, it seemed to me Allen Dulles made a serious mistake in judgment by darting off to Puerto Rico or elsewhere to make a speech on the very eve of the most serious undertaking of his career as Director of CIA. In my opinion, Allen should have known that a young, inexperienced Administration quite possibly would be influenced to make errors in judgment and this, of course, is just what happened. I do not criticize General Cabell or you for not accepting Secretary Rusk's offer that you appeal directly to the President after you learned of the President's critical decision of standing down the B-26s, which apparently was a critical mistake. However, if Allen had been in Washington and available, he might well have persuasively outlined the tragic results of the President's decision and quite possibly gone to the point of turning around the brigade before the ill-fated landing was attempted.
>
> The second responsibility rests squarely on the shoulders of President Kennedy, who apparently was persuaded by Adlai Stevenson and possibly others to "stand down" the B-26 air support which was vital to the success of the brigade landing. As you know, (and I know from those associated with you), the mission of the B-26s was to destroy the four or five operable aircraft then in Castro's hands, thus insuring that the brigade with all of its equipment, supplies, fuel, etc. could have been brought ashore unmolested by Castro's air capability. Standing down the air strike was, in my opinion, a reckless decision by the President and one that Allen Dulles, had he been on the scene, would not have stood for.
>
> Of course, Dick, there have been countless postmortems and opinions as to what "might have happened if" everything had gone off as planned. The brigade might have faced a three or four week battle rather than a three day skirmish, but that of course is conjecture.[46]

While the president's decision to cancel the air strikes on April 16 was certainly the gravest contributory factor in the operation's failure, the loss of information as reports worked their way through the bureaucracy to the White House was also important. Policies established by the administration just three days after Kennedy's inauguration partly explain the phenomenon. McGeorge Bundy, the new national security adviser, presented Kennedy with a five-page memorandum on reforming the national security apparatus. The reorganization altered the National Security Council's role within the bureaucracy in ways that augured poorly for the weeks ahead. Bundy envisioned a council, he told Kennedy, where a subject could be opened up "so that you can see what its elements are and decide how you want it pursued." In the process of reorganizing the council to fit the lean, activist bent of the New Frontier, Bundy dismantled the checks and balances that Eisenhower and his top aide, Andrew Goodpaster, had built into its bureaucracy. Its planning board was eliminated, as was the position of executive secretary. Furthermore, when Kennedy and Bundy also pulled the plug on the operations coordinating board, they eliminated half the staff of the National Security Council, greatly reducing the remaining staff's ability to perform oversight functions and analyze prospective plans and policies. More importantly, as John Prados points out, Bundy "transformed the NSC staff from the servants of the Presidency, to those of the President. Staff members became Kennedy's eyes and ears, no longer disinterested mediators working to push papers up to the NSC level."[47]

Without the staffing and regular reporting channels that characterized the Eisenhower White House, the incompleteness of communication between the CIA and the Joint Chiefs, not to mention our differences in opinion as to the likelihood of the operation's success, was not readily apparent. I found the change of structure liberating, but there is little doubt in my mind now that Eisenhower's staffing procedures, while cumbersome, had positive attributes. For example, the damaging information in Lemnitzer's February 3 memorandum should have been revealed at the February 8 meeting in the Oval Office, where many of the key players of Kennedy's newly assembled foreign policy team came together—Dean Rusk, Thomas Mann, Charles Bohlen, Robert McNamara, Paul Nitze, McGeorge Bundy, and myself among them—but it was not.

Reflecting on Bundy's reorganization, Andy Goodpaster comments: "Eisenhower at various times said, 'Organization will not make a genius out of a dunce.' That's a favorite of his. But organization can give the decision maker the facts he needs, presented in a way that would enable him to make wiser decisions and guard him from making serious mistakes. That was a very profound observation and President Kennedy fell victim to that in his early days." Arleigh Burke also felt that organizational failure was a key factor in our defeat: "What really happened in the Bay of Pigs . . . was a complete breakdown in governmental ability to take actions in a complex situation. . . . [W]hen the new administration came in, they wanted to do away with red tape. They didn't like the way government had been run. They didn't like the complicated and what they thought were delaying procedures that had been developed."[48]

The reticence of McNamara and Lemnitzer to speak up forcefully in presidential meetings may reflect what Morton Halperin and Arnold Kanter suggest is characteristic behavior of members of a bureaucracy, who informally perform a cost-benefit analysis of the risks involved in raising their profiles on any given issue or policy proposal. Halperin further suggests that "disputes over roles and missions affect the information reported to senior officials." He contends that there are many written and unwritten rules governing how information flows in a bureaucracy and how decisions are made. Those individuals or agencies "having the action" are "responsible for moving an issue through the government." Generally, they become advocates for a given proposal, and while other agencies may become involved in developing a policy or course of action, there is an unwritten rule that one respects the prerogatives of those that "have the action."[49]

In the Cuba operation, it was the CIA, above all other government agencies, that had the action. The Joint Chiefs did not have it. The operation was not theirs; they acted as advisers to the president. It is therefore not surprising that they would be reticent to comment too harshly on what another agency was doing. Their memoranda to McNamara had been responsive to the president's request for a review of the operation and its military aspects, and they probably felt no further critique or recommendations were necessary. Referring to the tendency of bureaucracies to tread lightly on one another's turf, McGeorge Bundy, an active participant at the White House meetings, sums up the attitude of the Joint Chiefs toward the CIA's plan by explaining that "it's the other fellow's property. . . . The Joint Chiefs really didn't regard this as their main business, and therefore if they responded honestly and straightforwardly to the president's questions, they didn't have a campaigner's need to go on and say, 'Please don't do this.' "[50]

In other words, another government agency had the action, and Kennedy's intense interest in the project only heightened the potential cost of dissent. Reframed within the context of bureaucratic prerogatives, McNamara's and Lemnitzer's behavior suggests that from their perspective a failure at the Bay of Pigs was a loss for the CIA but not necessarily for the Department of Defense.

In late autumn 1961 I went to the Philippines for a meeting of mission chiefs. At the last minute, John McCone decided that he would like to accompany me. I ran the meetings, but he was always present. It was in a session with station personnel from all over the Far East that I first recounted the story of the Bay of Pigs. The event was only a few months old, and I thought they should hear the facts from me, their boss. I don't remember there being a flurry of questions and I have no particular recollection of my account, but I am sure that in many ways it served as a confession for me.

Even that soon after the event, my supporters, the conservative commentators, liked to blame the whole thing on the president's last-minute decision to cancel the air strike. I know that when I reported to the agency personnel in the Philippines I did not say that we would have won if the air strikes hadn't been first cut back and then called off. My position there, and at other times as well, was that there would have been a significant difference between flying eight sorties and close to forty sorties, but that decision alone would not have ensured success. No one could say it would have.

Historians commonly note in early accounts of the Kennedy administration that the Bay of Pigs failure taught Kennedy valuable lessons that would later help him meet the challenge of the Cuban missile crisis. Arthur Schlesinger, for example, remarks in *A Thousand Days* that "no one can doubt that failure in Cuba in 1961 contributed to success in Cuba in 1962."[51] His statement implies that Kennedy underwent a metamorphosis because of the Bay of Pigs, but as documentary evidence and my own experience suggest, his attitude toward Cuba changed remarkably little, if at all, after the debacle.

On May 5, just days after the Bay of Pigs, the National Security Council concluded that U.S. policy toward Cuba should not be revamped in the light of a damaging and humiliating defeat; it should continue to "aim at the downfall of Castro." Furthermore, while the council decided that the United States "should not undertake military intervention in Cuba now," it determined that the administration should do "nothing that would foreclose the possibility of military intervention in the future."[52]

The summer of 1961 found the Kennedy administration growing increasingly concerned about Castro's continued military buildup. In response to its request for an evaluation of the perceived threat, the United States Intelligence Board concluded that the Cuban army and militia were augmenting their combat effectiveness and could be defeated only by a "modern substantial combined arms force."[53] There was no hope of deposing Castro by landing parties made up of Cuban exiles or by guerrilla operations of any kind.

Kennedy asked Edward Lansdale, who reported to Deputy Secretary of Defense Roswell Gilpatric, to examine the administration's policy toward Cuba. Lansdale had become a legend helping Philippine President Ramon Magsaysay achieve a counterinsurgency victory against the Hukbalahaps, and no doubt it was believed that his general knowledge of guerrilla and counterinsurgency operations would prove useful in helping develop a strategy to deal with Castro. Lansdale's review and subsequent recommendations ultimately served as the basis for Operation Mongoose. Lansdale proposed that the United States train Cuban exiles so that they would be able to overthrow Castro on their own. His idea was to infiltrate the men into Cuba, where they would organize cells to initiate guerrilla activity.[54] Needless to say, Operation Mongoose bore a remarkable resemblance to the CIA's original plan for the Bay of Pigs. I am still convinced that Lansdale's plan did not embody a concept radically different from that contemplated by the CIA in the summer and fall of 1960.[55] It was our inability to develop an effective underground and Castro's underestimated ability to eliminate resistance groups that redirected the CIA's activities in those crucial months from a guerrilla operation to an invasion—something whose planning and execution could not be left exclusively to Cuban leadership.

Despite national intelligence estimates showing that Castro's consolidation of power precluded successful guerrilla activity and despite the similarities between Lansdale's plan and the CIA's failed efforts, Kennedy endorsed the plan. He created an entirely new organizational structure, the Special Group Augmented, to maintain close control over Operation Mongoose and ensure that this time the plan worked. In addition to the regular members, Robert Kennedy and Maxwell Taylor were included in meetings of the Special Group Augmented. It was the group's responsibility to oversee how Lansdale, who was now in charge of Mongoose, and the CIA were carrying things out. For the most part, the group's members were the same men who had advised Kennedy on the Bay of Pigs operation. How much fresh insight and wisdom these men brought to deliberations simply by virtue of being placed in a new organizational structure is open to question. In any event, Kennedy seemed convinced that it was the lack of full information that had caused the Bay of Pigs failure and not simply the insufficient resources mobilized against Castro or a flaw in the policy itself. He therefore made it a requirement that, before authorization for a mission against Castro was granted, a highly detailed plan would be submitted to the group.[56]

Robert Kennedy experienced a transformation during this period. Prior to the Bay of Pigs, he had been skeptical of the operation; later, as a member of the Taylor Board, he became a highly vocal critic of the CIA and covert operations. Yet, by late 1961, he was pushing hard to move forward with Operation Mongoose. Perhaps because of his increased involvement with the project he had become more accustomed to the kinds of covert activities that were possible and had decided that the end really did justify the means. And perhaps the change had something to do with the fact that within a few months after the Bay of Pigs he and his brother found themselves confronting the same Castro-related problems that had inspired the Bay of Pigs.

The Church Committee's report reveals that in fall 1961 I was chewed out by the president and the attorney general in the Cabinet Room for "not doing anything about getting rid of Castro and the Castro regime."[57] I do not remember this meeting, but I do remember clearly that the Kennedys wanted action and they wanted it fast. Robert Kennedy was willing to look anywhere for a solution and was impressed by Lansdale's name and reputation, more so than by any concrete plans Lansdale evolved. I attended meetings where Lansdale outlined his approach, but looking back on my own unhappy experience with the Bay of Pigs, I thought his ideas impractical and never had much faith they would be successful. I was under a stern injunction, however, to do everything possible to assist him, which the agency did indeed try to do.

To understand the Kennedy administration's obsession with Cuba, it is important to understand the Kennedys, especially Robert. From their perspective, Castro won the first round at the Bay of Pigs. He had defeated the Kennedy team; they were bitter and they could not tolerate his getting away with it. The president and his brother were ready to avenge their personal embarrassment by overthrowing their enemy at any cost. I don't believe there was any significant policy debate in the executive branch on the desirability of getting rid of Castro. Everybody would have agreed; Castro did not have many defenders. Robert Kennedy's involvement in organizing and directing Mongoose became so intense that he might as well have been deputy director for plans for the operation. Richard Helms, too, recalls the depth of Robert Kennedy's interest: "The pressure from Bobby Kennedy was daily. . . . He would call people in charge of Cuban operations—anyone who could answer a question at the agency."[58]

It had become increasingly clear to me that he was the driving force behind a continued operation against Castro and that Edward Lansdale was his official instrument. I remember telephoning him at Hyannisport two or three times during the Thanksgiving weekend of 1961 to reassure him that the agency was trying to do everything possible to meet Lansdale's requests. These conversations were always polite but fairly deadpan. He didn't voice any objections or any particular approval, although there was a strong urging that things move more quickly. I believe that by late November 1961 Lansdale had not been working on the project long enough to have produced a specific plan of operations. His plan did not address the question of safe houses, secure communications, or any of the troublesome issues encountered in our operations during late 1960. Nevertheless, the Kennedys wanted to get more saboteurs, more trained guerrillas who could be infiltrated sooner, and, most important, results. I felt confident that we were moving as fast as possible, given the various external restraints, including plausible deniability.

President Kennedy continued to receive intelligence information indicating Castro was growing stronger, yet he permitted Operation Mongoose to move forward. In the guidelines for the operation that the administration adopted in March 1962, it was resolved that to overthrow Castro "the U.S. will make maximum use of indigenous resources, internal and external, but recognizes that final success will require decisive military intervention." Kennedy was incapable, however, of making the final decision to send in troops. Just as the Cuban missile crisis was beginning, Helms, who by this time had replaced me as deputy director for plans, received a memorandum from his assistant on Cuban affairs observing that "during the past year, while one of the options of the project was to create internal dissension and resistance leading to eventual U.S. intervention, a review shows that policy makers not only shied away from the military intervention aspect, but were generally apprehensive of sabotage proposals."[59]

Operation Mongoose was a more ambitious and more massive paramilitary activity than the Bay of Pigs had been. Its modus vivendi was entirely different, and it involved significantly more personnel, as well as hit-and-run raids. Almost all the targets of these raids (many of them on the north coast of Cuba) were industrial facilities such as petroleum refineries and storage tanks.

I never lost sight of the irony that the same president who had canceled the air strikes and ruled out open intervention was now having his brother put tremendous pressure on the agency to accomplish even more. If the Kennedys felt this strongly about waging war against Castro, relaxing the constraints that crippled the planners at the Bay of Pigs would have been much easier in the long run—not to mention far less expensive—than undertaking a successor project in the hope of achieving the same results.

Although some historians may contend that the CIA was a rogue elephant, the intensive oversight of Operation Mongoose (as well as of the Bay of Pigs) demonstrates otherwise. Operation Mongoose was closely monitored by the chief of state, and all actions received his explicit authorization. Whether it was a good operation or whether it served the long-term interests of the United States is very much open to debate. But it clearly was not a case of the agency's acting independently and without sanction from the top.

In fall 1961, shortly after John McCone, whom I had known through my wartime work in shipping, had become director of the CIA, I had a discussion with him in which it was agreed that I would tender my resignation from the agency at the end of December, as expected. Then his wife died and he called me from California and asked that I not make any move, as he was uncertain whether he would be able to go on with his task. As it turned out, he returned to Washington in early January and took firm hold of the reins of command.

Eventually he decided he wanted me to remain at the agency in the newly created position of deputy director of science and technology. He went first to Robert and then to John Kennedy for approval. They concurred, and I was strongly urged to accept. The position was one of reduced authority and level of importance within the CIA, and so, after careful deliberation, I declined. I felt the time to move on had arrived. In the aftermath of the Bay of Pigs, whatever possibility there had been of my becoming CIA director was a closed option in Kennedy's eyes and mine. Accordingly, I left the Central Intelligence Agency in February 1962 with successes and regrets and a legacy that still has not been put to rest historically and perhaps never will be.

On March 1, 1962, I was awarded the National Security Medal for my "outstanding contribution to the National Intelligence Effort." At a ceremony at the White House attended by my wife, Ann, two of my children, Ann Harriet and Winthrop, and McGeorge Bundy, Kennedy presented the medal and a statement I can't help but be proud of:

> As a senior official of the Central Intelligence Agency, Mr. Bissell has made a most distinguished contribution to the security of the United States. In vital areas of scientific intelligence collection, his achievements have been unique.
>
> During his more than twenty years of service with the United States Government, he has invested a rich fund of scholarship and vision. He has brought about returns of direct and major benefit to our country. In areas demanding the creation and application of highly technical and sophisticated intelligence techniques, he has blended theory and practice in a manner unparalleled in the intelligence profession. Mr. Bissell's high purpose, unbounded energy, and unswerving devotion to duty are benchmarks in the intelligence service. He leaves an enduring legacy to those in the intelligence service who will themselves be called on to advance further the frontiers of intelligence.

By mid-1962, I was president of the Institute for Defense Analyses, a think tank that had been formed by a dozen universities to recruit scientific personnel for the evaluation of weapons systems. Although no longer at the center of action on a high government level, I still managed to find myself enmeshed in controversy and interagency strife. Not much had really changed.

CHAPTER EIGHT

A Philosophy of Covert Action

The need for an institution like the Central Intelligence Agency in today's multipolar world is at least as great as, if not greater than, it was during the cold-war era. In the past, intelligence was mainly an area of combat between the major developed powers, but with the rapid spread of weapons of mass destruction our potential foes have multiplied and become more diverse. Such challenging and threatening circumstances require that the CIA have at its disposal all appropriate capabilities to counteract them. An analytic framework is necessary, therefore, to assist policy makers in determining why, where, and when we as a nation should intervene covertly in world affairs.

It is important to clear the decks of misleading concepts and maxims of policy. A case in point is the belief that covert activities are incompatible with democracy and that major powers can and should refrain from using such intervention. Allegedly, secrecy conflicts with the openness of a democratic society, but every organization has to enjoy the protection of privacy for certain deliberations, decisions, and actions. Otherwise, there can be no formal debate, no vigor in decisions. Democracy has to be compatible with privacy—that is, with "secrecy," and I believe it is.

The question can be raised as to what democracy requires in these matters. Not everything a government is doing, or even just thinking about and discussing, should be disclosed—that would be the end of skillful, subtly designed action. Publicity is the enemy of intellectual honesty, objectivity, and decisiveness. I contend that democracy requires that secret activities be effectively controlled at every stage from authorization to audit, that the control be by legally constituted authority, and that controls ensure conformity with national policy. In my view, authority should always rest with the executive branch, not with Congress.

There will never be unanimity as to what our broad interests are in the internal affairs of other nations. Nor will there be unanimity on the question of why it is necessary to intervene, but I would suggest that the following four broadly defined areas are a few of the most obvious and widely accepted reasons:

1. *Military Security*. The military strength both of our allies and of our foes has important balance-of-power ramifications that can affect our military security. We must be able to influence this balance in our favor.

2. *Economic Security*. For our nation to remain economically strong, we must have access to strategic materials and technologies. When nations attempt to limit our access to these resources, we must have a capability to circumvent their efforts.

3. *The International Order*. The United States seeks to foster an international order that promotes democracy, the assurance of reasonable liberties for the individual citizen, and the acceptance of social values conducive to honesty in public and private administration. When individual nations in this system are threatened by the forces of Communism, fascism, or totalitarianism, the values of our heritage demand we intervene to preserve democracy and protect human rights.

4. *Humanitarian Concern*. We are increasingly uncomfortable in a world in which there is a widening gap between the have and have-not nations. This discomfort is a product both of our concern for the less fortunate and of our fear that an increasingly unequal world will be unstable. It is our duty to promote policies and take action to address these imbalances.

It becomes overwhelmingly obvious that we are deeply concerned with the internal affairs of other nations and that, insofar as we make any effort to encourage the evolution of the world community in accord with our values, we will be endeavoring purposefully to influence these affairs. The argument then turns out to be not about whether to influence the internal affairs of others but about how.

Intervention in the internal affairs of another nation does not automatically mean covert action. Traditional diplomacy has long been an important means of influencing friends and foes alike in the pursuit of policies that we wish to promote. These objectives are sought openly. Making nations reduce their barriers to free trade and promoting human rights and democracy are examples. Diplomacy is even used to get countries to pay back their loans to American bankers. World opinion is courted through publicized negotiations, speeches at the United Nations, and so forth. We are even willing to threaten other nations with trade sanctions, embargoes, and war to effect a desired result.

Open diplomacy, however, has its limitations as a policy tool. There are times when a great power can best attain its objectives by acting in total secrecy. Quite often this action takes the form of secret diplomacy. On its simplest level, such diplomacy occurs when two nations discuss a topic or negotiate a treaty of such significant international sensitivity or balance-of-power ramifications that their discussions or negotiations take place without the knowledge of the international community. On certain occasions, however, a great power may seek to influence the internal affairs of another nation without its knowledge or without the knowledge of the international community. These circumstances require covert action.

I define covert action as influencing people, organizations, and events in other countries secretly, using a variety of inducements and pressures while attempting to conceal sponsorship. Yet if secrecy is how we measure the success of covert action, why have so many intelligence operations become public knowledge and what can we learn from those experiences?

The basic weakness in the agency's operations has been their tendency to be compromised either by project design or by insufficiently professional handling of the day-by-day flow of business. The clandestine service, especially in dealing with covert action, has been able neither to keep as many events, names, and relationships secret as it should nor to assess with sufficient realism its ability to maintain secrecy. These are of course mutually reinforcing shortcomings. Had the assessment of the feasibility of secrecy been more accurate, many activities might have been vetoed and the number of compromised activities greatly reduced.

To emphasize the significance of this form of failure, it is useful to ask how many of the covert activities criticized in the early sixties (after exposure) as ineffective, inept, or unwise for other reasons would have been so described if they had not been compromised. Had secrecy been preserved, how many operations would have been listed as failures in private reports to the president? The answer is that there would have been a list of failures, but it would not have included a fifth of those now so categorized and the cost of most of these failures would have been reported as negligible. The subsidies to a variety of international organizations, for instance, almost certainly would have been listed as major successes had they not been made public. Radio Free Europe would have been classified as a success, though an expensive one in dollars, had the CIA's hand remained unknown. Of the political and paramilitary interventions in Guatemala, the Congo, and Iran, at least two and probably three would have been classified as successful. Most of the interventions in elections would have been so classified.

Is it possible to discern practices or circumstances that have rendered the agency's operations more susceptible to compromise than they should have been? It is easy enough to recite certain practices that constitute good tradecraft; the difficulty is finding the way to practice good tradecraft within the constraints of particular operations and to train and indoctrinate case officers and agents to the point where they can practice it even where the application is unclear. Thus, to suggest a way of strengthening the clandestinity of certain activities is not simply to propose a policy change that can be carried out by the issuance of a memorandum but rather to undertake a laborious, difficult, and unending effort involving the selection and training of people and the exercise of operational judgment day in and day out. Such changes, then, are not readily effected once and for all (even assuming they are valid), and I advance these suggestions with appropriate diffidence.

It has been wryly observed that security is either a suit of armor or a fig leaf—in other words, that a fact is not secret if those disinclined to favor it politely refrain from mentioning it. Three degrees of clandestinity can be distinguished: *true secrecy,* meaning that no unauthorized person knows what, if anything, has happened; *plausible deniability,* meaning that the result or outward manifestation cannot be concealed but official sponsorship is; and *conventional disavowal,* the fig leaf. On the other hand, it is impossible to define in any given situation what is meant by clandestinity or security without asking the question *What* is to be kept secret from *whom*?

Certain of the activities that form part of any covert operation cannot be and are not intended to be kept secret from anyone. (A man takes a briefcase out of a parked car and walks away with it in broad daylight. The *act* is public; what is secret is the identity and motivation of the agent.) As to the identity of those from whom information is to be withheld, there is usually a very obvious "enemy," but compromising an operation in the eyes of the general public at home or in friendly or neutral countries is often more catastrophic than compromising it to the benefit of the obvious enemy. Confusion about what can and what must be kept secret in any given operation is the foe of effective clandestinity.

Certain covert operations are truly secret; that is, they are carried out in such a way that the enemy does not know what has taken place. (Papers are taken out of a briefcase, photographed, and returned without the enemy's knowledge; funds are passed to a politician through a Swiss bank account and no one else is any the wiser.) A second category of operations, though requiring the same rigorous security and the same professional tradecraft, involves activities (or outward manifestations of activities) that cannot be kept from the knowledge of the enemy (or, as a rule, the general public). These are deniable operations. The enemy knows that *something* is happening, often *what* is happening (that a political party is receiving funds from some source or that arms are being smuggled into a country), but has no knowledge of how the operation is being accomplished or by whom. The enemy may surmise that the United States or some other government is behind it, but unless and until the operation is compromised, the enemy cannot identify the persons or organizations through whom the operation is mounted and controlled, the communications links to the government supposedly involved, or any other specific evidence that would represent proof of involvement. Constituting a third category are activities and relationships that are neither secret nor deniable, only conventionally disavowed. Senior clandestine service officers on embassy staffs maintain thin diplomatic cover, yet their identities are known to colleagues, friends (often officially), and enemies.

It is worth reemphasizing that the deniability of those aspects or manifestations of an operation that cannot be concealed depends on preservation of the tightest security around those that can and must be truly secret. There should not be two levels of security—that which is secret must always be protected by the coat of armor. But when secret activities are stimulating, influencing, or controlling large overt forces or institutions, it is often extremely difficult to manage the interface between the secret operation and its sometimes embarrassingly visible manifestation or consequence. A number of the weaknesses discussed below occur at this interface.

Transfers of funds are central to most large covert-action operations. When funds are transfered from a case officer to an agent, as in a typical espionage operation, the transaction can be wholly secret and no special channel is needed. With many covert-action operations however, it is essential to have an ostensibly innocent source of funding. This need arises in two sorts of situations: one, where the recipient is a large public organization (political party, labor organization, corporation) whose accounts are audited or open to many persons and the *receipt* of funds must be explained, and, two, when the operation involves only support, not attempted control, and it may be desirable for the recipient to be ignorant of the true source of funds.

Unfortunately, with respect to relationships with private organizations, the agency became careless in its use of cut-out organizations, failing especially to preserve sufficient compartmentation between them—that is, using a single funding channel for several different organizations and doing so in such a way that many funding organizations became tied together in a network, so that the exposure of a few exposed them all. It is of course laborious to form corporate entities and foundations and to recruit individuals who can serve as funding channels. Nevertheless, these could have been more numerous, and realistic planning for possible compromise of a major supported organization might have led to a modification of funding arrangements to prevent compromise of others.

The agency should probably have endeavored to avoid or curtail the practice of making key individuals in supported private organizations aware of the source of their support. The importance of this recommendation, however, could hardly have been foreseen in the early 1950s, when non-Communist students, intellectuals, and labor leaders were, by and large, proud to be advancing their government's purposes so long as no effort was made to control their political attitudes, their associations, or their methods. Programs of financial support could be more effective if key recipients were witting. Security appeared to be enhanced by the presence, in the supported organizations, of individuals who were not being fooled about the source of funds. The "morality" of these operations seemed more solid and unquestionable when they were undertaken with the active consent of those who were assisted. Once they were started on this basis, it would have been difficult to refuse to cut in the successor to a witting organization leader who moved on. The system worked reasonably well so long as the prevailing values of the private citizens involved remained as they had been in the early and middle 1950s. As the corps of witting individuals expanded, however, and then as the prevailing sense of urgency about anti-Communist activity and of loyalty to the government declined, compromise became inevitable. Student organizations were particularly vulnerable to the changing climate of opinion. It seems clear with hindsight that many of these relationships should have been phased out early in the 1960s. If a need for financial support still existed, it could probably have been provided through newly selected financial channels, with recipients completely unwitting.

What is true of the much-publicized support of private national and international organizations applies to many other types of covert financial support, most of which, mercifully, received no publicity up to the late 1960s. When a politician, political faction, party, labor organization, group of army officers, or segment of the press is to be given financial support, a question that should always be carefully considered is whether the same purposes can be adequately served by strengthening the recipient organization without endeavoring directly to influence its behavior. In other words, should a quid pro quo be sought in return for help provided? Where the answer is yes, then of course support cannot be from ostensibly innocent and essentially passive sources. In many situations, however, little is gained by making the recipient specifically knowledgeable of the source of funds. Whenever this is true, it is good practice to expend ingenuity in developing a funding channel that will enable recipients to receive help without having to admit to themselves, let alone to associates or others, what the ultimate source may be.

Where the recipient individual or organization is knowledgeable, it is a cardinal rule that if secrecy is to be at all dependable there must be a true parallelism of interest between the agency and the recipient. This is not to deny that there is still great scope for the use of classic agents who do what they do for money (and perhaps the promise of asylum in the United States if they need it). But for a prominent politician, a political party, or a labor organization, this motivation is obviously ineffective. The recipient of support must be regarded and treated as an ally. These propositions are well understood and, on the whole, were skillfully practiced by the agency during my tenure.

The one respect in which there may be room for improvement has to do with planning for the termination of such operations. Sometimes termination is desirable because objectives have been achieved or are no longer accorded sufficient importance to justify continued activity. In the context of maintaining secrecy (the context within which all these comments and suggestions are offered), the real importance of a termination plan is that it may permit the secure liquidation of an operation that would become dangerously insecure if continued under altered circumstances. Secure termination is easier said than done, and for it to have a chance of success, there must usually be planning from the start of the operation. One of the great advantages of leaving recipients ignorant of the true source of their subsidies is that discontinuation cannot provoke reprisals that involve embarrassing disclosures. When recipients are witting, it is obviously desirable to arrange the transaction in such a way that disclosure will be more embarrassing to them than to the donor. In operations in which there is a single key agent or in which only an agent or two is capable of embarrassing the agency, it is usually worth a great deal of trouble to find jobs or provide political asylum for the individuals or in some other respect place them under obligation, and perhaps control, when the operation is to be terminated. Finally, there will always be times when an operation has ceased to be useful but it is the better part of valor to phase it out very slowly, or not at all, rather than run the risk of embarrassing compromise.

The transparency of official cover mitigates against the effective preservation of secrecy. It is not merely, or even mainly, a matter of rendering contacts between agency personnel and indigenous agents insecure. Perhaps the greatest damage is to the habits of thought of agency people who realize that their colleagues, their host governments, both friendly and hostile, and the enemy's intelligence services know what they are.

In every United States embassy or other foreign post there will always have to be a CIA command post whose members are visible. Surely, however, it should be possible to place a number of Americans under much deeper cover, some official and some unofficial, and thus to restore a degree of privacy to their activities. The value of unofficial cover is an ancient and controversial topic within the clandestine service. Although I believe unofficial cover has considerable potential (if ingeniously exploited), there is no doubt that it is costly, because much of the agents' time has to be spent living their cover, the process of building it is lengthy, and many activist individuals whose temperaments are otherwise suited to clandestine service find it galling.

At least on a limited scale, however, most of these obstacles can be circumvented. Unofficial cover might be more obtainable if the agency made more systematic use of alumni who have chosen to turn to other careers but are willing to place a career agent in their organizations. Proprietary organizations can provide cover, especially if they can be staffed with a mixture of active agents and more passive alumni. These could be businesses, consulting firms, research organizations, or nonprofit organizations. The opportunities for deep official cover may be harder to come by.

Another aspect of tradecraft with obvious relevance to the maintenance of secrecy is the practice of internal compartmentation for the purpose of reducing to a minimum the number of agency (and, of course, other governmental)

personnel aware of any given operation. The tight compartmentation of the early 1950s seems to have gradually but significantly relaxed. In theory, case officers need to be informed of relatively few operations other than those they are conducting; station chiefs or desk officers in Washington have to know everything that is going on within their countries but need not be aware of much elsewhere. The same principle applies up the line. In practice, however, by 1960 the general character of many of the agency's larger (and more sensitive) operations were known by many hundreds or perhaps even thousands of people. To a large extent, compartmentation was broken down by the agency's practice of personnel rotation. By the time a middle-rank officer had completed three tours of duty in different assignments, he might have been exposed to the whole range of operations in two or three different countries or might have served as a divisional staff officer with exposure to everything going on in a large region. While this was inevitable, there was also a less tangible relaxation. In the interest of improving the performance of clandestine service officers, it was considered prudent to provide them with a deeper background in their area of concern. The goal of this relaxation was worthy, but the result was reduced security.

The weakening of compartmentation internally was paralleled by an increase in the circle of individuals in other agencies knowledgeable about certain covert operations. Coordinating such operations with various assistant secretaries at the State Department was probably good government, but it produced a situation in which at least three, and often more, individuals at the heads of department bureaus were informed of everything going on in their areas and in which most of the desk officers were aware of many of the agency's operations in the countries for which they were responsible. The practice of country-to-country and bureau-to-bureau coordination largely replaced the securing of approvals through chosen liaison officers; the result was an increase in the number of people who were knowledgeable.

It is extremely difficult to determine how much damage was done through the weakening of internal and external compartmentation. My impression is that this development contributed to an atmosphere in which tight secrecy and careful tradecraft seemed less crucial than the possibility of an important accomplishment and the urgency of obtaining political approval. Nevertheless, it is not easy to suggest ways in which compartmentation could again be strengthened. One remedy might be to lengthen tours of duty in assignments both in Washington and overseas, so that there would be less personnel turnover. This would also improve the area expertise of CIA officers. It may be possible, too, to restrict more narrowly the number of officials in other agencies who have access to operational information. It is inevitable and useful that contacts at the bureau level occur; for some purposes they may be useful at the level of the country desk. But the contacts could involve many fewer individuals and those individuals could be under sterner obligation to limit the dissemination of any operational information to specified and authorized persons.

Large operations constitute a special category, both because it is difficult to maintain secrecy about them and because their compromise, if and when it occurs, is usually dramatic. Most large operations cannot be truly secret: if they involve many people (as in paramilitary activities) or a lot of money (as in political subsidies) or significant hardware development and employment (as in reconnaissance), the activities are simply too massive to be unobservable. The best exception that comes to mind was the Berlin tunnel. There is every evidence that the Russians had no knowledge that their telephone lines were being tapped until the inadvertent discovery of the connecting cables. Thus, although a large building had been erected and a sizable excavation made, true secrecy was successfully maintained. In general, however—as in Guatemala, the Bay of Pigs, paramilitary activities in Laos, and many political subsidies in Latin American and European countries, operations have been planned to be plausibly deniable.

The record of maintaining at least technical deniability in these activities has been quite good. In the largest and most controversial operations, such as Guatemala and the Bay of Pigs, however, what is so visibly taking place is unanimously attributed to the United States government simply because there is no other possible source of funds, logistic support, and organization. Thus, even if all direct connections are so well concealed that the enemy does not know how support is being provided and cannot prove U.S. involvement, this technical deniability is valueless.

The same is true of political support. Funding on a scale that could plausibly be attributed to "acceptable" sources can be deniable in the absence of compromise, but if enormous sums suddenly appear in a small country's election, it is usually evident whence they came and the act will be publicly attributed to the true source no matter how good the tradecraft has been. The conclusion is self-evident: in any given situation and for any given type of activity there is a limit to the scale on which an operation can be undertaken covertly and still remain, in any useful sense of the word, deniable.

It does not follow, of course, that such an operation should not be undertaken from time to time or that responsibility for it should be with an overt department of the government. Sometimes the government has to practice intervention that will inevitably be attributed to it and for which it will be blamed or praised but for which it cannot officially accept responsibility. (It is instructive to remember that many "liberal" observers wished the United States to intervene to overthrow Ngo Dinh Diem in Vietnam.) In these situations, clandestine tradecraft may prevent the appearance of clear evidence implicating the government, but this fig leaf is as much security as it can provide.

Although operations beyond a certain size can rarely be more than deniable and the meaning of deniability tends to break down with the largest of them, there are ways to minimize political and operational costs. First, there is surely room for improvement in modifying public reaction to activities that have come to be popularly attributed to the government. Denials of involvement, especially if they are elaborate, are so often disproved by events or so often appear false even in the absence of evidence that it is probably better to cultivate the habit of making "no comment." This is seldom easy, but it could be done more frequently than it is. Second, since it is almost always necessary to accept an operational penalty if an effort is made to maintain the deniability of an operation, the possibility of keeping it meaningfully deniable should be weighed before one accepts an excessive penalty. The penalty usually takes the form of limiting funds, logistic support, personnel, or the level of technology so as to render the supporting role of the clandestine service less obvious. If there is a good chance that despite all efforts deniability will be eroded to mere diplomatic fiction, then there is no point in jeopardizing the success of an operation for the sake of appearances. If the likelihood of such erosion is foreseen in time, it may be a valid reason for canceling the operation. But once an operation is irrevocably under way, there is no reason to continue to pay for deniability that is already lost.

Correct assessment of the risks of compromise, both their nature and their magnitude, is an integral part of the task of maintaining secrecy. Moreover, realistic assessment is absolutely essential to decisions about what activities and what specific operations are to be undertaken. Some of the worst mistakes of the 1950s and 1960s could be described as errors of assessment rather than of operational tradecraft. It is not surprising that this should be so.

The sponsors of operations (those responsible for their initiation and their continuation) within the clandestine service and among witting persons in other parts of the executive branch are apt to be temperamentally "operators." If they are to be good at their jobs, they must believe in the potentialities of covert operations. At each successive echelon in the chain of command within the clandestine service, the officer who presents a project for approval is bound to be its advocate and thus subject, at the least, to favorable bias. Many proposed projects are turned down at or below the division level, but those that reach the deputy director of plans or the director of central intelligence may express that bias by underestimating the operation's risks. Perhaps the worst failures of assessment have been those relating to large operations, where the risks of eroded deniability have been grossly underestimated. Another failure of assessment is the false sense of security engendered by successful maintenance of secrecy throughout the history of an operation. As early as 1962, anyone who had carefully reviewed the subsidies of private organizations—even without taking into account something so subtle as the changing mood of students and intellectuals—should have found cause for concern in the large number of persons known to be aware of them. The only plausible explanation for the failure to note an increasing risk of compromise is that compromise had been avoided so successfully for so long that there seemed no reason to fear the catastrophic loss of secrecy.

Such suggestions as can be made for increasing the realism of risk assessments can only be procedural. They should, however, recognize one basic principle. The professional competence of a clandestine service consists of, and is measured by, its ability to carry out operations secretly (or deniably), much as lawyers' competence consists in their ability to win cases, and doctors' in their ability to prevent or treat illness. The clandestine service may number among its members brilliant journalists, able warriors, and superior political analysts, but the professional skill for which, presumably, they are hired is the ability to organize and conduct operations covertly. This is a rather specialized skill not widely found outside of intelligence and internal security services. The task of assessing risk can be performed professionally only by members of the profession. For all practical purposes, it must be done predominantly inside the agency. The problem is to ensure that it is done realistically and that the results of the assessment are conveyed objectively to the policy makers who must weigh prospective benefits against prospective risks.

The primary responsibility must rest with middle-level and senior officers, but a strong case can be made for supplementing their efforts with assessment by staff (objectionable as excessive staff interference can be). A small group of experienced covert operators reporting directly to the deputy director for operations (covert action) could systematically scrutinize ongoing and new projects for the express and limited purpose of assessing the risk of compromise. Presumably, the deputy director of central intelligence or the director would have access to the group's conclusions.

Greater emphasis on the maintenance of secrecy and greater attention to assessment of the risk of compromise would have (and probably by now has had) effects on decision making within the agency and on the agency's relations with the rest of the executive branch. Fewer operations would reach the stage at which approval is sought through the formal or informal machinery of external control. The agency's professional judgment within the area of its special competence would acquire greater respect and there would be less inclination elsewhere in the government to question it. Operations might still be undertaken in which the risk of compromise was substantial, but at least there would be a record that the risk was foreseen and incurred deliberately. One must hope there would be another effect: that, rather than see the potentialities of covert operations too little exploited, the clandestine service would be stimulated to be more ingenious in the business of preserving true secrecy or deniability.

I believe there are ways to redeem the agency's credibility and operational privacy if there are senior people who deeply believe in so doing, but it is essential to have a director who wants to take that direction. It has been alleged that William Casey and other directors of central intelligence forced analysts to shape reports so as to arrive at conclusions that would be welcome to incumbent administrations. I have no knowledge of this and one would have had to be close to the situation to decide whether that kind of pressure was applied, but I am sure that public reports are exaggerated. If it did happen, I think it is a very grave failing of the agency's. I know that in my day Allen Dulles would not have stood for it, his deputy Pearre Cabell would not have willingly allowed it, and the Board of National Estimates would not have put up with it for an instant. The agency must again build a culture in which intellectual honesty is valued and professionalism esteemed. Most important, it must always be above politics.

There is general agreement that decisions to undertake or continue specific operations are ultimately political, not technical or professional, ones. Nevertheless, only professional covert operators can provide the assessments of capabilities, risks, and costs that define the choices open to policy makers. To estimate an operation's chances of compromise and its probable accomplishment is a professional judgment; to weigh the ultimate benefits (and disadvantages, if any) that might accrue from that accomplishment against the damage that might result from compromise is a political judgment. It has been claimed from time to time that the agency's representatives have presented misleading assessments of risk and probability of achievement because either they have been unable to make accurate judgments or (presumably in their enthusiasm) they have not presented them fully and fairly. If the political officers concerned come to suspect the professionalism or the honesty with which options are presented by the clandestine service, they will have no solid basis for choice and the process will tend to break down. Surely, therefore, the first requirement for sensible decision making is that operational risks and probable accomplishments be assessed as accurately as possible by the clandestine service and presented fully and fairly to the political authorities.

Estimates of operational success involve four explicit judgments or evaluations: the resource costs (personnel hours, dollars, etc.), the chances of compromise in the short run, the chances in the long run, and the impairment of the clandestine service's capabilities that would result from compromise or any other type of failure. There may be other estimates that would be useful, but these are obviously essential.

As to resource costs, it is worth emphasizing that the avoidable or "direct" costs of specific covert operations are small. A major part of the cost of the clandestine service is overhead—the cost of the staff, communications arrangements, and research and development. The prevailing and the only rational procedure is to treat the size of the service and the scale of supporting activities as matters for long-run decisions reviewed annually in the budget but unrelated to immediate operational requirements. Accordingly, although a sizable proportion of personnel hours and other inputs can be allocated to specific operations, the true cost of undertaking any particular operation is the operation's opportunity cost; that is, the value of the other activities that its undertaking will preclude. Subsidies to mass media or political parties are exceptions to this rule, mainly because the size of the operation measured in dollars can vary widely with no change in the required inputs of other resources. In such cases, therefore, direct (avoidable) costs can be a large proportion of the total, but except in a few massive undertakings of this sort, the sums involved are still minor compared to such items in the federal budget as new weapons systems or the operations and maintenance costs of even small military units. Thus, a weighing of effectiveness against resource costs is largely irrelevant in the process of approving or disapproving individual operations. Cost-effectiveness standards can be applied only for determining the size of the clandestine service as a whole or for allocating the resources of its major areas for major types of activities.

With respect to the professional judgment of chances of success, the main comment that needs to be made is that there should be a clear understanding as to the direct results desired or hoped for and that success must be defined as the achievement of these results. An estimate of the likelihood of obtaining a certain body of intelligence data, of exercising effective control over a newspaper or broadcasting station, or of securing the desired outcome in an election is a difficult judgment to make and one subject to a large margin of error, but it is a *professional* judgment of the sort that clandestine operators must try to make. A judgment of the effectiveness of the propaganda published in a newspaper or of the capacity of a friendly regime to promote orderly and stable development—these are essential political judgments (in the present context). What requires emphasis is that the operational success of the clandestine service can be measured only against the results it seeks and can hope to accomplish directly in an operation, not by the long-term significance of these results or the ultimate outcome of a complicated situation dominated by other influences and developments.

If the first requirement for intelligent decision making is that the clandestine service render these professional judgments as explicitly and accurately as possible and present them to the political decision makers honestly, the obvious second requirement is for an intelligent and orderly political assessment of the options thus offered. Broadly, there are two subjudgments to be made at this level, which are often confused but which it is useful to keep separate. First, what is the significance of success as it has been defined for purposes of professional evaluation of the project? Is a short-term accomplishment really worthwhile if all it does is buy time? Is there any chance that the time purchased can be put to good use? Is the intelligence really unobtainable from other sources? Will the failure of the operation, assuming no compromise, do serious damage? Has the alternative of doing nothing been weighed in determining the value of success? The second set of subjudgments concerns the consequences of compromise. Would a compromise of a specified sort at a particular time more than offset the benefits of a successful outcome? Would the combination of failure and compromise be catastrophic? How are the prospective political costs of compromise affected by its timing? If the cover begins to wear thin years after an operation is ended, how much damage will be done?

A third type of question that must be asked in the course of making judgments about cost effectiveness is whether there is some way to achieve the objectives by means other than a covert operation, thereby incurring no requirement of secrecy and no risk of compromise. The theoretical possibilities are self-evident; the difficulties that stand in the way of their wider employment are often practical ones connected with public and congressional opinion and the ability to obtain financial support.

If one group of people in the government makes professional estimates of resource costs and of the probabilities of success and compromise and a second group then makes the political judgments involved in evaluating the possible outcomes, their combined judgments should theoretically permit what amounts to a cost-effectiveness assessment. But this version of how decisions could and should be made gives an impression of greater tidiness and determinacy than is ever going to be possible. Estimates of the likelihood of operational success and of the dangers of compromise are bound to be vulnerable. The political judgments are even more indeterminate—how is anyone to decide that if Arbenz is overthrown in Guatemala and Castillo Armas put in his place the country will enjoy reasonable stability and sustained progress?

Many, probably most, successes were successes only in the short run. Arbenz, for instance, was overthrown, but the long-term problems of Guatemala were not solved. Elections were won in several countries, but political parties and political systems were not permanently rejuvenated. Most covert-action operations (like military operations) are directed at short-term objectives. Their success or failure must be judged by the degree to which these objectives are achieved. Their *effectiveness* must be measured by the degree to which achievement of the short-term objectives will contribute to the national interest. It can be argued that, although few uncompromised operations actually failed, the successful achievement of their short-term results made only a limited contribution to the national interest.

Covert political action is therefore usually an expedient and its long-term value, like that of all other expedients, can be questioned. The uncertainties surrounding such action will always be great enough to provide a good excuse for a negative decision. In the current mood of the country, it can be confidently predicted that too few risks will be incurred and too few short-term interventions will be attempted. Most of my thinking on covert action stems from, and was appropriate to, a period when perhaps the reverse was true. The real task of future administrations will be to regain a balance in this field and to reestablish at the working level a drive for accomplishment.

Considerable attention has been given to the question of how the executive branch's control of covert activities might somehow be made more effective. Should the agency's own inspector general report to someone other than the director of central intelligence? Should every project (of many hundreds) be reviewed by some external authority annually—or more often? Should the director of central intelligence establish additional review bodies within the CIA but external to the clandestine service to investigate the activities of the clandestine service?

This concern with levels of review, with an elaboration of the scrutiny to which every case officer, desk officer, and division chief's actions should be subjected ignores elementary principles of good organization and could give rise to highly damaging recommendations. The repetitive and overdetailed review of operators' judgment and their harassment by an increasing number of persons having the power to interfere with them is surely the wrong way to produce desirable results in almost any organization at almost any time.

Formal control, as I knew it, was exercised by an active senior cabinet committee that in effect provided an oversight by the State Department, the Defense Department, and the White House. Intimate relationships were maintained at the working level between the components of the clandestine service and the various assistant secretaries' offices in the Department of Defense. Thus, the senior representatives on the committee had the benefit of staff work on proposals that came before them. In addition to these interdepartmental arrangements, there was an annual financial review by the Bureau of the Budget. Finally, there was the President's Board of Consultants on Foreign Intelligence Activities, which had complete access to the CIA's affairs and reported to the president in confidence. At least one witness has characterized this whole set of arrangements as providing more detailed and authoritative control over the CIA than is exercised over any other component of the executive branch.

There have been many mistakes made by CIA operators, particularly under the heading of inadequate tradecraft. Risks have been assumed that were excessive in the light of promised benefits; operations have been mounted or continued when the exercise of good judgment would have suggested that they could not accomplish much of value. But the way to reduce the number of wrong decisions in the future is almost certainly not to increase the number of people outside the line of command who are involved in each decision. After all, an operation is typically designed by a case officer in Washington or in the field and then reviewed by the station chief and the desk officer in Washington. Only after such scrutiny is a proposal submitted for the approval of the deputy director for plans. Depending on the size and nature of the operation, it is next forwarded to the director of central intelligence for approval. In the course of this sequence of reviews up the line of command, the proposed project will probably have been coordinated in the field with a senior political officer of the embassy and will almost certainly have been discussed with either the desk officer or the bureau chief in the State Department. Finally, if it is a major project, there is a formal review by the cabinet committee, in preparation for which the State Department and Defense Department members will have been briefed by the appropriate members of their staffs.

If too many mistakes have been made over the years by all these people, surely the proper thing to do is to indoctrinate the decision makers differently or replace them rather than to have more people looking over their shoulders. If there is a need to heighten the professionalism that middle and junior officers apply to the perception of opportunities, the assessment of risks, the determination of proposed operational techniques, the selection of agents and other instrumentalities, and the performance of logistic and communications planning, the only way it can be done is by making every effort to maintain and raise the professional competence and professional standards of the service. More control and more reviews will not accomplish this result.

The way to ensure that senior officers in the line of command design operational programs consonant with national policy is to provide them both from above and collaterally, through the State Department, with appropriate guidance. Senior officers who are temporarily unable to adapt their view of the national interest to current national policy should be reassigned or fired. This sort of difficulty is incapable of being cured by a multiplicity of reviews.

The clandestine service, like any other operational organization, can be effective only if the decision-making process operating through its internal chain of command yields reasonably prompt and clear-cut decisions with a minimum of paperwork and of collateral coordination with administrative personnel and staff officers. By 1960 the agency exhibited the beginnings of bureaucratic habits of decision making. Administrative procedures were becoming too restrictive and people who should have been operators were spending too much time writing up voluminous supporting documentation for operational plans. The excuses for extreme caution, delay, and inaction were multiplying. Perhaps there was room for greater sensitivity and imagination in the perception of opportunities, for more realism in the planning and conduct of operations, and for better judgment in the approval and direction of activities by senior officers. But none of these things can be legislated by fiat, still less induced by superimposing review upon review. Indeed, nothing will more surely destroy them than the multiplication of procedural obstacles to action.

Nor can a country run covert activities out of a democratically elected legislature. Congressional oversight of covert operations today is far different from what it was in the 1940s and 1950s, when congressional committees did not expect to be told of all covert operations or to be responsible for their supervision. I think it was extremely merciful that Congress never tried to inquire into every political subsidy in Europe after the war. But if Congress had known more about the Bay of Pigs or the contras in Nicaragua, it might have blocked the actions and therefore they would not have failed. Congress cannot be blamed for the Bay of Pigs since it played no part in the plan. What has to be considered is whether it would have been worthwhile to pay the price of congressional advance knowledge in the hope that Congress would have been brighter and abler and more perceptive than the executive branch in canceling an operation that was not going to be a success.

The same has to be asked about the contras. There, I think, congressional oversight gravely impaired the effectiveness of the attempted covert operations. If Congress hadn't interfered, two outcomes might have been possible. One is that the contra operation might have proceeded more rapidly and more successfully and we might have effected an overthrow in Nicaragua sooner and more decisively, without leaving a whole Sandinista infrastructure in place. The other is that the operation might have ballooned up in size and been even more of a failure than it ultimately was. I am inclined to feel that congressional oversight before the fact of covert operations, whether intelligence or covert action, is simply not consistent with security and effectiveness. There are very few cases I have ever witnessed at close hand in which congressional advance knowledge was not leaked to the press.

If our intelligence service is to be vigilant, morale must always be at its highest level and management must be willing seriously to entertain new ideas about organizational structure, technology, and personnel. News reports suggest that the CIA of the 1990s may be lacking in these things. There are those who may find fault with some of the agency's programs in its golden age, the fifties, but there is no doubt that during this period it was a place where innovation flourished. To a large degree, it was Allen Dulles's management style that spurred its effectiveness, and Dulles worked actively to forge an effective collaboration with the scientific, academic, and business communities. The CIA as an entity had a fascination about it that made everything seem possible: ideas, procedures, public-private collaborations. This firmament of ideas was sustained by the constant injection of new personnel from outside the agency. Any serious reform of the CIA must seek to recapture that spirit, if not necessarily the policies, that animated the agency during those early years.

CHAPTER NINE

The Institute for Defense Analyses

I joined the Institute for Defense Analyses (IDA) as executive vice president on March 1, 1962, immediately following my departure from the CIA. I viewed my new job at IDA, which bridged the academic and military worlds, and more generally the area of U.S. foreign policy, as providing an opportunity to stay in Washington and continue working on problems that would prove interesting. My background was thought to be useful, particularly since I had had more academic experience than a good many of the people who might have been considered for the post. Jim Killian, my friend from U-2 days and the president of MIT, was a moving spirit in the formation of IDA. One of the reasons I was offered the position was that I had been on the MIT faculty and knew Killian reasonably well. Four and a half months later, on July 12, 1962, I became president of IDA, succeeding Garrison Norton. This was the beginning of a difficult two-year period that was to end in personal disaster.

The Institute for Defense Analyses came into being at the request of the secretary of defense in 1956 as a not-for-profit membership corporation designed to encourage increased interaction between university scientists and engineers on the one hand and a small group of analysts in the Office of the Joint Chiefs of Staff on the other. Five of the nation's leading universities—California Institute of Technology, Case Institute of Technology, Massachusetts Institute of Technology, Stanford University, and Tulane University—took the initiative and were joined in succeeding years by other prestigious schools like Columbia University, the University of Michigan, Pennsylvania State University, the University of Chicago, Princeton University, the University of Illinois, and the University of California. Their intent was to make available to the Department of Defense independent and objective evaluations on a wide range of issues related to weapons development. These evaluations would be made by able professionals, using advanced analytic methods.

The relationship that evolved between IDA and the Pentagon was very important for the development of the nation's weapons systems. The most controversial aspect of the relationship concerned the Pentagon's Weapons Systems Evaluation Group (WSEG) and IDA's Weapons Systems Evaluation Division (WSED). WSEG was an organization within the Department of Defense that conducted operational analyses and evaluations for the Joint Chiefs of Staff, the director of defense research and engineering, and the secretary of defense. It produced studies designed to assist the military in selecting and developing the best weapons systems for national defense. WSED supplied personnel directly to WSEG, which was housed in Pentagon offices and worked directly with Pentagon officials to provide military assistance in support of these projects. Conclusions reached by WSED were incorporated into WSEG reports, with the Joint Chiefs of Staff receiving quarterly updates. Because both study groups had a high profile, their conclusions and recommendations rippled through the Pentagon and defense-contracting community as a whole.

I became an active player within the defense establishment and found myself dealing with numerous issues having to do with choice of weapons systems, their technology, procurement, evaluation, and testing procedures. I was one of a large number of "intellectuals" who became involved in the military process after the election of John Kennedy and the arrival of Robert McNamara at the Pentagon. Henry Kissinger, who participated in a civilian capacity; Thomas Schelling of Harvard University, who applied game theory to military conflict; and Harold Brown, who became the Pentagon's director of defense research and engineering, were others. All were placed in positions of authority and used that authority to apply the sophisticated methods of analysis and management that McNamara advocated. This type of analysis was not widely practiced at the military academies or staff levels at the time, and as a result, many of the military personnel came to resent McNamara and his civilian professionals. The views of Thomas D. White, the former air force chief of staff, were fairly representative of this outlook: "I am profoundly apprehensive of the pipe-smoking, trees-full-of-owls type of so-called defense intellectuals who have been brought into this nation's capital."[1]

The appointment of McNamara and a number of his early actions in the name of efficiency aroused considerable opposition from the uniformed military services. Especially irksome were his innovations in decision making, his reliance on quantification, and his use of business-school managerial techniques. One notable example was his insistence that the navy and the air force collaborate in building the TFX, a next-generation fighter-bomber. Both services had wanted to produce their own aircraft. While McNamara viewed his decision as part of a policy of procurement and development, the military felt he was using the cause of efficiency to influence what should have been a purely military decision. As a result, the defense establishment became fraught with civilian-military tensions, which increased as time went on.

This was the situation that existed in the summer of 1962 when the so-called Bell Report was drawn up by a cabinet committee (of which McNamara was a member) and approved by the president as a formal policy document for the executive branch. The report sought to address the changing nature of government and its relation to a new breed of nonprofit institutions like IDA and Rand. The report explained:

> Not-for-profit organizations (other than universities and contractor-operated Government facilities), if strongly led, can provide a degree of independence both from Government and from the commercial market, which may make them particularly useful as a source of objective analytical advice and technical services.
>
> In the case of organizations in the area of operations and policy research (such, for example, as the RAND Corporation), the principal advantages they have to offer are the detached quality and objectivity of their work. Here, too close control by any Government agency may tend to limit objectivity.[2]

The report stipulated that there should be a clear line of demarcation between the roles of government staffs and research contractors. Its conclusion greatly influenced my tenure at IDA, since I worked toward implementing the outlined objectives. It appeared both to me and to a number of officials in the Department of Defense that to conform to these policies would require some modification in the relationship between IDA and the Pentagon.

When IDA was established in 1956, the nucleus of what later became its Weapons Systems Evaluation Division was formed by bringing in a group of scientists from civil service positions that they had held as employees of the Defense Department's Weapons Systems Evaluation Group. The head of this IDA staff also served as the technical director of WSEG, in which capacity he was a government employee without compensation and reported to military director of WSEG. The staff members continued to be housed with WSEG in the Pentagon; they generally identified themselves as members of WSEG and were so treated. Thus, their new status was virtually indistinguishable from their former one as civil servants (except for a more favorable pay scale). This was almost all there was to IDA in its early years. It was inevitable, therefore, that the corporate entity was widely regarded as merely a device to recruit and pay WSEG's civilian staff, with no pretense to being an independent research organization like Rand or the Stanford Research Institute.

By the time I became associated with IDA it had grown into an institution with three divisions in Washington working under contract for a number of offices in the Department of Defense (and occasionally for other parts of the government). I expected to find that it had evolved into a reasonably unified though multidisciplinary research institute and that its management's executive and technical direction of its activities was looked for and accepted by both its own staff and the government offices that it served. I assumed (naively, as it turned out) that the main concern of its clients would be with the quality and usefulness of its professional work and that its internal organization would be regarded as its own business.

What I actually found (as far as WSED was concerned) was a situation little changed from that of the early years. The WSED staff was still functioning as part of a government office (the Pentagon), looking exclusively to that office for guidance and vigorously resistant to the notion that the management of IDA should have anything to do with what tasks were to be accepted, how personnel were to be assigned, how work was to be done, and what professional standards were to be maintained. In truth, IDA was serving as little more than a hiring hall for WSEG.

Plainly, since the management did not in any significant sense direct or supervise WSED's activities, IDA was in no position to discharge a corporate responsibility for the quality and effectiveness of that division's work. Nor was it given such a responsibility. The WSEG contract specified not that the contractor would provide "evaluations and operational analyses" for the government but that it would furnish "competent personnel." Moreover, I soon found that IDA was not considered responsible for its own internal organization and that any changes in procedures, relationships, and even senior-level personnel within IDA that affected WSED were regarded as the business of the Joint Chiefs.

This sort of relationship was diametrically opposed to the objectives and values outlined in the Bell Report.

In an attempt to improve this system, I enacted a series of reforms and renegotiated IDA's Pentagon contract. The new contract stated that IDA's role was to provide the military with an objective source of analysis and that full responsibility for the quality of the analysis rested with IDA management. Changes were also made to stipulate how information would flow between the Pentagon and IDA and to establish that formal communications with the Defense Department would be maintained by IDA's senior management, not by "any subdivision of contractor"—that is to say, not by a division like WSED.

For the reforms to succeed, it was essential to communicate their purpose and importance to IDA's professional staff. I stated in a planning memorandum to the director of WSED that "IDA's clients have a right to expect that this organization will practice rigorous quality control. The Division Directors and other Officers must assure themselves as to the professional quality, relevance, and adequacy of IDA's work."[3] I wanted IDA to be able to make, and take responsibility for, its own reports, which might be parallel to or incorporated into WSEG's. I expected that our reports would go through WSEG, but only when IDA's senior officers had approved them in final form would they be sent to the appropriate senior people in the Pentagon. My aim was to run a professionally competent independent organization. I felt that what we were being paid to do was to bring an independent judgment on weapons. How good is an aircraft? Will it really achieve the promised range? How efficient is it as a weapon? We were hired not to give another military opinion but to exercise an independent judgment arrived at by competent scientists and technical people.

By fall 1962 I had worked out a series of agreements with the Pentagon and begun the implementation of new management policies. The agreements specified that tasks would be accepted and reports released only on the authority of the president of IDA and under the IDA imprint; they insisted, too, on IDA's prerogatives in the assignment of its personnel and the placing of projects in appropriate divisions. As a result, I felt that the planning, supervision, and review of IDA's research work would be more centralized than it had been in the past. Specifically, the acceptance and definition of tasks, the internal assignment of responsibility for them, the review and design of the attack on major projects, and the review of work as it approached completion would be regarded as corporate actions that received consideration and involved participation by senior officers at IDA.

To achieve these objectives, IDA's internal organizational structure had to be studied and modified. Divisions were not in the practice of consulting one another on projects, lending personnel as needed, or subcontracting appropriate kinds of work from one another. It was also clear to me that WSED was far too large for efficient administration as a single entity, yet the existing structure of subdivisions within WSED was neither rational in concept nor effective in practice.

IDA also had to press for consolidation of its Washington staff, including the major part of WSED, in nongovernment office space at the earliest feasible date. That move, I felt, would result in less immediate access to the Pentagon by members of WSED, more effective collaboration between the divisions of IDA, and a more cohesive structure. As these envisioned reforms had the potential to disturb officials at the Pentagon who found any change unnerving, I strove to make sure they would be evolutionary. McNamara provided his full support for the plan, and I moved forward with the confidence of one who was implementing policies widely sanctioned within the administration.

These far-from-revolutionary formal changes were, I think, initially accepted, but the process of accomplishing them engendered a many-sided suspicion of motives and intentions. From my perspective, subsequent events fell into two phases. First, a real and definable disagreement emerged between IDA and the Joint Chiefs of Staff concerning IDA's internal organization and procedures. The IDA management would have preferred to use professional staff members from all three of its Washington divisions to meet the needs of both the Joint Chiefs and the civilian offices (mainly the director of defense research and engineering) in the Pentagon. On the other hand, as stated in testimony to the Appropriations Committee, the Joint Chiefs wished to have all support to WSEG rendered by a separate and compartmented subdivision of IDA that would have a relatively stable personnel base. In the end, their position was substantially accepted by IDA, with, however, a reaffirmation of the responsibility (and authority) of the IDA management for normal supervision of the subdivision's work.

The controversy might well have ended amicably at that point, and indeed virtually no specific actions having to do with IDA procedures or the staffing or conduct of projects were taken or proposed. In the atmosphere that had developed, however, real disagreement on these matters blew up into an emotionally loaded controversy. This was the second phase. The IDA management was apparently suspected of planning to disregard its acceptance of the Joint Chiefs' position, to breach the compartmentation that surrounded work undertaken for the Joint Chiefs, and to undermine the close civilian-military cooperation that had always characterized the WSEG-WSED relationship. On the other side, the Joint Chiefs were suspected of endeavoring to break up IDA or to dictate its internal arrangements and frustrate its officers' exercise of their normal managerial functions.

It was no secret that this unpleasant situation was further complicated by the reactions of certain members of the WSED staff. Faced with a conflict of loyalties between the government office that sponsored their work and the corporate entity that employed them, they found their sympathies lay with the former. They not only wished to retain the integrity of the division and the compartmentation surrounding it but tended to resent the participation of the corporate officers in major decisions concerning the division and, to some degree, their supervision over its activities. Given WSED's history, environment, and tradition, this reaction was understandable, but the conflict of loyalties gave rise to justified apprehension over the stability and morale of its staff.

The "definable" disagreement in my opinion did not concern any effort on the part of WSEG to exercise direct control over the output of WSED. Rather it focused on the appearance of an effort to limit the degree to which and the manner in which the IDA management would be permitted to perform normal supervisory and managerial functions with respect to WSED. In this sense it concerned the control of that IDA division.

Actions I took may have contributed to the controversy. First was the institution of the formal changes adopted in 1962, and second the establishment within IDA of procedures that provided for much closer review and control of WSED's activities by the officers. I also considered, discussed with my IDA colleagues, and outlined in a memorandum to Harold Brown, the director of defense research and engineering, further changes in internal organization and procedures. Action on these was postponed because of opposition in WSED. Later, when it appeared that they would be unwelcome to the Joint Chiefs of Staff, they were dropped at the chairman's request.

In addition to the principles set forth in the Bell Report, the importance of establishing IDA's independence and objectivity was also underscored by McNamara. He told me in my initial interview after I joined IDA that there were grave deficiencies in the work of WSEG and WSED, that they were primarily a result of WSED's closeness with WSEG, and that he was seriously considering terminating the WSEG contract with IDA unless IDA's management took action. Viewing IDA's relationship with the Pentagon in the context of the Bell Report, I had to agree with McNamara's assessment.

The autumn of 1962 saw an escalation of the cold war that came as a complete surprise to me. Although for years I had been intimately involved with matters relating to Cuba, I was unprepared for the disclosure that the Russians were initiating a capability to launch missiles from Cuba to the United States. On October 24, I wrote my son Winthrop at boarding school: "This has not touched IDA or me particularly because the kind of work we do is not related to immediate crises. Most of my friends in the government have been so busy that they have not even been free for lunch. All in all, I feel very much an outsider."

Once the showdown in Cuba was resolved and things got back to normal, I was able to continue working in earnest to reorganize IDA. By spring 1963, it became evident that the military establishment was not responding well to either the reforms at IDA or the principles of the Bell Report that had preceded them. Maxwell Taylor, chairman of the Joint Chiefs of Staff, had the dubious distinction of leading the forces of reaction against the IDA reforms. He explained in a letter to me that, although the Joint Chiefs understood my desire to reorganize IDA, my objectives were not in the interests of national security. As a former deputy director of the CIA, I understood well the role of security in achieving a policy end; I was certain, however, that security was being invoked merely as a rhetorical device and was not a reasonable issue. Taylor concluded by noting that he had the support of McNamara.[4]

Taylor's letter was cause for concern. I had been working at IDA for almost a year to implement what I understood to be the wishes of both Secretary McNamara and President Kennedy. To have the management reforms attacked and to have the attack invoke the support of the secretary of defense was disturbing to me. To clarify my situation, I met with McNamara three days later and asked whether Taylor's letter should be construed narrowly or broadly. Was the request to IDA simply that WSED should continue to exist as a component of IDA, or did the request carry the additional implication that WSED should be a semi-independent entity over which the IDA management exercised little or no supervision? In raising this question I reminded the secretary of our initial interview and his statement that he looked to the IDA management to remedy the deficiencies in the divisions' work. He said that the request contained in

Taylor's letter was not intended to restore what he described as a "Kelly girl" situation, one in which IDA furnished people to work in WSEG but exercised little authority over them and assumed little or no responsibility for their work. He reaffirmed his understanding that WSED was a component of IDA and that IDA management should exercise normal managerial functions with respect to it. Reaffirming the views he had expressed ten months earlier, he noted that the first draft of Taylor's letter had more directly implied a curtailment of the authority and responsibility of IDA management and that he had insisted on changes of wording to eliminate that implication.

I next spoke with Taylor and began our discussion with the question I had raised with McNamara. In explaining how he came to write the letter he did, he outlined the background of events as they had unfolded within the Pentagon. Although the Joint Chiefs understood the nature of the Bell Report, they valued stability over reform. They wanted a stable cadre of professional civilians who would work regularly in close contact with the Pentagon's WSEG, period. I explained to Taylor, as I had to McNamara, that when IDA was consolidated in a new building I proposed to make certain organizational changes that would affect WSED but would not impair its continuing existence. Like McNamara, he raised no objection. At the end of our discussion, I showed him a draft of my reply to his letter. He read it through and said that it "read perfectly well" to him. I explained that I felt compelled to emphasize the authority and responsibility of IDA's management because I felt that their possession by the officers of IDA had never been fully accepted by WSEG. In parting, I told him I would like to feel free to talk to him from time to time about the work of IDA, to which he agreed.[5] In my formal response to him, I reiterated the degree of importance I placed on IDA's new directive—that is, on its exclusive responsibility for the work performed by its staff and for the form and content of completed studies.

Although relations with the Pentagon were strained, I was hopeful that any conflict was a result of misunderstanding and that my discussions and exchange of letters with Taylor and McNamara had clarified my position and served to dispel the atmosphere of mistrust. I felt that by moving forward I would be able to enact the reforms expected of me by McNamara and improve relations with everyone concerned. Unfortunately, another situation manifested itself shortly afterward, when Robert F. Rinehart, the director of WSED, wrote to me and the IDA board of directors complaining bitterly about what he characterized as the rapidly deteriorating relationship between IDA and the Pentagon. Unaware of the extent of my efforts to restore relations and unencumbered by the responsibility given to me by McNamara to implement the directives of the Bell Report, Rinehart concerned himself with a microlevel view of tense dealings between WSED and WSEG members. The problem, as he saw it, arose from "certain of the policies and managerial philosophy and practices of current IDA management, which are about to destroy, among other things, the close military-WSED cooperation which has been one of IDA's unique and valuable assets."[6]

Rinehart's letter implied that the alternatives facing IDA were to adopt policies acceptable to the military or forfeit its cooperation. Although Rinehart reported to me in my capacity as president of IDA, it was apparent that his stronger allegiance was to the concerns of the Pentagon. I now had to reconsider whether Taylor had indeed accepted the resolution of our brief disagreement, how fully he accepted McNamara's support of my position, and the possibility that, while he had said yes to us, he might very well have conveyed dissatisfaction down the military chain of command to Harvey Alness, the air force general who served as director of WSEG and who had a close working relationship with Rinehart. The reason for the mutiny was not hard to understand. If IDA's management began to exercise the corporate authority that it was vested with, it would mean a diminution of Rinehart's freedom of action.

I wrote a long *eyes-only* letter to Rinehart asking directly what it was about IDA's philosophy of management that was so distasteful not only to him but to the Pentagon and specifically to Alness. Was it Alness's fear of what would happen if officers of IDA continued their (necessarily very limited) participation in decisions and in the supervision of WSED's substantive work? On the basis of the record to date, it seemed to me the worst Alness could say of IDA was that we occupied some hours of Rinehart's time to little effect.[7]

While mutiny by Rinehart was disturbing, a frontal attack on IDA by Alness was most dangerous to the organization and any hope of reform. Alness was, in truth, a very difficult person to get along with, someone who tended to cast events in the mold of a military-civilian confrontation. He suspected and disliked civilians and civilian interference, but the very essence of his job in WSEG was to develop a close working relationship between military and civilian people and organizations. As I assessed what was becoming an increasingly frustrating situation, I had to wonder if my task was ill-fated from the start.

Soon a campaign of leaks and inference began that was reminiscent of the guerrilla tactics used by General Somervell in his attempt to wrest control from the War Shipping Administration during World War II. By August 1963 the conflict had caught the attention of the national press. *Newsweek* reported:

"The root issue in the conflict is the question of just who should decide how the U.S. can get the best possible arsenal at the least possible cost." Seen as an impediment to the military's shopping list, I had become the victim of what *Newsweek* described as "that old reliable bureaucratic weapon—the side of the mouth." I had "arrived just in time to become a handy target for the deep and increasing hostility of the military to the ascending role of the civilian policy makers." I think this was true. Since it would hardly have been prudent for the generals to aim their guns at the secretary of defense, perhaps they thought the man who had managed the planning for the Bay of Pigs would make a more vulnerable target. The article concluded that the "episode seemed to prove nothing, except that there is a valuable role to be played by an independent evaluation agency, with close ties—but no chains—to the Pentagon brass."[8]

As the situation at IDA continued to deteriorate, another shock hit in late November. I wrote to my daughter, Ann Harriet, in early December to comment on the events of the previous few days: "I was in Pennsylvania Station in New York on Friday afternoon waiting for a train to Trenton when I first heard a rumor of the assassination. It was a garbled report and seemed too fantastic to believe and it wasn't until I overheard another passenger on the train who had his own small radio with him that it was confirmed. . . . There is no point in trying to describe my feelings; everyone had the same experience and similar feelings. The only time in my life I had even faintly comparable feelings was when I heard the news of the Japanese attack on Pearl Harbor." I had written my son Richard a few days earlier with more or less the same message but had added something about my situation at IDA: "Just to compound matters, my office crisis has finally been resolved—at my expense. The decision is that I shall leave IDA, probably in about six months' time. This may be wise from Mr. McNamara's point of view and it may turn out in the long run to be the best outcome for me. Nevertheless, it is a defeat and this is never a happy result. It may mean that we will leave Washington entirely, if I find an attractive opportunity elsewhere."

Both Alness and I were asked to resign, I by the chairman of IDA's board of directors and Alness by the chairman of the Joint Chiefs. As I look back on this period, I feel that perhaps I was not as good a president as I could have wished. There were many relatively minor things that did not get done or that were not done as well as they could have been, but this did not really worry me. A more serious matter was my sometimes undiplomatic display of energy in attempting to reorganize IDA on the model proposed in the Bell Report, an effort based on what turned out to be an overreliance on the support of Robert McNamara. I believe McNamara made great contributions to American strategic thinking in the early sixties, but the manner in which he chose to resolve this conflict indicated to me that he was all too willing to sacrifice both personnel and principle to assuage his military counterparts. Although I was deeply hurt by his actions, I felt less abandoned by him than by Harold Brown, the senior technical civilian officer at the Department of Defense. I think he should have been more supportive of my position as a civilian dealing with the military personnel at WSEG.

My years at IDA and the manner in which I departed were symptomatic of a much broader problem developing in the military establishment. McNamara's position as secretary of defense was never in question during this period, but his visibility at the top masked an inability to penetrate effectively the establishment below. While McNamara espoused managerial efficiency, I became increasingly disturbed by Pentagon decision-making procedures that discouraged technical innovation, lengthened the lead times needed to take a weapon from concept to production, and inevitably contributed to inefficiency. It is a simple fact of life that, as the number of levels and points at which a proposal or program is subject to review and modification increase, the total decision-making process becomes slower and vastly more cumbersome. In many ways the protracted development of weapons systems and the consequent cost overruns we see today had their procedural birth in this period. It may even be said that the failure to resolve many of the civilian-military issues that emerged at this time directly contributed to this condition.

Perhaps the problem had its roots in views on military technology shared by McNamara and Brown. They believed that the United States had reached a plateau in military technology and that, although there would be steady progress in the design of most weapons, we need not anticipate major new technical developments of a sort that would render the balance of power fluid and uncertain. Holding these beliefs as they did, they naturally viewed the conflict over IDA as secondary. After all, if IDA was involved in the development of weapons system and that technology had plateaued, it would hardly make sense to waste their political capital fighting the Joint Chiefs over my reforms.

What I think McNamara and Brown failed to realize was the degree to which their skepticism discouraged innovators. Coupled with the multiple-review process, it resulted in stagnation. For creative and ingenious people concerned with military technology, the atmosphere in Washington during this period was much less exciting than it had been in the fifties. During Eisenhower's presidency there was a feeling of urgency and a willingness to give sympathetic consideration to all kinds of radical proposals. This was missing in the sixties, and its absence contradicts the popular image of Kennedy's administration. I believe that over the long run this change in climate had serious consequences for our military—something that we saw played out in the seventies. Our creativity in military technology didn't have its renaissance until the Reagan years, when the renewed cold war gave birth to a sense of urgency not seen since the Eisenhower days. With the fall of the Soviet Union and the development of the Star Wars technology that in some ways precipitated it, the views of McNamara and Brown seem sadly off the mark.

Partly to cheer me up, partly to dispel the chill one can experience in Washington as people distance themselves from those about to lose power, Ann arranged a whirlwind of social events. I shared my feelings with Win: "We have no very dramatic family news, but we seem to have been rather busy the last several weeks. We went out to dinner three times last week and the week before your mother had a rather formal dinner party with the Allen Dulleses and the Wolfers. This week we go to a formal dinner party at the Wisners tomorrow night and have some more people over to dinner a week later. I think one reason your mother has been spurred to activity is that quite a few of our friends and acquaintances have acted as if our departure from Washington was imminent and she decided to show that we are still very much in business here."

A couple of years after my departure from IDA, Maxwell Taylor became its president. By then I was in Connecticut and had very little contact with the organization. A year or two later, however, I was there on some sort of business and Taylor stopped me as I was walking past his open door and asked if I wanted to come in and talk. He had his deputy with him (a civilian who was something of a friend of mine) and his chief scientist. What followed was a conversation among the three of them in which Taylor said some things that brought cheer to my heart. "If I had known at the time what was going on, believe me, you would not have left," he said to me. "Whenever a problem arises, we go to the files and usually find memorandums from Bissell on the subject, all of which are, without exception, excellent. In effect, the policies that you outlined in writing and that you stood and fought for were policies we admire as correct and are following now." He had no cause to say this; he didn't know me very well and we certainly weren't friends. Although this may be a self-serving story, its truth has been a consolation to me whenever I reflect on this time.

CHAPTER TEN

Private Life

I had been badly spoiled by the succession of jobs I had held in the government, beginning with my position with the War Shipping Administration soon after Pearl Harbor. All of them had been exciting, difficult, and intellectually challenging, particularly since I believed deeply in what I was trying to accomplish. They involved a mix or alternation of two different emphases, one on organization building and the other on the substance of the current activities of whichever agency I was with. The intense, urgent, time-limited projects like the U-2, where the focus was on substance, provided excitement; the opportunity for organization building in the Marshall Plan apparatus and later in the CIA was remarkably unencumbered by inherited or imposed frustrations. I also enjoyed in a wholly different fashion my two academic interludes, at MIT after the war and with the Ford Foundation in the early fifties. What all my activities in the government had in common was that they were related to major national problems, primarily those subsumed under the heading of "national security." The decision to leave Washington and seek a career in the private sector was one I made with difficulty and a lot of soul searching.

I began by trying to characterize what my role (as distinguished from my formal position or responsibility) had been in my various jobs. It seemed in almost every case to have involved an ability to deal with the diverse aspects of an enterprise, its finances, internal organization, external relations, and technology. I realized that I had enough ability to understand the technical presentations of engineers, physicists, economists, and lawyers (without myself being professionally competent in any of their fields) to be able to make judgments of the kind that transcend any one discipline or departmental function. What this often enabled me to do was to sort out the relationships between the means that were under consideration and the ends that justified the enterprise. I reached the conclusion that if I had made any contribution to the success of the ventures in which I participated, it was not only through the possession of knowledge and the exercise of judgment but because I had been willing to make decisions (good or bad) reasonably promptly and cleanly and to accept responsibility for them.

I began a serious employment search in early 1964, and I received firm offers from companies like Polaroid, Perkin-Elmer, and United Aircraft through colleagues and friends. Other possibilities I considered were with Litton Industries, the World Bank, RCA, the Defense Research Council, Joel Dean Associates, United Nuclear, and Harvard. I wrote to Ann Harriet in mid-March 1964 that, much as I knew the family preferred to stay in Washington, I thought it unlikely we would: "I have a horror of hanging on here in a job that is not the center of things, as so many people do."

One offer I was inclined to turn down was from Erle Martin, vice president for research and development at United Aircraft in East Hartford, Connecticut. Its Pratt & Whitney division had produced the J-57 engine for the U-2 and I knew Perry Pratt quite well and respected him. Although I declined Martin's offer in June, citing as one of my reasons "the pull of long-established personal relationships in another direction," my response was not taken as final and negotiations continued over the summer. In mid-August Ann and I decided to take a three-week trip with Ann Harriet and Winthrop to give them their first exposure to Europe. On September 2, while we were in Venice, I received a telegram from Martin telling me that the board had approved my job. The decision had been made. I joined United Aircraft Corporation as director of marketing and economic planning. I would be reporting to Martin, and my duties were to provide economic guidance in expanding areas of nongovernment business, as well as in new technical programs under investigation.

We did not make the official move to Connecticut as a family until mid-November, and in the interim I continued to undertake consulting assignments while making quick trips on behalf of United Aircraft. In October 1964 I accepted a brief assignment from John McCone at the CIA, which involved looking into the very highly classified business of another agency of the government. My job was to write a report on what I had learned from visits and interviews with authorities on the problem.

My ten years at United Aircraft were, on the whole, unfulfilling. Although management direction at the time was not very strong and I could give it as an excuse, I must accept a certain part of the blame. Somehow I never took much initiative in creating a role for myself that would have been stimulating or innovative, although I easily could have.

The job was very different from previous ones I had held. I think I made significant progress toward the degree in amateur engineering that Kelly Johnson offered to confer on me during the U-2 project, and I certainly continued to learn about market research; but while it was interesting to see a different kind of large organization from the inside, I served in a purely staff role, something I found frustrating. I was used to a faster pace and a much closer relationship to and participation in active decision making. It was not easy playing a less active, more peripheral role. It has to be said, however, that, contrary to the belief of many, both decision making and actual accomplishment, move more slowly in industry than in government. Perhaps the reason is that industrial accomplishments have to be solid—the development of a new aircraft turbine or the opening up of a new market—whereas government programs produce their results (good or bad) in the form of procurements, new institutions, or the execution of major operations, all of which, with enough money and energy, can be accomplished rather quickly. I had to fight from drifting into a state of mind where everything I did from eight to five was an unavoidable, unchallenging routine. That would have been more of a reversal of my personal values than I could have tolerated.

My tenure at United Aircraft was satisfying, however, in the sense that I found it most agreeable to associate with people of outstanding ability. With the permission of Erle Martin, I also continued to pursue a number of outside interests. Some included Washington, but others involved organizations like the Scientific Engineering Institute in Waltham, Massachusetts, headed by James Wakelin, and assignments closer to home. United Aircraft agreed to an arrangement, for example, where I worked one day a week as budget director for the University of Hartford, receiving compensation directly from the university in place of my United Aircraft salary. I also became a member of the board of directors of the Covenant Mutual Insurance Company, headed by John Alsop (Joe and Stew's younger brother), and continued to attend meetings of the Institute of Foreign Affairs in Washington and discussion groups of the Council on Foreign Relations in New York whenever I could. My main reason was that these were lively and fascinating people whom I had known previously and wished to keep in touch with. I also served on various committees on diverse subjects and began to receive requests for interviews on aspects of my government career.

By the time I was nearing retirement, United Aircraft had become United Technologies Corporation under the leadership of Harry Gray, who wanted the name change to reflect a more diversified image. The aerospace industry in the early 1970s was in a declining phase, and while United Aircraft had not been hit as hard as Boeing had, the corporation was shrinking steadily and was expected to do so more rapidly in the near future. Inevitably, a major corporation reorganization was on the horizon.

In March 1974 my position, along with my staff of five, was eliminated. Since I was due to retire in September at age sixty-five, it suited both the company and me for me to leave six months early. Among my staff members who faced a relocation search was my secretary of four months, Frances T. Pudlo. Although we were still in the process of getting to know each other, I asked her if she would be willing to join me in a venture I had been contemplating with three friends. The plan was to open an office in Farmington and try our hand at management consulting, with Fran serving as secretary and staff. She agreed without hesitation, we rented space in a newly constructed office building called The Exchange, and the two of us moved in on April 1, 1974. As it turned out, however, my three potential partners never joined the enterprise—one died unexpectedly, one took a job in Washington, and one decided to stay with his present position. Fran and I were left to conduct our "so-called business" (as I always referred to it) alone, which we did quite happily for the next twenty years.

This office was a vital part of my later life. Throughout my career I had had extremely competent secretaries and assistants who handled all aspects of my business and personal affairs, something I very much wanted to continue. More importantly, I needed to maintain a challenging, stimulating existence. The greatest horror I could imagine was to retire to warmer climes to play shuffleboard and sit in a rocking chair. It was fortunate, however, that I received retirement income from various former employers, because the net earnings from the office would have placed me well below the poverty line. Fran and I worked hard on various mutual and individual endeavors, but we managed to have a lot of fun, too.

My continuing part-time assignments for the University of Hartford and Covenant Insurance, plus other, nonrecurring tasks, made variable demands on my time during the first couple of years, and I often found myself heavily overemployed. I also entered into an arrangement with John H. Hoagland, a friend of mine who had a more serious consulting business in Wellesley, Massachusetts, and gave me assignments largely commissioned by a firm in New York that sold specialized industry reports and analyses to companies interested in industrial markets. These assignments, which would take a year or more to complete, involved the writing of an extensive report or a book and covered subjects as diverse as the air-cargo industry, the use of advanced compositions in the aerospace industry, applications of organic rankine cycle systems for waste-heat recovery, liquified natural gas, electronic warfare, and nuclear power plants. Although I was basically ignorant about such topics when I began, with a little reading and research I managed to turn out results that gave the impression of being much more learned than they actually were. On occasion, I also assisted Hoagland in smaller jobs that were more nearly management consultancies. In the meanwhile, it was good for me to be employed after a fashion, and I found it enjoyable to have to dig into one topic after another and try to educate myself sufficiently to produce an acceptable product.

Marketing myself was never one of my strengths, so I depended heavily on Hoagland and whatever independent periodic assignments came my way. I undertook a peculiar one in late 1976 for Yale's president, Kingman Brewster, the purpose of which was to establish the feasibility and cost-effectiveness of a new process for recovering energy and activated carbon (together with other byproducts) from municipal waste. Unfortunately, the assignment never reached a viable stage and was terminated after a year and a half.

My agency career caught up with me in 1975. In April of that year I spent some three hours with the Rockefeller Commission, first in discussion with its chief of staff and then giving testimony to the commission itself. These sessions were rather demanding, but all in all they seemed to go well and they were less embarrassing than I feared they might be. They were followed by four or five trips to Washington to testify before the Senate Select Committee on Intelligence, a most unwelcome and unrewarding task. As a result of these inquiries, my name appeared in public print far more than I might have wished. These efforts were time-consuming, occasionally hard and unpleasant, but not too damaging. I found myself, however, profoundly depressed by the state of the intelligence community because of the attacks on it and by the state of the nation because of the strength of pacifist and isolationist sentiments in Congress.

The furor of the midseventies died down eventually, but not the requests for interviews from historians, writers, television producers, and students. These have continued at an ever-increasing pace over the years, and although I sometimes find them repetitive and tiring, I feel an obligation to respond to such requests and almost always to comply.

In September 1978 I took on an unexpected consulting assignment for the Space Research Corporation, a facility straddling the border of Vermont and Quebec that specialized in chemical, electronic, and shell-loading ordnance. I was asked to use my Washington connections to find out why the issuance of an export license authorizing the company's transfer of certain military technology to the Israeli government was being delayed. The company's president and founder, Gerald V. Bull, and his executive, Colonel Rodgers Gregory, were concerned that the decision on the license might have been influenced by allegations that had appeared in the press, both in the Caribbean and in Canada, to the effect that military materiel, including significant quantities of artillery ammunition, had been transshipped from the company's test range in Antigua to South Africa, possibly for use in Rhodesia. Such action would have been illegal under the regulations of the government of Antigua and in violation of the United Nations embargo.

I made a couple of trips to the Space Research Corporation plant and one trip to Washington to find out what I could about the charges, but by December the customs service had gathered enough evidence against the company to convene a federal grand jury investigation. Both Bull and Gregory were eventually prosecuted and found guilty.

My role in this affair was brief and peripheral, but interestingly enough, Bull resurfaced and made headlines again in March 1990, when he was mysteriously assassinated outside his apartment in Brussels. He was regarded by some as the world's greatest artillery expert and a ballistics genius, but evidently "his lifetime obsession died with him: the dream of building a Supergun, a huge howitzer able to blast satellites into space or launch artillery shells thousands of miles into enemy territory."[1] It was alleged that the Supergun was destined for Iraqi leader Saddam Hussein. In fact, a prototype was discovered in the mountains north of Baghdad after the Gulf War. United Nations inspectors said that the 360-foot-long howitzer had been tested and was capable of firing nuclear, chemical, and biological warheads.

Gradually the phase of what I would call true consulting ended in the early 1980s and I became more and more involved on a daily basis with community affairs in Farmington and greater Hartford. Being retired and having my own office and assistant, I was especially popular, particularly since any commitment on my part always included Fran without cost. In 1973 I served as president of the Farmington Historical Society, followed by a stint as secretary that included the period of the national bicentennial in 1976. I found myself responsible for putting in place the apparatus for planning an appropriate town-wide celebration that included both ceremonial and social events.

I began a six-year involvement with the World Affairs Center in Hartford, first serving as vice president and then as a director. My main role was to offer suggestions and guidance on obtaining speakers. On one occasion I arranged for a three-part lecture series on the CIA, giving one of the talks myself. I also served as a trustee of the Mark Twain Memorial. The house where I was born had been restored in the 1970s to its appearance when the Clemenses lived there, and it is now one of Hartford's most popular attractions.

The project that continues to take up most of Fran's and my time is a small not-for-profit organization called the Friends of Hill-Stead, which provides volunteer, financial, and community support for a beautiful turn-of-the-century house in Farmington that serves as a museum. Situated on a 160-acre site, it contains a small but impressive collection of French Impressionist art, as well as furniture, silver, Chinese celadon, Japanese prints, and works by Barye. I came on board as vice president of the Friends in 1976, went on to become president from 1980 to 1984, and then served as treasurer or assistant treasurer until 1994, when my term expired and could not be renewed. During the early 1980s, under my guidance, the Friends undertook a major capital fund-raising campaign that netted slightly over $1 million, two-thirds of which was to be invested as endowment. The Friends were also responsible for numerous capital improvement projects at the museum, and we initiated programs for children, concerts, and varied events to help promote the museum to the public.

Continuing in a financial role, I was invited in 1981 to become treasurer of a life-care retirement community in Bloomfield that was still in the planning stages. Over the course of my seven-year involvement I learned a great deal about budgets, financial controls, bond issues, and many other matters on which I should long since have been better informed.

Beginning in September 1991, I finally faced the inevitable and began working away slowly on this memoir. I am pleased to accomplish this task finally and hope that it offers something to historians and those concerned with the period it covers.

When I look back on my life, I think it can be said that I was something of an opportunist. I had no grand plan for advancing myself or any offices to which I particularly aspired. I did want to lead a challenging life and, if I could, participate in the key issues and events of my time. To attain this end, I seized those opportunities that came my way and made the most of them. Some of my accomplishments I am very proud of, others less so, but I take pride in knowing that I did my best.

How This Book Was Written

Mr. Bissell passed away peacefully at home in his sleep on February 7, 1994. A deteriorating heart condition had sapped his physical strength, but his ever-sharp mind and intellect never faltered. He worked on this memoir until the last days with the same interest and resolve he put into all tasks throughout his career. He was not a man who was comfortable talking about himself or his accomplishments, but he recognized a duty to historians and scholars to try to give some insight into the period in which he worked and the actions for which he was personally responsible. He was capable of looking back in a detached manner, yet he never spent much time dwelling on past mistakes. They happened; he had given his best effort; he did so with the best of intent and integrity.

This is a book that Mr. Bissell never really contemplated writing. His reluctance had nothing to do with keeping secrets; rather it reflected his feeling that his career had not been sufficiently important or interesting to be the subject of memoirs. He was chided, however, by family, colleagues, and friends who convinced him that he had been uniquely positioned to observe at close range, and often to play an active role in, some of the major events of the last fifty years. Persuaded he could no longer postpone this project, he began working on it at the age of eighty-two, in collaboration with Frances T. Pudlo and Jonathan E. Lewis.

After twenty years of close association with Mr. Bissell, Fran was finely attuned to his style of writing and personal preferences, and she mainly served as an editor on this manuscript. Her familiarity with Mr. Bissell's files, papers, and contacts was essential to the completion of this work. Jonathan became part of this effort in September 1991. He interviewed Mr. Bissell on the Marshall Plan at McGeorge Bundy's suggestion while working toward an M.A. in history at New York University. It was during this meeting that Mr. Bissell and Fran broached the subject of working together to produce a memoir. Jonathan agreed that day to begin work on this project.

Mr. Bissell established the priorities and scope of the project from the very beginning. For the most part, he wanted to write extensively only about those events that he believed would benefit from his personal perspective. As a result, certain topics either receive cursory treatment or are not discussed at all. For example, he wished to discuss the assassination plots against foreign leaders and the development of an executive action capability as little as possible. He also did not want to probe too deeply into his personal life, although he accepted the fact that his upbringing deserved attention because of the impact it had on the rest of his life.

There are several unstated themes throughout the memoir that shape it and reflect Mr. Bissell's priorities and goals—the impact of the bureaucratic process on policy making, effective management of government programs, intragovernment tensions between civilian and military agencies, efficient systems development and procurement, democracy and secrecy. These are the themes around which his discussions naturally gravitated.

The foundation of the memoir rests on a series of one-on-one interviews Jonathan conducted with Mr. Bissell between fall 1991 and summer 1993; Mr. Bissell's personal files and papers; interviews with former colleagues (or "witnesses," as Mr. Bissell referred to them); and research conducted by Jonathan. The taperecorded interview sessions, which ranged from three to over six hours, were generally informal and focused on a specific topic or grouping of topics. Jonathan developed a list of questions and talking points, which would be pursued by Mr. Bissell until he was satisfied that he had nothing more to contribute to the subject. The research for these interview sessions was derived from both primary and secondary sources and is reflected in the endnotes. The best example of how this process worked can be found in the section related to America's policy toward Cuba. Mr. Bissell's main goal was to provide an insider's account of the personalities and historical forces that led to the Bay of Pigs and Operation Mongoose. His second goal was to step away from the historical narrative and evaluate those aspects of the bureaucratic process that contributed to the invasion's failure. He and Jonathan spent a number of hours reviewing many of the original planning documents and memoranda obtained from the John F. Kennedy Library in an attempt to reconstruct how the national security bureaucracy operated during this period.

Interviews of Mr. Bissell's colleagues were conducted at Mr. Bissell's direction as a double check on his memory when the available literature proved inadequate and also so that Jonathan and Fran would get a different perspective on his life. While it is somewhat unusual for a memoir to include other people's memories and viewpoints, it was clear that some of the material from these interviews was too valuable not to include.

In gathering background material, Jonathan, acting on Mr. Bissell's behalf, was allowed access to certain classified histories written by the history staff of the CIA and to documents from the CIA's directorate of plans.

The working procedure that evolved between Mr. Bissell, Jonathan, and Fran began with the taped interview sessions. Mr. Bissell was able to expound at great length, without fatigue, and with remarkable precision. The tapes (as well as those of the other interviewees) were transcribed by Fran, and once topics had been covered in sufficient depth, Jonathan integrated the transcripts, material from Mr. Bissell's personal papers and files, and research into a draft.

Mr. Bissell reviewed each draft with a critical eye. Working with Fran, he eliminated anything he considered too personal or irrelevant, added details from his files, and did general editing. He would dictate changes and fill in gaps in the draft, relying on Fran to ensure that the result was consistently in his voice and style.

By late 1993, the memoir was virtually complete. Although there weren't any extended interview sessions at this point, Jonathan would call Mr. Bissell several times a week to consult and ask follow-up questions. He also conducted research and interviews to amplify ideas and recollections related to the development of the CIA's overhead-reconnaissance capability and the planning for the Bay of Pigs that occurred under Eisenhower's command. The chapter on the Marshall Plan no doubt could have benefited from archival research, but Mr. Bissell was comfortable that the material gathered from the *Foreign Relations of the United States* series was suitable.

In January 1994, the chapters concerning Mr. Bissell's career with the CIA ("Overhead Reconnaissance," "Crises," and "Cuba") were sent to the agency's Publications Review Board for clearance. In the months following Mr. Bissell's death, Jonathan completed the assignments that he and Mr. Bissell had outlined in late 1993 and early 1994, including interviews with Andrew Goodpaster, James Reber, Lawrence Houston, Leo Geary, Stanley Beerli, and Walt Rostow; a research trip to the Eisenhower Library; and review of additional material from the Kennedy Library. Fran completed transcribing the tapes. Though complete at the time of his death, the chapters "Transition: The Ford Foundation to the CIA" and "A Philosophy of Covert Action" were in a rougher stage of draft. Mr. Bissell was pleased with the Marshall Plan chapter and was in the process of a final review at the time of his death. "Private Life" is the only chapter that was written entirely after Mr. Bissell's death. This chapter was produced by Fran, who relied heavily on letters from Mr. Bissell's private papers and her own memories and experiences of working with him during those years.

When, in late 1994, Yale University Press accepted the memoir for publication, Jonathan and Fran began detailed editing. Research from the Eisenhower Library was incorporated, as were interviews conducted during 1994, research from the Kennedy Library pertaining to counterinsurgency doctrine (and *Foreign Relations of the United States* documents on Laos and Vietnam), reports from the CIA, and information from secondary sources suggested by readers.

Mr. Bissell rarely referred to the secondary literature and relied heavily on his own memories. Nevertheless, Jonathan found a number of studies helpful for his interview sessions with Mr. Bissell. *Bureaucracy, the Marshall Plan, and the National Interest* by Hadley Arkes, *The Marshall Plan: America, Britain, and the Reconstruction of Western Europe, 1947–1952* by Michael J. Hogan (Cambridge: Cambridge University Press, 1987), *The Marshall Plan and Its Meaning* by Harry Bayard Price, and *The Marshall Plan Revisited* by Imanuel Wexler provided an overview of the plan's organizational structure its intellectual antecedents and its programs. *The European Payments Union* by Jacob J. Kaplan and Gunther Schleiminger is the most complete study of the subject.

Eisenhower: Soldier and President and *Ike's Spies: Eisenhower and the Espionage Establishment,* both by Stephen Ambrose, were invaluable for an understanding of Eisenhower and his approach to national security and intelligence issues. *Keepers of the Keys: A History of the National Security Council from Truman to Bush* by John Prados offered insights into how the National Security Council did and didn't operate under Eisenhower and Kennedy. *Mayday* by Michael Beschloss, *Deep Black* by William E. Burrows, and *American Espionage and the Soviet Target* by Jeffrey Richelson threw light on issues related to the U-2 crisis and overhead reconnaissance.

John Ranelagh's *The Agency: The Rise and Decline of the CIA* (New York: Simon and Schuster, 1987) was especially useful for the breadth of material it covers. Its broad historical sweep dovetailed nicely with the focused analysis of covert operations contained in *Presidents' Secret Wars: CIA and Pentagon Covert Operations since World War II* by John Prados.

The Bay of Pigs by Haynes Johnson, *Bay of Pigs: The Untold Story* by Peter Wyden (New York: Simon and Schuster, 1979), and *The Perfect Failure: Kennedy, Eisenhower, and the CIA at the Bay of Pigs* by Trumbull Higgins were important sources. An interesting (and overlooked) source on the Bay of Pigs is *Operation Puma: The Air Battle of the Bay of Pigs* by Edward B. Ferrer (Miami: International Aviation Consultants, 1982). Ferrer was one of the Cuban pilots who participated in the air campaign, and he provides an important insider's account, rich in detail about recruitment, training, Cuban-American relations at the camps, and the operation itself.

It is hoped that the endnotes will serve as an adequate reference for any readers who are concerned with how this book was assembled and who wish a more complete bibliography. Certain works are singled out as helpful for obtaining a general understanding of the period, but other important books were not mentioned. If, after consulting the endnotes, readers have questions about sourcing, they may write to Jonathan Lewis through Yale University Press for further details.

Notes

CHAPTER ONE

The Early Years

1. George F. Bissell, "An Example of Family Patriotism in Revolutionary Times," undated. Papers of Richard M. Bissell, Jr.

2. "Secret of the Purple Heart," *Sunday Star Magazine,* 23 February 1930.

3. Hawthorne Daniel, *The Hartford of Hartford: An Insurance Company's Part in a Century and a Half of American History* (New York: Random House, 1960), 126.

4. George Nicholson to Rev. Endicott Peabody, 3 May 1922. Papers of Richard M. Bissell, Jr.

5. Joseph Alsop with Adam Platt, *I've Seen the Best of It* (New York: W. W. Norton, 1992), 58–60.

6. Geoffrey C. Ward, *Before the Trumpet: Young Franklin Roosevelt, 1882–1905* (New York: Harper & Row, 1985), 189.

7. Richard M. Bissell, Jr., "The Yale House Plan," *Harkness Hoot,* 7 October 1931, 19.

8. "Bissell, Jr. Hurt in Fall over Cliff," *Hartford Courant,* 18 March 1931.

9. Charles A. Lindbergh, *The Wartime Journals of Charles A. Lindbergh* (New York: Harcourt Brace Jovanovich, 1970), 411.

10. Justus D. Doenecke, ed., *In Danger Undaunted: The Anti-Interventionist Movement of 1940–1941 as Revealed in the Papers of the America First Committee* (Stanford: Hoover Institution Press, 1990), 215.

CHAPTER TWO

The War Years

1. Robert Paul Browder and Thomas G. Smith, *Independent: A Biography of Lewis W. Douglas* (New York: Alfred A. Knopf, 1986), 165.

2. S. McKee Rosen, *The Combined Boards of the Second World War* (New York: Columbia University Press, 1951), 107–08.

3. Browder and Smith, *Independent,* 168.

4. Herman Miles Somers, *Presidential Agency OWMR: The Office of War Mobilization and Reconversion* (New York: Greenwood Press, 1950), 94–95.

CHAPTER THREE

The Marshall Plan

1. Robert Marjolin, *Europe and the United States in the World Economy* (Durham: Duke University Press, 1953), 3–4.

2. McGeorge Bundy, ed., *The Pattern of Responsibility* (Boston: Houghton Mifflin, 1952), 46.

3. Stanley Hoffmann, *The Marshall Plan: A Retrospective* (London: Westview Press, 1984), 101–02.

4. Harry Bayard Price, *The Marshall Plan and Its Meaning* (Ithaca: Cornell University Press, 1955), 39.

5. Paul Nitze, interview by Jonathan E. Lewis, tape recording, Washington, D.C., 24 January 1992.

6. U.S. Department of State, *Foreign Relations of the United States,* 1948, 3:390–91.

7. U.S. House Committee on Foreign Affairs, *Emergency Foreign Aid: Hearings,* 80th Cong., 1st sess., 1947, 16–17.

8. Hadley Arkes, *Bureaucracy, the Marshall Plan, and the National Interest* (Princeton: Princeton University Press, 1972), 191.

9. U.S. Department of State, *Foreign Relations,* 1948, 3:408.

10. Ibid., 414–15.

11. Ibid., 414.

12. U.S. Senate Committee on Foreign Relations, *Extension of European Recovery: Hearings before the Committee on Foreign Relations on S.833,* 81st Cong., 1st sess., 1949, 338–39.

13. Lincoln Gordon, interview by Jonathan E. Lewis, tape recording, Washington, D.C., 24 January 1992.

14. Paul Nitze was the principal witness when Congress was deciding whether or not to have a Marshall Plan, and I was the principal witness for procuring its funding each year.

15. Vaughan Gary to Richard M. Bissell, Jr., 21 January 1952. Papers of Richard M. Bissell, Jr.

16. When Harriman arrived in Paris in April 1948, his first order of business was to requisition a building to serve as the headquarters for his staff of five, as none had been designated. He chose the Hôtel de Talleyrand, an eighteenth-century mansion built for a count. A boudoir became the office of the director of information, a stable the snack bar, and a reception salon Harriman's office. Within a year, the staff had grown to 767 employees (Hoyt Price, "The ECA in Europe," *American Foreign Service Journal* 27, no. 8 [1950]: 19).

17. U.S. Department of State, *Foreign Relations,* 1948, 3:649.

18. Ibid.; Imanuel Wexler, *The Marshall Plan Revisited: The European Recovery Program in Economic Perspective* (Westport: Greenwood Press, 1983), 97.

19. U.S. Department of State, *Foreign Relations,* 1948, 3:668, 688–89, 670.

20. Wexler, *Marshall Plan Revisited,* 106.

21. Theodore Geiger, interview by Jonathan E. Lewis, tape recording, Washington, D.C., 21 February 1993.

22. U.S. Department of State, *Foreign Relations,* 1948, 3:486–87.

23. Marjolin, *Europe and the United States,* 15.

24. U.S. House Committee on Foreign Affairs, *The Economic Cooperation Act: Hearings on H.R. 7378 and H.R. 7797,* 81st Cong., 2nd sess., 1950, 493–94.

25. Jacob J. Kaplan and Gunther Schleiminger, *The European Payments Union: Financial Diplomacy in the 1950s* (New York: Clarendon Press, 1989), 24.

26. House Committee, *Economic Cooperation Act,* 495–500.

27. Price, *Marshall Plan,* 121.

28. Geiger, interview.

29. Kaplan and Schleiminger, *European Payments Union,* 368; Geiger, interview.

30. William Wade, "Real Obstacles Hamper Britain's Union with Europe," *Foreign Policy Bulletin,* 18 November 1949.

31. Blair Boles, "West European Unity No Panacea for Economic Ills," *Foreign Policy Bulletin,* 11 November 1949.

32. U.S. House Subcommittee of the Committee on Appropriations, *Foreign Aid Appropriations for 1951: Hearings,* 81st Cong., 2nd sess., 1950, 8, 11.

33. Kaplan and Schleiminger, *The European Payments Union,* 91–92.

34. U.S. Department of State, *Foreign Relations,* 1951, 1:1615–19.

35. Ibid., 1950, 1:308.

36. Ibid., 1951, 1:903–04, 907–08, 911.

37. Ibid., 285–86, 287.

38. Richard M. Bissell, Jr., to Averell Harriman, 25 January 1952. Papers of Richard M. Bissell, Jr.

39. For a fuller discussion of these issues, see Richard M. Bissell, Jr., "Foreign Aid: What Sort? How Much? How Long?" *Foreign Affairs,* 31, no. 1 (1952): 15–38.

CHAPTER FOUR
Transition

1. James L. Cochrane, *Industrialism and Industrial Man in Retrospect: A Critical Review of the Ford Foundation's Support for the Inter-University Study of Labor* (Ann Arbor: Monograph Publishing, 1979), 42.

2. Richard M. Bissell, Jr., "Notes on U.S. Strategy," unpublished, 1952–53. Papers of Richard M. Bissell, Jr.

3. Cochrane, *Industrialism,* 46.

4. Walter LaFeber, *Inevitable Revolutions: The United States in Central America* (New York: W. W. Norton, 1984), 111–13.

5. Richard H. Immerman, *The CIA in Guatemala* (Austin: University of Texas Press, 1982), 58–59; Cole Blasier, *The Hovering Giant: U.S. Responses to Revolutionary Change in Latin America* (Pittsburgh: University of Pittsburgh Press, 1985), 154–55.

6. Immerman, *CIA in Guatemala,* 59–60.

7. U.S. Department of State, *Foreign Relations of the United States,* 1952–54, 4:1031.

8. Ibid., 1071–72, 1074.

9. Ibid., 1093.

10. Ibid., 1096, 1112.

11. Ibid., 1174–76.

12. G. J. A. O'Toole, *Honorable Treachery: A History of U.S. Intelligence, Espionage, and Covert Action from the American Revolution to the CIA* (New York: Atlantic Monthly Press, 1991), 461.

13. Burton Hersh, *The Old Boys: The American Elite and the Origins of the CIA* (New York: Charles Scribner's Sons, 1992), 348.

14. John Prados, *Presidents' Secret Wars: CIA and Pentagon Covert Operations since World War II* (New York: William Morrow, 1986), 104.

15. Ibid., 105.

16. Dwight D. Eisenhower, *The White House Years: Mandate for Change, 1953–1956* (New York: Doubleday, 1963), 425–26.

17. Hersh, *Old Boys,* 351. Piero Gleijeses explains that Guatemala's generals betrayed Arbenz well before the weapons were distributed. Fearing a confrontation with the United States, they avoided meeting Castillo Armas in battle and resigned themselves to overthrowing Arbenz (*Shattered Hope: The Guatemalan Revolution and the United States* [Princeton: Princeton University Press, 1992], 321–28).

18. Gregory F. Treverton, *Covert Action: The Limits of Intervention in the Postwar World* (New York: Basic Books, 1987), 62–63.

19. Gleijeses notes that before his downfall Arbenz enacted a successful reform that gave 500,000 peasants land. Castillo Armas reversed virtually all Arbenz's reforms, and by 1957, when Castillo Armas died, only 200 peasants remained in control of their land. Gleijeses concludes that since 1954 Guatemala has been "a foreboding world of repression and violence; it holds the macabre record for human rights violations in Latin America" (*Shattered Hope,* 381, 383).

20. Richard M. Bissell, Jr., to Allen Dulles, 6 August 1954. Papers of Richard M. Bissell, Jr.

CHAPTER FIVE

Overhead Reconnaissance

1. Jeffrey Richelson, *American Espionage and the Soviet Target* (New York: William Morrow, 1987), 139–40; Clarence L. "Kelly" Johnson with Maggie Smith, *Kelly: More Than My Share of It All* (Washington: Smithsonian Institution Press, 1985), 120; Ben Rich, interview with Richard M. Bissell, Jr., tape recording, Farmington, Conn., 8 July 1992.

2. Andrew J. Goodpaster, Memorandum of Conference with the President, 24 November 1954, ACW Diary, November 1954 (1), Box 3, Ann Whitman Diary Series, Eisenhower Library; James R. Killian, *Sputnik, Scientists, and Eisenhower: A Memoir of the First Special Assistant to the President for Science and Technology* (Cambridge: MIT Press, 1977), 82.

3. Larry Houston has a somewhat different recollection. He says that the money did not come out of the CIA's contingency fund. Instead, "the air force said, 'We have funds for

procurement for such occasions and we'd be glad to make them available and we can make available $22 million.' " According to Houston, the air force funds were covertly transferred to the CIA, and the agency handled the rest (Interview by Jonathan Lewis, tape recording, Washington, D.C., 11 February 1994).

4. Ibid.

5. Ibid.

6. Leo Geary, interview by Jonathan Lewis, tape recording, Denver, Colo., 27 February 1994.

7. Arthur Lundahl, interview by Jonathan Lewis, tape recording, Bethesda, Md., 23 January 1992.

8. Ibid.

9. Ibid.

10. Stephen Ambrose, *Ike's Spies: Eisenhower and the Espionage Establishment* (Garden City: Doubleday, 1981), 267–68; Dino Brugioni, *Eyeball to Eyeball: The Inside Story of the Cuban Missile Crisis* (New York: Random House, 1991), 11.

11. Lundahl, interview.

12. Michael Beschloss, *Mayday* (New York: Harper & Row, 1986), 143.

13. Lundahl, interview.

14. James Reber, interview by Jonathan Lewis, tape recording, Chevy Chase, Md., 11 February 1994.

15. According to Chris Pocock, about sixteen men died in the program from 1955 through 1960 (*Dragon Lady: The History of the U-2 Spyplane* [Osceola: Motorbooks International, 1989], 204–05).

16. Lundahl, interview.

17. Andrew J. Goodpaster, Memorandum for Record, 9 September 1958, Intelligence Matters (6), Box 14, White House Office, Office of the Staff Secretary, Subject Series, Alpha Subseries, Eisenhower Library.

18. Ibid.

19. Ibid., 21 June 1956, Intelligence Matters (1).

20. Ibid., 3 July 1956, Intelligence Matters (2).

21. Leo Geary, interview by Jonathan Lewis, tape recording, Denver, Colo., 27 February 1994.

22. Unofficial Translation, 10 July 1956, Intelligence Matters (2), Box 14.

23. Goodpaster, Handwritten Memorandum of Conversation, 15 November 1956, Intelligence Matters (3), Box 14.

24. Andrew J. Goodpaster, interview by Jonathan Lewis, tape recording, Washington, D.C., 10 February 1994.

25. Pocock, *Dragon Lady,* 39.

26. Beerli, interview.

27. Brugioni, *Eyeball to Eyeball,* 34.

28. Goodpaster, interview.

29. John S. D. Eisenhower, Memorandum of Conference with the President, 22 December 1958, Intelligence Matters (7), Box 15.

30. John S. D. Eisenhower, Memorandum for Record, 12 February 1959, Intelligence Matters (8), Box 15.

31. Goodpaster, Memorandum of Conference with the President, 11 April 1959, Intelligence Matters (10), Box 15.

32. Goodpaster, Memorandum for the Record, 8 February 1960, Intelligence Matters (13), Box 15.

33. Rich, interview.

34. Beschloss, *Mayday,* 241–42.

35. Goodpaster, interview; Lundahl, interview.

36. Goodpaster, Memorandum for Record, 25 April 1960, Intelligence Matters (14), Box 15.

37. Francis Gary Powers with Curt Gentry, *Operation Overflight: The U-2 Spy Pilot Tells His Story for the First Time* (New York: Holt, Rinehart and Winston, 1970), 74–75; Rolf Tamnes, *The United States and the Cold War in the High North* (Brookfield: Dartmouth Publishing Company, 1991), 135; Beerli, interview.

38. Powers, *Operation Overflight,* 75.

39. Norman Hannah to Christian Herter, Telegram, 18 May 1960, U-2 Incident, vol. 1, May 1960 (7), Box 25, White House Office, Office of the Staff Secretary.

40. Beerli, interview.

41. Dwight D. Eisenhower, *Waging Peace, 1956–1961* (Garden City: Doubleday, 1965), 546.

42. Robert King, interview by Jonathan Lewis, tape recording, Washington, D.C., 27 May 1992.

43. Geary, interview.

44. Discussion at the 444th Meeting of the National Security Council, 13 May 1960, Ann Whitman File, Box 12, NSC Series, NSC Summaries of Discussion, Eisenhower Library; Goodpaster, Memorandum of Conference with the President, 26 May 1960, U-2 Incident, vol. 1, May 1960 (8), Box 25, White House Office, Office of the Staff Secretary.

45. Gordon Gray, Memorandum of Meeting with the President, 1 June 1960, 1960 Meetings with the President, vol. 1 (3), Box 4, White House Office, Office of the Special Assistant for National Security Affairs, Special Assistant Series, Presidential Subseries, Eisenhower Library.

46. Rich, interview.

47. Goodpaster, Memorandum for Record, 2 June 1960, Intelligence Matters (15), Box 15.

48. Thomas P. McIninch, "The Oxcart Story," *Studies in Intelligence,* 26, no. 2 (1982): 26.

49. Johnson, *Kelly,* 135.

50. Brugioni, *Eyeball to Eyeball,* 39.

51. Johnson, *Kelly,* 137–38; Ben R. Rich and Leo Janos, *Skunk Works* (Boston: Little, Brown, 1994), 200.

52. William E. Burrows, *Deep Black: Space Espionage and National Security* (New York: Random House, 1986), 154; Rich and Janos, *Skunk Works,* 203.

53. Rich and Janos, *Skunk Works,* 204; Johnson, *Kelly,* 139.

54. McIninch, "Oxcart Story," 32.

55. Rich and Janos, *Skunk Works,* 241.

56. Lundahl, interview.

57. Jeffrey Richelson, "The Keyhole Satellite Program," *Journal of Strategic Studies* 7, no. 2 (1984): 124–25; Paul Stares, "Space and U.S. National Security," *Journal of Strategic Studies* 6, no. 4 (1983): 35.

58. Stephen E. Ambrose, *Eisenhower: Soldier and President* (New York: Simon and Schuster, 1990), 449–50.

59. Richelson, "The Keyhole Satellite Program," 126.

60. Burrows, *Deep Black,* 104.

61. Walter A. McDougall, *The Heavens and the Earth: A Political History of the Space Age* (New York: Basic Books, 1985), 180–81.

62. Burrows, *Deep Black,* 109–10.

63. McDougall, *The Heavens,* 224.

64. Richelson, "The Keyhole Satellite Program," 127; Brugioni, *Eyeball to Eyeball,* 53; Burrows, *Deep Black,* 90.

65. McDougall, *The Heavens,* 329.

CHAPTER SIX
Crises

1. Henry F. Jackson, *From the Congo to Soweto: U.S. Foreign Policy toward Africa since 1960* (New York: William Morrow, 1982), 23.

2. Ernest W. Lefever, *Crisis in the Congo: A United Nations Force in Action* (Washington: Brookings Institution, 1965), 4–5, 8–9, 11–12.

3. U.S. Senate, *Alleged Assassination Plots Involving Foreign Leaders* (Washington, D.C.: GPO, 1975), 14–15.

4. Ibid.

5. Len E. Ackland, "No Place for Neutralism: The Eisenhower Administration and Laos," in *Laos: War and Revolution,* ed. Nina S. Adams and Alfred W. McCoy (New York: Harper & Row, 1970), 149–50, 152.

6. John M. Newman, *JFK and Vietnam* (New York: Warner Books, 1992), 9–10.

7. Ibid., 10.

8. W. W. Rostow, *The Diffusion of Power: An Essay in Recent History* (New York: Macmillan, 1972), 169; Rostow, oral history interview by Richard Neustadt, 11 April 1964, John F. Kennedy Library.

9. National Security Action Memorandum 124, 18 January 1962, National Security Files: Meetings and Memoranda—NSAM 124 Establishment of the Special Group (Counter Insurgency), Box 333, John F. Kennedy Library.

10. Memorandum to the Special Group (CI) from General Lemnitzer, 30 January 1962, National Security Files: Meetings and Memoranda—NSAM 124 Establishment of the Special Group (Counter Insurgency).

11. U.S. Department of State, *Foreign Relations of the United States,* 1961–63, 1:321, 343; Marilyn B. Young, *The Vietnam Wars, 1945–1990* (New York: HarperCollins, 1991), 79–80.

12. U.S. Department of State, *Foreign Relations,* 532–34.

13. Richard Reeves, *President Kennedy: Profile of Power* (New York: Touchstone, 1994), 261.

CHAPTER SEVEN

Cuba

1. Andrew J. Goodpaster, Memorandum of Conference with the President, 26 January 1960, Cuba (2), Box 4, International Series, White House Office, Office of the Staff Secretary, Eisenhower Library.

2. Andrew J. Goodpaster, Memorandum of Conference with the President, 18 March 1960, Intelligence Matters (14), Box 15, Subject Series, Alpha Subseries; "A Program of Covert Action against the Castro Regime," 16 March 1960, CIA Policy Paper Re: Cuba, Box 4, International Series.

3. Trumbull Higgins, *The Perfect Failure: Kennedy, Eisenhower, and the CIA at the Bay of Pigs* (New York: W. W. Norton, 1987), 61.

4. Synopsis of State and Intelligence Material Reported to the President, 18 October 1960, Intelligence Briefing Notes, vol. 2 (6), Box 14, Subject Series, Alpha Subseries.

5. Discussion at the 464th Meeting of the National Security Council, 24 October 1960, Ann Whitman File, Box 13, NSC Series, NSC Summaries of Discussion, Eisenhower Library.

6. U.S. Senate, *Alleged Assassination Plots Involving Foreign Leaders* (Washington, D.C.: GPO, 1975), 126–27.

7. Doris Mirage, interview by Jonathan E. Lewis, tape recording, Washington, D.C., 23 January 1992.

8. Discussion at the 467th Meeting of the National Security Council, 21 November 1960, Ann Whitman File, Box 13.

9. Richard M. Bissell, Jr., to Edmond G. Thomas, 14 November 1960. Papers of Richard M. Bissell, Jr.

10. Gordon Gray, Memorandum of Meeting with the President, 5 December 1960, 1960 Meetings with the President, vol. 2 (2), Box 5, Special Assistant Series, Presidential Subseries, White House Office of the Special Assistant for National Security Affairs.

11. "Special National Intelligence Estimate Number 85-3-60: Prospects for the Castro Regime," National Security Archive, *Cuban Missile Crisis, 1962* (Alexandra: Chadwyck-Healy, 1990), microfiche.

12. Gordon Gray, Memorandum of Meeting with the President, 9 January 1961.

13. Whiting Willauer to Livingston Merchant, Memorandum, 18 January 1961, 1960 Meetings with the President, vol. 2 (2), Box 5, Special Assistant Series, Presidential Subseries.

14. McGeorge Bundy, Memorandum of Discussion on Cuba, 28 January 1961, "Taylor Report," Annex 8, National Security Files, Cuba, Box 61, John F. Kennedy Library.

15. Lyman Lemnitzer to Robert McNamara, Military Evaluation of Cuban Plan, 3 February 1961, "Taylor Report," Annex 9, 1–3, 10, 26–27, 31–32, 6.

16. John F. Kennedy, Memorandum for Mr. Bundy, 6 February 1961, National Security Files, Meetings and Memoranda, Box 328; McGeorge Bundy to John F. Kennedy, Memorandum for the President, 8 February 1961, President's Office Files, Box 115, John F. Kennedy Library.

17. Thomas Mann to Dean Rusk, Memorandum, 15 February 1961, National Security Files, Cuba, Box 35.

18. Bundy to Kennedy, Memorandum for the President, 8 February 1961, President's Office Files, Box 115.

19. McGeorge Bundy, Memorandum of Meeting with the President on Cuba, 9 February 1961, National Security Files, Cuba, Box 35.

20. McGeorge Bundy, interview by Jonathan E. Lewis, tape recording, New York, N.Y., 25 March 1992.

21. Stanley W. Beerli, interview by Jonathan E. Lewis, tape recording, Hillsboro, Oreg., 25 February 1994.

22. Lyman Lemnitzer to Robert McNamara, Memorandum for the Secretary of Defense, 11 March 1961, "Taylor Report," Annex 10.

23. "Proposed Operation against Cuba," 11 March 1961, "Taylor Report," Annex 11. 7–9.

24. McGeorge Bundy to John F. Kennedy, Memorandum, 15 March 1961, National Security Files, Cuba, Box 35.

25. David W. Gray, Memorandum for Record, 9 May 1961, "Taylor Report," Annex 16.

26. Paul Nitze, interview by Jonathan E. Lewis, tape recording, Washington, D.C., 24 January 1992.

27. Robert Amory, oral history interview by Joseph E. O'Connor, 17 February 1966, 114, John F. Kennedy Library.

28. According to Cecil Currey, Edward Lansdale was the person in the Defense Department most actively at work to obstruct cooperation with the agency. Currey concludes that Lansdale's "influence was such that many . . . came to share his pessimism and cooperated slowly" (*Edward Lansdale: The Unquiet American* [Boston: Houghton Mifflin, 1988], 210–11).

29. Robert King, interview by Jonathan E. Lewis, tape recording, Washington, D.C., 27 May 1992.

30. Richard Helms, interview by Jonathan E. Lewis, Washington, D.C., 23 January 1992.

31. Arthur M. Schlesinger, Jr., *A Thousand Days* (Boston: Houghton Mifflin, 1965), 248; Amory, interview, 19 February 1966, 23–24; 17 February 1966, 120–21. It was not unusual for Amory to be cut out of a major covert operation. He was never briefed about PBSuccess either (Piero Gleijeses, *Shattered Hope: The Guatemalan Revolution and the United States* [Princeton: Princeton University Press, 1992], 244).

32. Information Reports, 10 March 1961; 16 March, 6 April 1961, CIA Directorate of Plans Files.

33. Leo Geary, interview by Jonathan E. Lewis, tape recording, Denver, Colo., 27 February 1994.

34. Haynes Johnson, *The Bay of Pigs: The Leaders' Story of Brigade 2506* (New York: W. W. Norton, 1964), 72.

35. Arthur M. Schlesinger, Jr., interview by Jonathan E. Lewis, tape recording, New York, N.Y., 25 February 1992.

36. Dean Rusk and Richard Rusk, *As I Saw It,* ed. Daniel S. Papp (New York: W. W. Norton, 1990), 211–12.

37. Beerli, interview.

38. W. W. Rostow, *The Diffusion of Power: An Essay in Recent History* (New York: Macmillan, 1972), 209; Rostow, oral history interview by Richard Neustadt, 11 April 1964, John F. Kennedy Library.

39. Rostow, interview.

40. Geary, interview.

41. Richard E. Welch, Jr., *Response to Revolution: The United States and the Cuban Revolution, 1959–1961* (Chapel Hill: University of North Carolina Press, 1985), 104. The private market firm of Sindlinger & Company conducted the analysis. The results were based on the responses of 4,000 Americans.

42. Arthur Lundahl, interview by Jonathan E. Lewis, tape recording, Bethesda, Md., 23 January 1992.

43. Allen W. Dulles Papers, Box 138, Box 244, Princeton University. Used by permission of the Princeton University Libraries.

44. Paul L. Kesaris, ed., *Operation Zapata: The "Ultrasensitive" Report and Testimony of the Board of Inquiry on the Bay of Pigs* (Frederick: University Publications of America, 1981), 36–37.

45. John A. McCone to Richard M. Bissell, Jr., 19 August 1985. Papers of Richard M. Bissell, Jr.

46. John A. McCone to Richard M. Bissell, Jr., 19 March 1986. Papers of Richard M. Bissell, Jr.

47. John Prados, *Keepers of the Keys: A History of the National Security Council from Truman to Bush* (New York: William Morrow, 1991), 100–02.

48. Andrew J. Goodpaster, interview by Jonathan E. Lewis, tape recording, Washington, D.C., 10 February 1994; Arleigh Burke, oral history interview by John T. Mason, Jr., 12 January 1973, Columbia Oral History Project, Eisenhower Library.

49. Morton H. Halperin and Arnold Kanter, "The Bureaucratic Perspective," in *International Politics,* ed. Robert J. Art and Robert Jervis (New York: HarperCollins, 1992), 406–08; Morton H. Halperin, *Bureaucratic Politics and Foreign Policy* (Washington: Brookings Institution, 1974), 49, 104–07.

50. Bundy, interview.

51. Schlesinger, *A Thousand Days,* 297.

52. "Record of Actions by the National Security Council at Its Four Hundred and Eighty-Third Meeting, Held on May 5, 1961," National Security Archive, *Cuban Missile Crisis, 1962* (Alexandria: Chadwyck-Healy, 1990), microfiche.

53. "The Military Build-up in Cuba: A Report Prepared by an Ad Hoc Committee of the United States Intelligence Board," *Cuban Missile Crisis, 1962.*

54. *Alleged Assassination Plots,* 140–41.

55. Cecil Currey suggests that Lansdale gave little consideration to the agency's failed attempts to form an indigenous Cuban guerrilla movement (*Edward Lansdale,* 236–58).

56. *Alleged Assassination Plots,* 140, 144.

57. Ibid., 141.

58. Helms, interview.

59. "Guidelines for Operation Mongoose," *Cuban Missile Crisis, 1962*; *Alleged Assassination Plots,* 146.

CHAPTER NINE
The Institute for Defense Analyses

1. "Special Report," *Business Week,* 13 July 1963, 58.

2. "Excerpts from Report to the President on Government Contracting for Research and Development, Released May 1, 1962," 22 May 1962. Papers of Richard M. Bissell, Jr.

3. Richard M. Bissell, Jr., to Robert F. Rinehart, 8 August 1962. Papers of Richard M. Bissell, Jr.

4. Maxwell D. Taylor to Richard M. Bissell, Jr., 12 March 1963. Papers of Richard M. Bissell, Jr.

5. Richard M. Bissell, Jr., Memorandum for the Record, 25 March 1963. Papers of Richard M. Bissell, Jr.

6. Robert F. Rinehart to Richard M. Bissell, Jr., 8 April 1963. Papers of Richard M. Bissell, Jr.

7. Richard M. Bissell, Jr., to Robert F. Rinehart, 10 April 1963, Papers of Richard M. Bissell, Jr.

8. "Game to the End," *Newsweek,* 12 August 1963, 23–24.

CHAPTER TEN
Private Life

1. Kevin Toolis, "The Man behind Iraq's Supergun," *New York Times Magazine,* 26 August 1990, 46.

Index